WHEELS OF FORTUNE

Francis Seufert

WHEELS OF FORTUNE

by

FRANCIS SEUFERT

edited by

Thomas Vaughan

with a

Photographic Portfolio

by

Gladys Seufert

To Johnson & Nova
For Francis Seufert
Gladys Seufert

Oregon Historical Society
1980

Rear cover illustration by James Longstreth.

Printed in the United States of America.

Frontis: Francis Seufert, pictured
in this photograph by Gladys
Seufert, about 1940. (Gladys Seufert photo)

CONTENTS

ILLUSTRATIONS

INTRODUCTION

We know that the Hudson's Bay Company sent barrels of Columbia River salmon to the London market in the early 19th century. And we know Captain John Dominis of the Boston brig *Owyhee* carried 50 hogsheads of salted salmon back home where he sold it in the mid-1820s for 10 cents a pound—maybe $3,000 worth of salmon.

Captain James Scarborough wrote of his salmon casks laid into the Hudson's Bay schooner *Cadboro* in the summer of 1846. This colorful sailor had a feeling about the teeming Columbia fisheries below his fir-covered homestead, which in two decades would be known across North America and Western Europe. Perhaps great runs of salmon had not always entered the vast Columbia River system, but archeological findings suggest that Indian tribes had gathered along the river banks for at least two thousand years of dependable fishing. Through generations, a complex culture developed and elaborate fish-taking weirs and cedar nets of enormous size gradually came into play in the river narrows.

Of course there were great salmon runs that entered other rivers along the western American coast-line, including the Sacramento, the Rogue, Umpqua, Siuslaw, and Siletz, and a hundred smaller streams along the Washington coast up to the Canadian Fraser River and north to Cook Inlet and Kodiak Island.

But somehow none quite excited the imagination and the palate like the several runs into the Columbia, especially the summer bluebacks and the "June hogs." Moving up from the brackish estuary, threading the lower islands and the seal packs, the salmon hordes gradually sorted themselves into the lower rivers such as the Cowlitz, the Kalama and Lewis, the larger Willamette system, and a score of finger streams running down from the Cascade Mountains. Other fat-bellied fish pushed up through the roaring cataracts of the lower Cascades and through the long, foamy basalt channels of Celilo Falls under the watchful eye of *Spilyai*, the legendary coyote. From there substantial runs moved into the Snake or up the main stream to Kettle Falls, living on the diminishing fat of their bodies as they urged themselves up the thousand miles into the Canadian Rockies. The Chinook salmon moved in long recognized cycles and it was simply understood that such huge fisheries would never diminish, would never die. The choices were, did you prefer a twelve-pound silver or the steaks from a fifty-pound June hog or a six-pound blueback for two?

The great Sacramento River fishery had finally failed in the early 1860s, but that could be explained. Enormous placer mines, spewing water and mud across the mountain slopes, had eventually destroyed the graveled spawning beds below. Three enterprising persons who noted this were Andrew S. Hapgood, the pioneer lobster canner from Maine, and his partners William and George Hume. They had separately left the Kennebec River in Maine only to meet frustration in the muddy Sacramento in 1864.

Immediately after the Civil War, William Hume moved north on a scout from the soil-polluted Sacramento River. What he found were the clear, boiling currents of the Columbia estuary alive with salmon runs that would feed the new canning processes forever. By the winter of 1866-67 the Maine men were firmly established on the north bank of the Columbia, a few miles downstream from the historic Oak Point area, which was earlier laid out by the Abernethy brothers. The bays and rivers were soon filled with elaborate salmon traps, set traps and purse and drag seines sometimes pulled by powerful horse teams or by oarsmen. All these techniques stemmed from the first seine net brought out from the Kennebec where the Humes' father and grandfather had won their livelihood by fishing.

In the first ten years the salmon packed in the newly developed cans introduced by the Hume enterprise expanded from 4,000 cases (48 one-pound cans) in 1867 to 450,000 cases in 1878. By 1880, salmon canning was the second largest export from the Oregon and Washington territories. Needless to say, such activity attracted an ever larger fishing industry all the way up the river to the falls.

Fortunately for the story in our own time, among others who came north from California was the Seufert family. Francis Anthony Seufert (1853-1929), a butcher, arrived in 1880, followed soon by his brother Theodore J. (1859-1947). Based on the success of their first fishwheel installed in 1884, the brothers purchased the Whitcomb fishing business in 1885.

My own association with this publication was fortuitous. In the 1930s times were hard along the lower Columbia River. Money was scarce and people did not move about casually, nor were they accustomed to the easy travel patterns that followed World War II. But even in lean times there were occasions made for family outings. A special place for my family was down the north shore of the Columbia, from the Cowlitz River valley toward the long-established village of Cathlamet. Just short of that old Hudson's Bay depot we would reach abundant fish in the rips between Abernethy Creek and Oak Point. Once a famous native village site, the sandy beach and the little coves beyond the solid rock promontory had then become the renowned Hume fishing and cannery site. Between Oak Point and Eagle Cliff the shoreline tidal beaches were impregnated with the weedy pilings of long-abandoned Hume canneries and moorages. Heavy thickets screened the tailings left by a hundred Chinese cannery crews brought in following the first big successes of Andrew Hapgood and the Hume brothers, the cannery kings of Eagle Cliff. And there one could also see the remains of William Hume's great house on the water's edge. In my mind I can see the house in desuetude, a somewhat carpenter gothic construction. But most of all I remember as an eight year old a vast amount of paper records littering the floors and fluttering about the sand hummocks and through the hoary orchard trees outside. This did not make much impact upon me as a small boy, but later when I returned as an adult in search of the house and its significant records, all had vanished, along with much else: the fish traps, the nocturnal fleets of purse seiners and the busy buying stations along the Columbia and its icy tributaries were the ordinary scene of years long ago.

Later, when returning east to school, I took my first drive up the now hard-pressed Columbia River Gorge; then there was scarcely a village or the disfiguring scar of the developers' heavy machinery. The radical geographical change at the east end of the Gorge cutting through the Cascades was a physical experience to remember forever. There, on a brilliant September morning, in the midst of looming hills, I first spied through its radiating mist the middle cataracts of the Columbia—Celilo Falls, flanked by stilled fishwheels, and teeming with hardworking natives of the Columbia tribes. Who would have believed the roaring waters and the vaulting fish, the entire scene, would so quickly fade in the next ten years, and that the tumultuous falls themselves would be submerged behind yet another dam?

Of the riverine processes downstream much has been recorded, and yet so much important data have vanished. William Hume never wrote a personal word. Since it would all last forever, why bother with grubby details? Well, fortunately for us, the mid-Columbia is well served by the Seuferts—a family imbued with deep historical perception. From the first years of their fishing operation in the late 1880s, down to the last day of corporate operations in the 1970s, the most accurate records were faithfully maintained through three generations. This, combined with the magnificent visual record carefully preserved and substantially enlarged by photographers Francis and Gladys Seufert, and their son Frank, will come into play when the statistical records available are again analyzed for the re-established fisheries of the future.

Francis and Gladys Seufert came downriver to Portland to see me just twenty-five years ago. They were concerned that the story of the mid-Columbia fisheries would be lost. We discussed a preservation plan in detail.

Thanks to them a substantial part of that record is now forever preserved in the collection of industrial records they faithfully kept, as well as thousands of photographs these skillful photographers either took themselves or preserved from earlier generations. They became in effect guardians of the Gorge heritage as had native Indians of countless generations back through time.

As our friendship flourished, it became ever more apparent that there was a special story lying submerged just below Francis Seufert's occasional recollections. It was also apparent that his memory of the fisheries was brilliant, but it would never get on paper. We needed a system, and I needed a partner who would stand by Francis through thick and thin, the hard places and rough patches of writing down a piece of history ''which everyone already knows.'' That person is Francis' wife, Gladys. Of course the story I refer to was the development of the world-famous fisheries and the canneries owned by the Seufert family at Seufert, Oregon, just upstream from The Dalles on the Columbia.

But first we had to get a small sample registered with Francis to show that it could be done; something to establish the level and atmosphere that it seemed to me necessary to embarkation on such a long-term voyage of reconstruction. I then posed a certain range of questions for a most reluctant Francis, to suggest something about what we hoped he might do. I think that you will sense the pleasure I experienced upon receiving from him the little vignette that opens this book.

Through the last 150 years, many men and women have written about the Columbia River, attempting to capture its grandeur. The legends of the Indians and their immemorial forebears recorded special qualities of "the river" in stone and legend; but as yet no one has quite succeeded in capturing the river's flow through the abiding hills, even as the huge dams of the 20th century will never harness the spirit of the magnificent stream. The harder the Columbia works and the more that is demanded of it, in some final sense the more elusive it becomes. A part of that grandeur not captured by writers or engineers will ever be undiminished. One senses this in a series of lonely mountain passes of the Canadian Rockies, from whose ice fields the river first emerges, and at the wide and rocky jaws on the Pacific where the boiling river joins the cold ocean mass.

The rise and fall of the snow waters from the north, the startling change as one leaves the vernal cliffs of the Gorge, and the runs of beautiful fish, all appeared permanent in times of great change. Today we perceive with some regret the evanescent dimension, the swift physical changes determined by a few, per-

haps for the benefit of the many. We can also more easily perceive that the rugged grandeurs of the spectacular Columbia River Gorge are now threatened by persons who have no thought for anything beyond the pleasures of their own time. Francis Seufert often acknowledged that more than ever before we had to work with the very finest kind of long-range planning, or we would lose banks and hills as well as the fish.

But I was not asking Francis to describe the grandeur of the cataract at Celilo Falls. What I wanted was a record of what happened there during the 75 years the Seufert family owned and operated the fishwheels and seines that annually—and almost predictably—garnered a silvery fortune. And I had a prototype.

Years ago I had the pleasure of serving as the research assistant to a great American novelist, Thomas W. Duncan. He was immersed in mid-19th century background material in preparation for a giant work dealing with every aspect of logging and rafting on the upper Mississippi River. For two years I mined the archives to find out how the "piney boys" worked, those robust men who felled the white pine forests that once covered the hills and river valleys of Michigan, Wisconsin and Minnesota. And what a grand job it was, resurrecting their rough and rollicking life of a century ago. In every sense it was my meat and drink, and a great American novel came from Duncan's vast talents.

But it was not easy. I could find out what they ate, what they drank, what time they started to work "daylight in the swamp," or what they sang and groused about. As with untutored William Hume, their letters were few and far between but once in a while a special trove of letters would surface in some inspired historical society, in a family archive, or obscure publication. But somehow no one ever sat down and wrote back to the old country, or Down East, to describe a week on the town after a long winter in the ice-clad forest. There were few personal revelations or introspections. A lad might describe how the huge logs were ox-dragged to the frozen river banks, but not a hot night in a whorehouse on the banks of the Little Eau Claire. The everyday, basic facts of life were always the most elusive. Evidently no one ever used an outhouse. None was noted. Clothes were always clean, the food good and no lice problems. It was curious. Surely someone got drunk, or lost all of his money, or ended up at the madam's—or in her back alley.

The Indians who once roamed the forest, where were they? Who made the tools, who stole the logs, not to mention the land, who got sick? Who died to be stuck in what icebound ground, who had a fever or flux, who got the clap, what were the simple facts of elimination, especially in the middle of the night at 30° below? Maybe here was another chance to find out from a keen observer who had watched the rise and fall of a great American industry—all the questions, the dreams and disappointments.

So that was the wonder of grandson Francis Seufert. The fisheries had come and gone, but in 1955 he remembered everything, man and boy. History and the basic traditions of the mid-Columbia salmon runs will live forever because Francis Seufert sat down and faithfully tried to answer every question put to him. At least a hundred of them must have seemed a bit odd at the time, but he put his encyclopedic mind to it and with the help of Gladys tried to answer every one with special care and accuracy.

And now we have it, thanks to the enlightened understanding of the historical process so generously perceived and supported by them. We finished our work together just before he died of cancer in a Portland hospital. He was pleased and proud.

With very few exceptions, the work appears as it came out of the written questions and taped answers that Francis read to Gladys' recorder, and were then transcribed in The Dalles. I retained only enough questions to clearly reveal the system that we found most workable and brought the greatest yield of solid facts into our wide-cast nets.

Thomas Vaughan
Executive Director
Oregon Historical Society
March 1980

XV

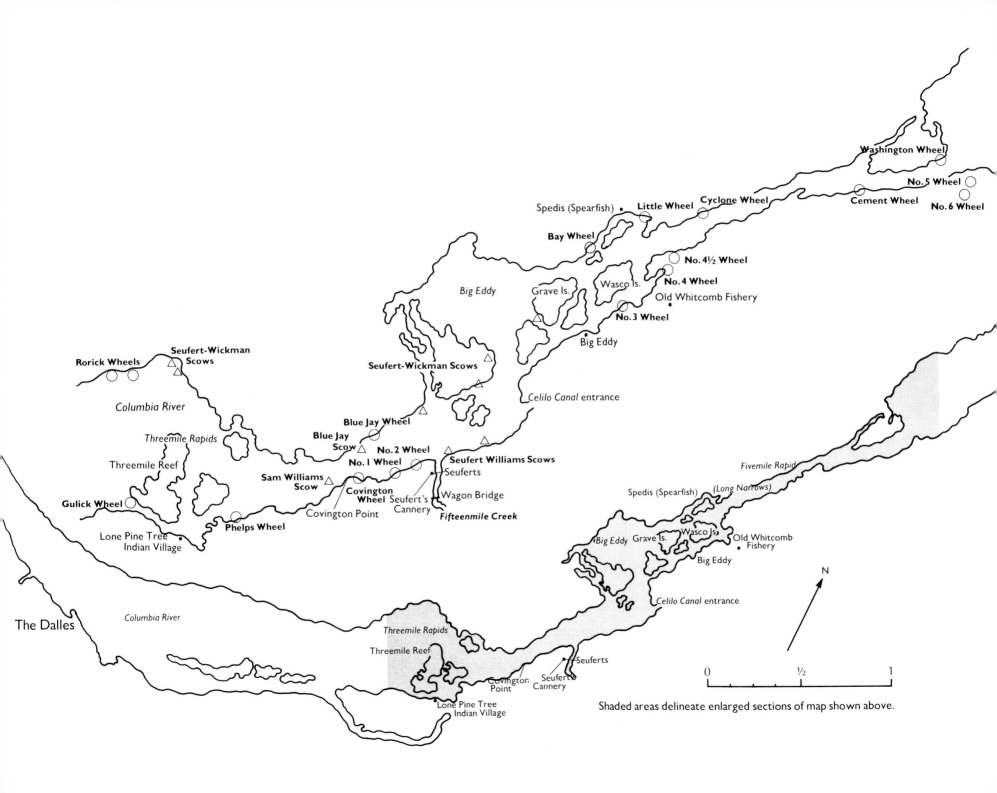

Washington Wheel

No. 5 Wheel

Cement Wheel

No. 6 Wheel

Cyclone Wheel

Spedis (Spearfish)   Little Wheel

Bay Wheel

No. 4½ Wheel

No. 4 Wheel

Big Eddy   Grave Is.   Wasco Is.   Old Whitcomb Fishery

No. 3 Wheel

Big Eddy

Seufert-Wickman Scows

Rorick Wheels   **Seufert-Wickman**
Scows

Celilo Canal entrance

Columbia River

Seufert-Wickman Scows

Threemile Rapids

Threemile Reef

Blue Jay Wheel

Blue Jay
Scow

No. 2 Wheel

Seufert Williams Scows
Seuferts

Sam Williams
Scow

No. 1 Wheel

Gulick Wheel

Covington
Wheel   Seufert's
Cannery

Wagon Bridge

Covington Point

Phelps Wheel

Fifteenmile Creek

Lone Pine Tree
Indian Village

Fivemile Rapid

Spedis (Spearfish)   *(Long Narrows)*

Big Eddy   Grave Is.   Wasco Is.   Old Whitcomb
Fishery

Big Eddy

The Dalles

Columbia River

Celilo Canal entrance

N

Threemile Rapids

Threemile Reef

Seuferts

Covington
Point   Seufert's
Cannery

Lone Pine Tree
Indian Village

0   ½   1

Shaded areas delineate enlarged sections of map shown above.

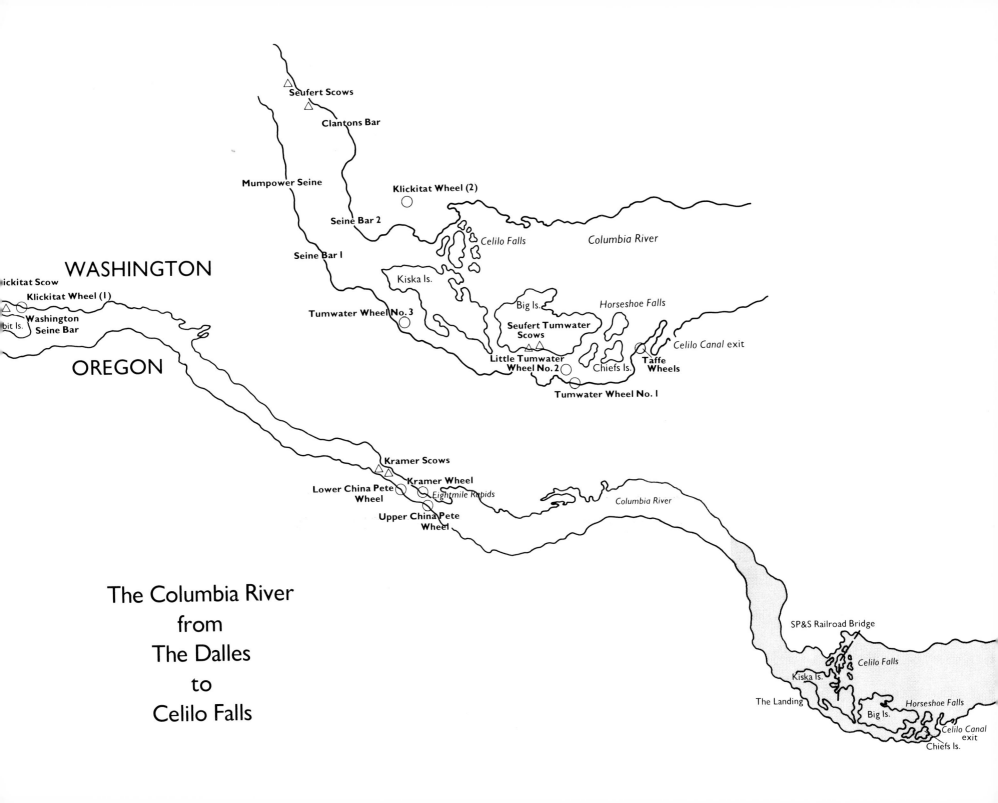

The Columbia River
from
The Dalles
to
Celilo Falls

WASHINGTON

OREGON

Seufert Scows

Clantons Bar

Mumpower Seine

Seine Bar 2

Klickitat Wheel (2)

Celilo Falls

Columbia River

Seine Bar 1

Klickitat Scow

Klickitat Wheel (1)

Washington
Seine Bar

bit Is.

Kiska Is.

Tumwater Wheel No. 3

Big Is.

Horseshoe Falls

Seufert Tumwater
Scows

Celilo Canal exit

Little Tumwater
Wheel No. 2

Chiefs Is.

Taffe
Wheels

Tumwater Wheel No. 1

Kramer Scows

Kramer Wheel

Lower China Pete
Wheel

Eightmile Rapids

Columbia River

Upper China Pete
Wheel

SP&S Railroad Bridge

Celilo Falls

Kiska Is.

The Landing

Big Is.

Horseshoe Falls

Celilo Canal
exit

Chiefs Is.

WHEELS OF FORTUNE

BY

FRANCIS SEUFERT

RIVER EVENING

My fondest memories of Oregon are of the Columbia River, the fishing industry and the people connected with it.

As the years ago by, in each late September, during the period of Indian summer with the warm quiet days and cool nights, when the air is smoky from the fires burning in the forest, I am always reminded of evenings such as these nearly 40 years ago when I was buying salmon at the Columbia River at Seufert's Big Tumwater Fishwheel.

It would be in the middle of September when the big fall salmon runs were on and I was at the base of the Big Tumwater Fishwheel, at the back side, away from the river, where we would be receiving salmon. It was generally about 6:00 P.M. on one of those wonderful September nights by the river; warm, not a breath of air moving, peaceful, quiet, nothing to be heard except the muffled sound of the river as it flowed downstream.

My only companion was Jack Johnson, an old time Seufert's employee, who had been fishwheel foreman for years. In the fall he worked the Tumwater fish house. We would be in a little rock cove, the rock walls rising to the west, coarse river sand at our feet, with fish scales for weighing the salmon, the wooden fish box, fish slips and pencil and pike pole.

Jack was not much of a talker, but then on an evening like that there was not much need for talk. A beautiful evening, a joy to be by the river, both of us content, just enjoying life and passing time until the Indians started to bring in their salmon.

We would hear the Indian fisherman before we would see him. We would hear muffled footsteps made by feet wearing gumboots walking over the rough rocks. Often the Indian would have a rope over his shoulder pulling the salmon, still in the river, with a rope strung through the salmon's mouth and gills. With a final grunt the salmon were pulled up on the rocks, and the squaw would put the salmon in gunny sacks, and swinging the sacks over her shoulders, would walk over the rocks making not a sound with her moccasined feet.

It was probably 50 feet to our fish scale set back in the rock cove. The squaws would dump the sack of salmon on the ground, and as the fish fell from the gunny sacks, there would be the sound of firm salmon striking the rocks.

1

By now the Indian would come up and Jack would always speak, calling the Indian by name. The Indian would always reply, "Hello, Jack." Now the salmon were put in the fish box on the scale. I would make the weights by lantern light, and write out the fish ticket, giving it to the Indian fisherman. The Indian would look at his fish ticket, carefully fold it and put it in his pocket. Then the fisherman would say, "Go home now, get some sleep." And Jack would always reply, "You go home, get plenty sleep, tomorrow lots of salmon." The Indian would walk down to the water's edge followed by his squaw and disappear into the darkness.

By now other Indians were arriving with their salmon and the process and words were repeated over and over again with each Indian fisherman. Then about 8:00 P.M. or so it was all over, the last Indian fisherman had left for the village.

We were through buying salmon, no more muffled footsteps on the rocks, just Jack and me, the night quiet and as lovely as ever.

It was time to go home.

THE DALLES

A portage town like The Dalles was always a supply town, a railroad town, a fishing town, an outfitting town for the back country. Of course, for the men working out of The Dalles or in the back country, the town offered girls, card rooms, saloons and later, beer halls. The men working for Seufert's and on the river did visit the local houses. The houses were always run by a white woman who was the madam. The madam of course was always well known, or, if you will, notorious. There were at least three whore houses in The Dalles in those days, sometimes more. These local houses were always upstairs in a local hotel. I would say the best description of these hotels would be to call them working man's hotels. These whore houses had a number of girls working at the same time. The Crescent Rooms had at least three girls, the Washington Hotel always had at least two. The madams considered these first-class whore houses, since they had several girls for the customers to choose from. Up at the Tourist Hotel the madam usually had only one girl at a time. These girls only stayed a week so the customer then had a new choice. The madam at the Tourist Hotel apparently had come from Portland, as the older men always spoke of knowing her years ago in Portland. One thing that no girl ever did was to speak to or recognize one of her customers on the street.

The local whore houses were all respectable operations, no liquor sold on the premises, and no man was ever robbed or rolled on the premises. The entire operation was run with one thought, to satisfy the customer. The madams all knew that if they didn't run a house that the men could trust, word would soon be all over town and they would be out of business.

The men in the cannery and in the fishing operation visited the girls from time to time. How often, I don't know, but these men were always well informed about a new girl being in one of the houses, and all the latest gossip about local houses. In fact, the goings on at the whore houses were always important bits of gossip that had to be thoroughly discussed. One of the men who worked for Seufert's lived with one of the madams for years. She was always referred to as "his girl" and he was quite proud of the fact that at that particular house he got his fun for free while the other men working for the Company had to pay. Of course, the local whore houses were strict in drawing a color line.

3

The girls were all white and the customers were all white. Apparently the whore house operations at The Dalles were profitable because the business flourished until the federal government closed them down during the building of The Dalles Dam. Although the old madams closed up shop and left town, they simply relocated around the dam site on the Washington shore and outside of any town; from that time on the whore houses were real clip joints.

The west wind blew up the Columbia River all summer long, a heavy wind of gale proportions. It blew during all daylight hours, although oftentimes after dark it would quiet down. Sometimes it howled all night long. Out on the rocks or around the cableways, the fishwheels, the seines and so on, you watched your step and your balance when the wind was blowing. To have the wind blow a man off balance was something that seldom happened, but if it did, he could take a nasty fall. When this heavy wind was blowing a gale on the seining bars it created a heavy moving cloud of sand called blow sand. It got into everything, your bed, your clothes, your food, and of course any machinery that had the slightest coating of oil on it. The machinery would become coated with oily dirt. This constant heavy blowing wind was by far the most annoying thing about being out and around any fishing operation. It was tiring and drove the men in on themselves.

In the original fishing operations and around the cannery, of course, they used horses, and where you had horses, flies were a nuisance.

Out around the river on the Indian fishing sites, moisture seemed to take care of the fly problem. They really were not a great nuisance there. But around the mess houses in the spring and summer, flies were a real nuisance, and with the coming of cool weather in the fall, flies moving into the mess houses were a bad problem. The flies were thick and into everything and everywhere. You just put up with the flies, cussed and tolerated a bad situation. When the men entered the cook house in the fall of the year they made jokes such as, "Today the flies are bad so today we get raisin cake." On the seine bars when the wind blew and the dust and sand got in everything, that was the day the men said they would get spice cake. Another favorite joke for the men was that chocolate pudding was called liver pudding. You could say the men had a crude sense of humor, but needless to say, none of the cooks ever appreciated such humor.

4

SALMON

Salmon were always referred to as fish. All Chinook salmon were fish. A steelhead, blueback or a silverside was always referred to by its proper name. If you talked to a fisherman and he said he had fish, you knew he was talking about Chinook salmon. If he had a steelhead on the boat, he would tell you he had steelhead. In the salmon cannery, of course, you sold canned salmon or canned fish. What you really were referring to was the fact that you were offering canned Chinook salmon. If you sold a buyer canned salmon, you knew he was talking about canned Chinook salmon and under no conditions would you ever sell him or ship canned steelhead or bluebacks or silversides. Canned steelhead salmon and canned silverside salmon were always offered to the buyers and sold to the public simply as choice Columbia River salmon.

In the salmon cannery none of the workmen knew the niceties that distinguished a fancy Columbia River Chinook salmon from a choice Columbia River Chinook salmon or a standard Columbia River Chinook salmon. So in the cannery they were always referred to as No. 1s, No. 2s and No. 3s. No. 1s were fancy Columbia River salmon, No. 2s were choice Columbia River salmon and No. 3s were standard Columbia River salmon.

On the cooler, if there was no mark, it was a fancy Columbia River Chinook salmon. If the Chinamen tied a little piece of tin and looped it over the edge of the cooler, it was a No. 2 salmon, and if they tied a piece of burlap string on it, it was a No. 3 salmon. Steelhead and silverside salmon were distinguished by taking a piece of baling wire and twisting a small piece of it around the edge of the cooler. The Chinamen knew no English and the white crew knew no Chinese so of course marking the coolers with a string or piece of tin was an easy way for both sides to communicate.

All canned salmon were sold to the consumer on the basis of color. The redder the meat in a can of salmon, the higher the price, and as the color of a can of salmon became whiter, the quality and the price of a can dropped. Now the reddest of all salmon was the Columbia River blueback running in the spring. He was of the sockeye or red salmon species, although a Columbia River blueback was a native of the Columbia River, spawning in the lakes of the Upper Columbia and Snake rivers. Wallowa Lake was at one time a big producer of bluebacks. Of course, this source of prime Columbia River bluebacks was destroyed when Wallowa Lake's lower end was dammed to supply water for irrigation. These Columbia River bluebacks were rich in oil with a pleasant mild flavor. Dams and irrigation had pretty much destroyed the bluebacks on the Columbia River by the middle 1930s, although some appear from year to year.

Columbia River Chinooks had beautiful color, although not as red as the bluebacks. I think they had a better, richer flavor. The salmon were large and the meat flaky. You could actually lift one layer of salmon flesh from the other after you had emptied the salmon from the can, and of course a Columbia River spring Chinook salmon was really rich in oil. The Columbia River spring Chinook was the top quality salmon of the canned salmon business, and though a very big percentage of the pack went to New York City, the demand was never really satisfied. The Columbia River fancy spring salmon spawned in the headwaters of the Columbia River.

In August the Chinook salmon on the Columbia River produced what we called a choice Chinook. They had a nice color, but not as nice as the spring Chinook. And though a nice flavor, still not as rich as the spring Chinook. And while they had plenty of oil, these August and September Chinooks were not as rich in oil as the spring Chinook. But although they brought a lower price, they made up half the salmon pack on the Columbia River and there was a market for them. Seufert's sold carloads of choice Chinooks under different brand names year after year in both the Memphis, Tennessee, and New York City markets. These choice Chinooks in the 1940s made up the backbone of the Co-

lumbia River salmon pack, but these choice Chinooks, too, were finally destroyed along with the Columbia River fishing and cannery business when The Dalles, McNary and Lower Snake River dams were built. These choice Chinooks spawned from above Arlington, Oregon, to Pasco, and on up the main stem of the Columbia River and the Lower Snake to Lewiston.

These dams formed large stagnant pools of slack water above them, permitting the Snake River and the Columbia River to drop their loads of silt on the spawning beds behind these dams. Once these gravel bars used for spawning were silted over, the salmon had no place where he could reproduce his kind. The dams with their quiet pools of backwater behind them completely changed the habitat that the Columbia River salmon needed: a free-flowing river, gravel bars and cool water to reproduce their young. When Man changed the Columbia River from a free-flowing stream to a series of quiet water pools, the Columbia River salmon were doomed. No amount of propaganda nor money will ever bring them back. With the completion of McNary Dam, the Columbia River salmon quality rushed downhill and has continued to deteriorate ever since. I say in regret it is not uncommon today to get a Columbia River Chinook that tastes muddy.

The salmon caught by Seufert's at The Dalles in spring and fall were in their prime. Probably nowhere else on the Columbia River were the salmon in such prime condition. These fish had left the sea and had been in fresh water long enough so that their bodies were free of all sea lice. Their stomachs were empty of all food, since a salmon does not eat any food after he enters fresh water. The cold river water had firmed-up the flesh so the salmon were firm and hard. At The

6

Dalles the salmon had many miles of river ahead to reach the spawning grounds on the Upper Columbia and Snake rivers, so their bodies were rich in oil. As they passed The Dalles in their prime they were unsurpassed by any other salmon in the world. Spring salmon caught at The Dalles and brought to our cannery were often so firm that it was nearly impossible to pack them into salmon cans. A fresh salmon slice would actually jump up on one side of the can when you pushed the slice down on the other side. It was common practice to leave such salmon unbutchered on the cannery floor overnight so it would lose some of its firmness. The Chinese salmon packers could then push it into the cans the next morning. How the crews cussed when they had to hand pack such firm fish. When you pitched them onto the cannery floor the salmon actually sounded the same as when a man strikes his leather riding boots with a buggy whip. There hasn't been fine salmon like this on the Columbia River for years.

Prime steelhead salmon in the Columbia River also came up the river in August and September, with September being the big month at The Dalles. These steelhead were fine fish. In fact, no other stream on the Pacific Coast produced a steelhead salmon that could begin to compare to the Columbia River steelhead in quality. It was a nice size salmon, firm, with good color and a nice flavor and nice oil. Another important thing about a steelhead, it kept its color after canning. In some respects a Columbia River steelhead was an all-round ideal salmon for processing. It would ship well to the fresh-fish market when packed in ice. Also a steelhead was a top salmon for freezing, probably freezing better than any other fish; and of course a steelhead produced a nice can of salmon. All of these canned steelhead were sold as choice Columbia River salmon. From the Company's standpoint when you bought a steelhead from a fisherman you got just what you purchased. A steelhead could be used either for fresh shipping, freezing or canning. Of course in the spring steelhead were of poor quality and we never bothered with them if we could help it. In the spring a steelhead salmon was returning downriver to the sea, having just spawned. They were long, narrow and of poor quality. We always referred to these spring spawned-out steelhead as snakes.

In the 1920s there were almost no Chinook salmon at The Dalles during the fall seasons that started on September 10. Some years there was not one single Chinook caught at The Dalles, and when any were taken in the fall at The Dalles it was a rarity. It was not until 1933 that the big fall Chinook run showed up on the Upper Columbia River. Why they came then, or from where, no one knows. Everyone was taken completely by surprise. No one had ever seen anything like it before. These fall Chinook at The Dalles were of good quality, and the size of the fall Chinook salmon runs surpassed any fall salmon runs that had ever been seen on the upper river before, but at the same time the steelhead and the silversides that used to make up the fall salmon runs just disappeared. They were completely replaced by these fall Chinooks. There were a few steelhead left, but the silversides just completely disappeared. In 1945 I had a salmon cannery foreman call me over, point to a silverside, the first I had seen in years, on the fish house floor, and the foreman asked me what kind of salmon it was—he had never seen one before. The big fall Chinook salmon completely dominated the fall salmon runs at The Dalles after that 1933 run, at least as long as Seufert's was in the fish business at The Dalles.

On the Columbia River in commercial fishing we always spoke of seasons. The spring season opened on May 1st and continued to August 25th. From 6:00 P.M. Saturday night until 6:00 P.M. Sunday on each weekend during the season all fishing gear had to be out of the river. Closure was strict. Then at 6:00 P.M. Sunday night you could start fishing again until the following Saturday evening. These 24-hour closed periods were to allow sufficient salmon to pass up the Columbia River to perpetuate the run. They did accomplish their purpose, for the spring salmon runs did hold up in volume year after year until the U.S. government started building dams on the Columbia River. It was customary that although fishing gear had to be pulled from the river by 6:00 P.M. Saturday nights, the states of Oregon and Washington would allow you reasonable time to deliver your catch to a buying station. I would say one hour was generally considered a reasonable time for a fisherman to deliver his salmon to a receiving station. Any fisherman who had salmon in his possession after that time was considered guilty of having illegally caught the salmon in his possession and was subject to arrest.

During the spring fishing season on the Columbia River all salmon caught were considered spring salmon until August 1st. This date was generally agreed on with the fishermen's union because salmon caught after that date were no longer considered prime spring salmon and they brought a lower price. The Columbia River Chinooks by August 1st were not prime fish. They had started to lose their fine color, and were not so rich in oil. These August salmon were canned and sold as choice Chinooks. Now the big August run of choice Chinooks that entered the Columbia River at Astoria about August 10th did not reach The Dalles until September. In other words, Astoria canneries canned choice Chinooks in August, while at The Dalles we canned choice Chinooks in September, although the salmon were from the same run. But even at The Dalles by the middle of August the salmon were no longer prime spring Chinooks.

All salmon fishing on the Columbia River ceased at 12 noon on August 25th. The season remained closed until September 10th. The season then opened on September 10th at 12 noon and continued into the winter. There was no closed period for the fall run. You could fish 24 hours a day, seven days a week until the salmon were gone because of cold weather. This season regulation was the most successful on the Columbia River. The salmon runs under this regulation lasted for over 50 years, the salmon runs holding at their usual or expected volume all that time. The August run of salmon at Astoria was huge and at The Dalles September always produced a lot of fish. The thing about this particular salmon regulation that differed from the usual practice was that the closed season came at the middle of the run. The Astoria fishermen took huge amounts of August Chinook salmon out of the first part of the run, and on August 25th the season was closed until September 10th, thus allowing the middle of this huge run to pass up the Columbia River to the spawning beds unhampered by any commercial fishing. Then on September 10th, after the bulk of the center of this salmon run had passed Celilo Falls, the commercial salmon season reopened and the commercial fishermen at both Astoria and The Dalles were permitted to put their fishing gear back into the river again. This particular closed season allowed the escapement of the heart of the August salmon run. Commercial fishing on both the Lower and Upper Columbia took only the first half of the run and the end of the run. This balanced out the escapement and the run continued at its normal size all through the years. This was the only escapement program that allowed the middle of the salmon run to pass, and it did perpetuate the great August Chinook runs of the Columbia River.

On the Columbia River up until the early 1930s you always heard the term Royal Chinooks. The term Royal Chinook was used to describe the big June Chinook salmon on the Columbia River. Up at Seufert's the men often referred to such salmon as channel fish. These Royal Chinooks were big salmon, starting at 30 pounds and on up. These salmon were not necessarily long, but the body was deep from the top of the back to the bottom of the belly. It was this depth of the fish that gave them their weight and size. These fish came in June, huge in size and in prime condition. Downriver they were called June hogs. Because of their size, when you packed them into cans, only one slice of salmon was necessary to fill the can. When the customer purchased this can of Royal Chinook salmon and took it home and emptied it, he found just one nice chunk of salmon the size of the can, rich in oil, fine color, excellent texture and superb flavor. This salmon really deserved to be called Royal Chinook. It had no peer in the canned salmon markets of the world.

These Royal Chinooks were going to travel a thousand miles or so before spawning in the upper reaches of the Columbia River beyond the Canadian border. These huge salmon were plentiful. You would often get several tons a day during June, but this entire run of salmon was wiped out and destroyed when the federal government built Grand Coulee Dam. No provision was made by the federal government to try to save this fine run of prime Chinook salmon on their way beyond the Canadian boundary to spawn.

The fishermen claimed that these huge spring Chinook came up the Columbia following the steamship channel, and of course the regular passage of the steamships up the Columbia River channel to Portland hindered the gillnet fishermen from fishing continually in the main river channel. When a fast moving steamer came up or down the channel, the gillnetters would have to pick up their nets and get out of the way. Anyway, after the federal government built Grand Coulee Dam, these runs of Columbia River Royal Chinooks were destroyed forever.

In the spring, Chinooks were a fine color so you didn't have to worry, but by late September, they would lose their color. When you canned these Chinooks you had to sell the can as a standard Chinook for less money than if they had graded out as a choice salmon. You always watched the salmon the fishermen delivered to you. As a general rule a bright fish was a good salmon and you could depend on his color, but if at any time you questioned the salmon's color you got your pocket knife out and started cutting.

When fishermen were out on the river, both white and Indian, the salmon they caught had to be delivered to the fish buyer in prime condition—fresh, with the skin moist. The hot summer wind of The Dalles could dry out a salmon lying on the rocks in no time. The hot sun would actually cook a salmon lying on the rocks, and hunks of meat would fall off the salmon when you picked him up. Just as soon as a fisherman took a salmon from the river and laid him on the rocks or in a fish box, he immediately covered the fish with a wet gunny sack. From time to time all day long he would have to moisten the gunny sacks covering the salmon, but as long as he kept the salmon under the moist sacks the salmon would stay as fresh as the moment they were taken from the river. I might add that all the fishermen kept their salmon moist and cool using these wet gunny sacks, so that when they delivered their salmon to you there was no chance you would reject a fish and lose just that much money. If you would not buy a fish that had been spoiled by the wind and the sun, the fishermen knew no one else would buy it either.

We had one more species of salmon in the Columbia River and this was a silverside salmon. Up to the early 1930s silversides were common in the Columbia. Then after that date they just disappeared around The Dalles. They were a good salmon, medium red color with a nice flavor and rich in oil. Silversides canned at The Dalles were sold as choice Columbia River salmon. In fact, in selling choice Columbia River salmon, unless the buyers specified the species, we would use either choice Chinooks or steelhead or silversides. The trade would accept any of these three species as choice Columbia River salmon, apparently having no preference.

Another thing should be mentioned about the quality of the Columbia River salmon before the dams were built on the river. This Columbia River salmon was, as I have said, all hand packed, rich in oil, the salmon producing all the natural oil needed. The only thing added to those cans of salmon was a pinch of salt.

Today on the Columbia River, the salmon are so dry and have so little natural oil in their bodies that some canneries actually add salmon oil to the cans to produce a halfway passable product. But this salmon with oil added in no way qualified as the strictly fancy Columbia River Chinook, if you use the fancy Columbia River Chinook salmon standards of the days before the dam-building on the Columbia River. And I might add that the old-time Columbia River canned salmon buyers in the big New York City wholesale houses would not have had a can of salmon in their warehouses that was of such poor quality that you had to add salmon oil to it to make it presentable to the public. But that was long ago.

I want to talk about "the big day," the day that you took the most salmon of any day of the fall fishing season. The commercial season opened at 12 o'clock noon on September 10th. There were always lots of salmon in the river and everybody fishing would do well. Without fail September 11th would produce more fish than the day before. September 12th would always produce more fish than September 11th, and September 13th more than the 12th. Year after year and without exception, September 13th was the biggest day of the fall salmon season. By September 14th the height of the salmon run had passed. Each day would then fall off some, although the salmon catches would remain large. Then on September 20th (or the 21st or 22nd), the fall equinox would usually produce stormy weather. It would generally rain. This rain seemed to signal the salmon to rush up the river. By September 21st the fall salmon rush would be over. From then on you would get fish but not a whole lot each day. From that time on the gillnetters would leave one after another

10

and the Indian fishermen would leave for their reservations. By October 1st most would be gone. There would still be some salmon left in the river and Seufert's would continue their operations down to the time the seine was catching a ton of salmon a day. Then Seufert's would pull the seine off, generally the first week of October or so. By this time nearly all the fishermen had left the river and it hardly paid to get steam up at the cannery to can the few salmon being taken from the river. By the second week in October, Seufert's generally closed the cannery and their entire fishing and packing operation for the year.

Then came the winter fishing. That was really from November 1st to May 1st. Seufert's fishing operation fully stopped by November 1st and didn't start again until the following May 1st. As far as Seufert's was concerned, there were no fish in the river during the winter months, at least not enough fish to fool with, even for the fresh-fish market. The fishermen, too, felt there were just no fish during the winter months. Because of the cold and miserable weather around The Dalles in the winter, no price for salmon was high enough to get any fishermen out on the river. I understand that once or twice the Indians tried to fish at Celilo in the winter but they could fish all day long and not take a single salmon during those cold, miserable months. Seufert's did put in the Little Tumwater Wheel during one winter, but it caught nothing.

FISHWHEELS

Francis Seufert, March 17, 1971, continuing to answer questions that were sent to him by Mr. Vaughan from the Oregon Historical Society about the Seufert Brothers Company, salmon packers, The Dalles, Oregon.

The first fishwheels were built by Seufert's at The Dalles. Seufert's Fishwheel No. 1 was built in 1884-85, and fished in 1885. It was built directly in back of Seufert's Cannery located three miles east of The Dalles on the Oregon side of the Columbia River, at Seufert's, Oregon. Fishwheel No. 1 was the only fishwheel Seufert's ever had that killed a man. F. A. Seufert and my grandmother were sitting on some rocks along the river bank watching the workmen construct this wheel. An A-frame used for hoisting timbers collapsed, striking one of the workmen and killing him. Fishwheel No. 1 was never much of a financial success. It never really caught enough fish to pay for the fishwheel licenses. It was destroyed in the high water of 1894. Grandfather Seufert then rebuilt the wheel in 1895 and it fished until 1914 when it was completely worn out. It was never fished again.

The next was known as Seufert's Fishwheel No. 2, and was built in 1885, directly behind Seufert's China-house. It was just west of where Fivemile Creek emptied into the Columbia River. Fishwheel No. 2 was not much of a financial success either, and really got very few salmon. It too was destroyed in the high water of 1894. Fishwheel No. 2 was not rebuilt until the fall of 1912 and the spring of 1913, and it first fished in the 1913 season and continued until 1926. It was a very poor wheel also and hardly caught enough salmon to pay for the license. Financially it was more-or-less a failure and was kept in operation just because it was there.

In 1886 Seufert's built fishwheels No. 3 and No. 4. They were built on the old Whitcomb Fishery property about a mile upriver east of Seufert's Cannery. No. 3 was built opposite Big Eddy, and I am speaking now of the Big Eddy buildings that were built by the Army Engineers upon the completion of The Dalles-Celilo Canal in 1915. No. 3 was a good wheel, caught very well as a high-water wheel. The next was No. 4, built in 1886. It was about half-a-mile upstream from No. 3.

It was a fine high-water wheel and it caught real well. Both No. 3 and No. 4 were also destroyed in the high water of 1894, and were rebuilt and fished in 1895. They continued in operation until 1926.

Seufert's built a small fishwheel outside of Fishwheel No. 4 on a small channel out toward the main stem of the Columbia River. This was called Fishwheel No. 4½. It was built in the winter of 1893 and 1894, and was destroyed in the 1894 flood and never rebuilt. In fact, the high water of 1894 destroyed it before it could ever do any fishing.

The most famous fishwheel on the Columbia was Seufert's Fishwheel No. 5, built in 1887 on the Oregon shore at the head of Fivemile Rapids. This was the most successful financially. It was the wheel that all the fish wars were fought over and talked about. No. 5 was the big money-maker of all the wheels Seufert's ever owned. It was also located specifically where the original old Fort Dalles east boundary line extended to the Columbia River.

In 1889 and 1890 Seufert's built No. 6 at Tumwater, Oregon, opposite our present Celilo Falls site. In those days Celilo Falls was known as Tumwater Falls, and the station that Seufert's had on the railroad opposite this fishwheel was called Tumwater. Tumwater Wheel was a good wheel although she was a low-water wheel and often fished in the low-water springs. After a bit this wheel was called Tumwater No. 1. A small wheel was built outside of No. 1 and was called Tumwater No. 2. It was a small removable wheel located on the river. It had to be rebuilt each fall and taken down at the end of every fall so that it wouldn't wash out in spring. Downstream a short distance, Tumwater

No. 3 was built in the early 1890s by Seufert's. It was destroyed by ice in 1899 and never rebuilt. All of Seufert's fishwheels were destroyed by the famous 1894 flood except No. 5 and it was badly damaged.

Seufert's then built No. 6 between No. 5 and the Oregon shore. It was built high up on the rocks in a place that would only fish if there was another flood like 1894. This fishwheel never operated because there never was another 1894 flood. There was enough water to operate this wheel in 1948, but by then the fishwheels had been outlawed; the fishwheel did run because it got away when the high water reached it, but of course it didn't catch anything.

Seufert's built one more wheel, called the Cement Wheel, downstream from No. 5 on the Oregon side of the Columbia River. It was called the Cement Wheel because it was the first Seufert's ever built using concrete. It was a low-water wheel, one that you built in the summer and fished in the late summer and fall. When the fishing season was over it had to be removed because, if not, it would wash away in the spring floods.

Seufert's had many other fishwheels, but they were built by other people. Seufert's later bought and operated them, but the wheels I have just mentioned were the only ones Seufert's actually built and installed themselves.

In answer to other questions from Mr. Vaughan: Who designed the wheels?

As far as I know these fishwheels were probably designed from those originally built at Cascade Locks. I understand these wheels at Cascade Locks were probably built in 1878 and 1879. By the time F. . Seufert was in The Dalles, in 1881, he apparently had gone to Portland many times on the passenger train. He passed these fishwheels and saw them operate in the Cascades and there had gotten his idea about building and operating fishwheels at The Dalles. The early pictures we have of the old fishwheels that were built between 1884 and the 1894 flood show them to be identical in design to those built at Cascade Locks. After 1894 when Seufert's rebuilt their wheels, the design was different. All the fishwheels down at Cascade Locks had only four gin posts. Those that Seufert's had at The Dalles had at least eight gin posts, and there was a very distinct difference in their appearance. I assume that Seufert's fishwheels had the eight gin posts because where they were located the river rose much higher to the deck of the wheel. With eight posts it was much easier to raise the wheel out of the water and keep all the operating parts out of the water when the floods were on, and a fishwheel with eight gin posts was less complicated, easier and probably cheaper to build.

As far as I know the timbers for the fishwheels came from Portland or Cascade Locks and were shipped to The Dalles on the railroad. All of the iron work, I would assume, came from fabricators and wholesalers in Portland. The wheel itself was assembled on the chosen site. All of the working parts of the fishwheels were made locally and they were built by local people who lived in The Dalles and were hired by Seufert's during the construction.

Who did the iron work for the wheels?

Well, Seufert's always had their own blacksmiths and all of the iron work on the wheels was done in Seufert's blacksmith shop. Actually there was very little iron work on the early fishwheels other than the long bolts that were made on a blacksmith's forge. Nearly everything else was wood. Seufert's always had a carpenter on the payroll. Anything that you wanted to build was in those days made out of wood and the carpenter put it together. If there was any iron work to be done then the blacksmith made it and it was attached to the woodwork.

While Seufert's always had their own blacksmith, The Dalles had a number of excellent blacksmiths who could do any kind of work, and our work would be taken to the local blacksmith in The Dalles where at that time they also had their own local iron works. This was owned locally and could turn out almost any kind of work. They even repaired steam locomotives in The Dalles iron works.

Did someone in the local railroad yards work on the construction of the wheels?

If you had difficult wheel work that an ordinary carpenter or blacksmith couldn't do, they then hired men from the old railroad shops in The Dalles to come out and do that particular piece of work.

How were the wheels lowered into the water?

The wheels were attached to a long cable and went over a sheave directly above the fishwheel. This cable went over to another sheave and from there the cable dropped down to a box. This box was called a counterweight. It was a box about twelve feet long and about two feet deep and two feet wide. You tossed scrap iron into the box until the scrap iron weight just about countered the weight of the fishwheel. When they were just about in balance it was very simple and easy to lower and raise the fishwheel out of the water.

The fishwheel, that is, the wheel itself, rode in a sash. Attached to the sash was a heavy cable that went directly above the sash to the top of the gin post where there was a sheave that directed the cable along just above the gin post and caps. This cable went down to the lower end of the fishwheel structure. Here another sheave was located and the cable rode over it and down to the counterweight. At the sheave directly above the counterweight, its shaft or axle extended out and over the fishwheel deck some two feet. Attached at the end of this shaft was the bullwheel, a sheave some three or four feet in diameter. Around this sheave and riding in the sheave's groove was a rope. The ends of this rope dropped down to the fishwheel deck and by pulling on this rope you caused the sheave at the upper end of the rope to turn; as it turned the cable from the counterweight was either raised or lowered. The weight of the balanced counterweight, plus the pull of a man on the rope passing around the bullwheel, was enough to raise or lower the fishwheel with little effort.

Fishwheels had a wheel, the wheel had arms, and the arms formed three dips. A fishwheel fished in a channel. The lower end of the channel was open, the upper end of the channel had a drift gate to keep the driftwood out when the wheel was operating. The fishwheel had a deck and maybe a watchman's shack. The timbers above the deck and on each side of the channel used to support the fishwheel when it was raised were called the gin posts. On top of the gin posts were the caps. A fishwheel operated by the current flowing downstream through the fishwheel channel. The arms of a fishwheel were attached to a flange. The flange was attached to the shaft. The shaft at each end fitted

into bushings. These bushings were in a sash. A sash was built the same as a window sash, only larger and much sturdier. A fishwheel was raised by the bullwheel and the line that lifted the fishwheel was called the cable. Inside the fishwheel dips, between the second and third arms of the dips, was the fish chute. The salmon were caught in the dips. They slid down and out the fish chute into the fish box. From the fish box the fish were brought up to the fishwheel deck in an elevator. A ladder led down from the fishwheel deck to the fish box. After the salmon were caught by the fishwheel and slid down the wheel chute into the fish box it was thought to be, by the uninformed, an efficient method of fishing with a minimum of human effort.

Only now the real work began. You climbed down the interior ladder into a fish box sometimes fifty feet deep. With a pike pole you piked the salmon from the fish box into the elevator. If the wheel caught a fifty-pound salmon while you were in the fish box (some four feet or so square and wet and slippery), the plunging salmon could knock you down or beat your legs black and blue. Anyway, you got the big salmon into the wheel elevator and then climbed back up the fifty feet of wet ladder, no lights, to the fishwheel deck. All you have to do is hoist the elevator. If the company furnished a gas engine to operate the elevator, not so bad. If no gas engine, you wound the elevator up on a hand winch. Before long you knew just how much time it took to lift those salmon fifty feet to the deck, plus a lot of sweat and hard work. Anyway, once the salmon were on the fishwheel deck you climbed back down into the fish box and started over again. So much for the ridiculous statement about a fishwheel being efficient and using a minimum of human effort. And of course there was always the danger of jabbing the steel point of the pike pole into your foot.

Fishwheel dips were covered with wire netting. The men called it fishwheel wire. Fishwheel wire cam in rolls and the men cut it to size. Fishwheels were greased, never oiled.

When the drift gate was lifted up so the driftwood could drift down through the channel and float out into the open river, the drift gate was said to be pulled. When the drift gate was lowered, it was then said to be put back. Just before a drift gate was pulled, the wheel was lifted, and then the jammed up driftwood would float down the channel unobstructed and, hopefully, out into the river. The drift gate then was put back into place and the wheel was lowered and could start operating again. People think that fishwheels operated continually, hour after hour after hour. If the river was full of driftwood, it would pile up behind the drift gate. And at least once every 30 minutes you would have to stop the wheel, lift it out of the channel, pull the drift gate, let the drift pass down into the channel and out into the river, then return the drift gate and put it back, lower the wheel and start fishing again.

The fishwheel channels were excavated with black powder and later with dynamite. About the only modern tools employed when the wheels were erected was a block-and-tackle and an A-frame, and that's not so modern. The main ingredient was simply a strong back.

Seufert's was involved in a federal tax case in Portland. One of the contractors that had worked on The Dalles-Celilo Canal and built a fishwheel channel for Seufert's testified in court that a fishwheel channel cost twice as much to build as it did to dig the rock out of The Dalles-Celilo Canal. He testified that when he worked on the main channel of The Dalles-Celilo Canal he could use modern equipment, and in the confined space of Seufert's channels he had to do everything by hand. When the fishwheel channels were blasted out of solid rock, above them wooden cribs were often built and filled with rock about the size of a man's head. It was trucked in little hand trucks, one rock at a time, out to the channel and dumped into the cribs. In later years some of the old cribs started to rot and were covered with concrete.

A fishwheel and its parts were never painted nor were the wooden cribs painted. The smell of paint would drive the fish away from a fishwheel channel. In fact, the first year after a fishwheel channel had been blasted out of the rock, the lingering smell of powder and fresh concrete would prevent a fishwheel from fishing well until all the odor had been washed out of the channel. Still, a fishwheel deck could be washed off with a hose and the water from the deck would flow into the channel to be immediately flushed away down the channel with no effect upon the salmon entering the channel.

A fishwheel always fished well in clear water for several reasons. One, the salmon swimming in the channel saw the tip of the wheel approaching. The dip between the last arm of one dip and the first arm of the following gave an unobstructed way upriver and he could pass the turning dips. But when the dips swung down and blocked the channel to the salmon's upstream passage, the salmon dropped downstream into the advancing dips. Now the lower end of the dip was down and below the salmon, rising now to the surface behind him, and the salmon was caught in the dip.

When the river was muddy and the salmon swam into the dip, instead of dropping back and being caught, he simply spooked, turned and raced madly downstream and beat the dip before it could rise to the surface and entrap him. A salmon caught in clear water in a fishwheel simply saw an obstruction in the water ahead of him and would slowly back away, and slowly backing away was too late. Of course when a wheel was off bottom the dips were above the channel floor. When the salmon saw the dips moving toward him, he simply ducked under it and swam on up the channel and out into the open river. Once the fishwheel was off bottom, it caught very few salmon.

A fishwheel operating properly would make three to five complete revolutions a minute. All the parts are bolted together. If something got in the wheel and started to break the wheel apart, it would break clean at the bolts, as you would break a match or a stick. If you used spikes, the wood split sometimes for many feet. About the only tools a man needed on the fishwheels were a crescent wrench, a hammer and a crowbar.

You always fished a fishwheel with her shaft just above the water, but when night time came and the river was rising, you raised the wheel so the shaft was at least a foot or two above the river. When you came back in the morning the shaft would then still be above the water. A good fishwheel foreman would know, or at least be able to guess intelligently, whether river was going to rise or fall during the night.

Fishwheel parts were generally standard and in-terchangeable. The length of the arms when they were made standard was 20 feet, but at one time Seufert's tried to use 24-foot arms which made a 48-foot wheel; but when this wheel was lowered to operate, it was found the arms would only go 20 feet into the water, after which the wheel would float. After this experiment, Seufert's always left their fishwheel arms at 20 feet. After the passing of the high water when the channel had no water flowing through it, you then said her channel was dry. If during high water the fishwheel itself was off bottom, you then said she can't fish, her wheel is off bottom.

As I said earlier, the first fishwheel Seufert's had that used concrete was called the Cement Wheel. Henry Wickman told me that when they worked on this wheel none of the men had any experience pouring concrete. They thought the concrete had to be thick, like mud, so they actually shovelled all the concrete into that wheel. None of it was poured. If the water flowed through that fishwheel channel too fast, it would tear the wheel apart. The way you slowed down the water was to go in the channel above the wheel and place huge concrete beams or baffles. They were generally about two feet by three feet laid square across the channel. You put in as many as needed to slow the water down and wherever you thought they would do the most good. If you found that you were in error, the concrete beams could then be knocked out with a jack hammer and you did no damage to the fishwheel channel whatsoever.

Once a fishwheel was built, under the law, another fishwheel couldn't be built by you or anyone else within 800 feet above or below that wheel. After Seufert's built a wheel and it was successful the Company always bought the land downstream from the good wheel. This was simply to protect the good wheel so that no one could change the shoreline and the water conditions below to affect her fishing ability.

Here are some other deck terms that were used around a fishwheel. A small wheel with a grooved rim to guide the cable was called a sheave. A winch with a crank turned by hand (used to raise or lower anything on the deck of a fishwheel) was called a crab. Crabs had no brakes, a rope turned several times around the shaft of a crab if pulled tight by hand acted as a brake; it was very efficient. After something was hoisted with a crab, a 2x4 put between the spokes served to lock the crab into position. When some heavy object was being lowered with a crab, sometimes the men (after removing the 2x4) would let the crab run free. The handle on the crab would spin at a high rate of speed, so fast it was almost a blur when it turned. You stood well back and away from the crab at this time as a flying handle had broken more than one man's nose or arms. Working on a fishwheel was not dangerous, but carelessness could result in a serious injury, or at least a painful one.

I will now talk a wee bit about the fishwheel channel. Fishwheel channels were wider at the upper end or entrance than the wheel channel itself. The wheel channel was that part of the channel that the wheel turned in. The upper end of a channel was some two feet on each side, or some four feet wider than the wheel channel. The wheel channel was one foot wider than the fishwheel. That is, a fishwheel turning in a channel had six inches of clearance between the channel wall and the wheel on each side. The down end of

the channel was never wider than the upper channel. This must be emphasized. Salmon were attracted to a fishwheel entrance by the volume and velocity of water. You never had too much of either as long as the salmon could swim into the channel. It was not uncommon to narrow the lower end of a channel where it entered the river just to speed-up the velocity of water leaving the mouth.

F. A. Seufert had a son, Willie, who ruined No. 5 fishwheel. While F. A. Seufert was in Los Angeles for the winter, his son took a crew up to No. 5 and blew the mouth off. He thought if No. 5's channel entrance was twice as wide, twice as many salmon would enter. After that fiasco, No. 5 was ruined and she never fished well because wheels were voted out by the state of Oregon before No. 5's channel could be restored to its original effectiveness.

Yes, it was a quiet business. A fishwheel ran very silently. There was no sound at all except the gentle slap, slap, slap, of the wheel as the cross braces entered the water. The watchmen always talked about how silent the wheels were at night, how lonely it was and how long the nights were.

On a fishwheel, all the wooden parts were continually being submerged in the river and the wooden arms and other wooden parts were not only soaked but very nearly waterlogged. Even if two wooden parts rubbed or moved against each other the slightest bit, this continuous soaking made the wood soft and their working or rubbing together would produce no sound. Any piece of wood which rubbed against another piece of wood or steel and made a shrill squeaking of any kind around a fishwheel channel might scare the fish.

18

Noise of any kind was just not tolerated and any man working around a fishwheel, down in the fish box, down in the wet, always wore gum boots that made no noise. And of course no one shouted around a fishwheel. A loud shout meant trouble or was a warning. No one raised his voice except in an emergency around the wheel or any fishing gear. Loud talking also scared the fish, so any man doing such a thing would be told to shut up and if he didn't he would be sent to the office for his time. Also, we were living in a day and age where when men worked, they didn't talk. A man who talked all the time was considered a poor worker. After all, if he spent all his time talking how was he to get anything done?

Seufert's fishwheel scows were operated on shares for years by Henry Wickman. The Company furnished the fishwheel scows ready to fish, as well as the pick-up boats, the fishwheel licenses and the fishing sites. Henry Wickman fished for so much a pound for salmon delivered to the cannery. The Company furnished the fuel for the pick-up boats but Wickman hired and selected his own men to help operate the fishwheel scows. Wickman was a highly skilled swiftwater boatman and fishwheel operator. He operated Seufert's fishwheel scows until the 1934 closure. During the rest of each year, Wickman supervised all of Seufert's heavy construction work, having built Seufert's scows and rebuilt all of Seufert's fishwheels.

When Seufert's built a fishwheel scow they found that the planking on both the deck and the bottom had to run across the deck. This kept the scow's hull stiff. At one time they built several fishwheel scows with the planking running lengthwise from bow to stern, and these scows were not much good. The hull was too limber and constantly worked loose and leaked badly.

A fishwheel scow was just a wooden scow with a fishwheel on one end, always on the stern of the scow. A fishwheel scow fished well in muddy water because a salmon couldn't see the dip before it caught him; in clear water the salmon could see the dip clearly, so he darted to one side to avoid the dip and swam on his way. There is no end to stories of how fishwheel scows caught so many salmon that they sank under the weight of the fish. These are nothing more than old wives' tales. Because the wheel was on one end, scows were easily sunk. The weight of the wheel at the end of two arms extending some 20 feet from the scow's stern put a tremendous weight on the stern itself. The leverage created by the weight of the arms made scows very unstable, sinking very low in the water at the wheel end with the bow of the scow raised clear of the water itself. The fish box was also in the stern of the scow, directly in back of the fishwheel itself. If the scow wheel was catching well, a ton and a half of salmon in the fish box would add enough additional weight at one end of the scow to sink her. If you were in charge of the fishing scow's operation, you were always told in no uncertain terms not to let her sink. When the weight of the fish box was forcing the hull of the scow deeper into the water you pulled the wheel up until her fish box was emptied. Then you lowered her wheel and started fishing all over again.

A few terms used on fishwheel scows. When they leaked, which they all did, they were bailed, never pumped. All that was needed to bail a scow was a strong back. Each scow was equipped with an old-fashioned farm kitchen pump with a long handle. After the water had been pumped out and the pump started to suck air, you got down on your hands and knees and bailed water with a five-gallon kerosene can. When you were through bailing you said she was dry.

Prior to 1915, Seufert's fishwheel scows in the winter were beached in the cove just above the Lone Pine Tree Indian village. Upon completion of The Dalles-Celilo Canal, Seufert's scows were wintered in the canal basin at the fishery. On a windy day with the west wind blowing as the scow wheel turned, drops of water were blown from the wheel wire onto the deck. It wouldn't be too long before the amount of water blown on her deck would cause her to start to sink. To prevent this, a large tarp or canvas was hung up back of the wheel on the gin post of the scow. Any water flying through the air would strike the tarp and drain back into the river instead of into the hull. Scows were made of wood, and in the dry climate around The Dalles they would often leak like sieves.

One of the simplest ways of stopping a leak in a scow was to take an old half-pound wooden cannery case, nail a long wooden handle to the case, then fill the case with sawdust. This was lowered over the side by hand near where you thought the leak was. The water flowing through the leak into the hull would carry the sawdust into the opening, which was generally planking of the hull that had lost some of its oakum. The sawdust collected in the opening, expanded with water, and then the hull was tight. If a leak was too big to be stopped by this method, the next thing to do was to place a salmon cannery case beside the leak inside the hull of the scow and simply fill the cannery case with concrete. As soon as the concrete set the leak would be stopped. This was only used as a last resort, but it always seemed to work.

You always tried to fish the scow over a large boil of water. As the river boiled up, salmon were lifted up into the wheel itself.

Any time you hear men talk about the days of fishing around The Dalles you will hear many terms used such as channels, points, reefs, and so on. I will try to give you some idea of what they were talking about.

They would often talk about a rocky point, a jut of rock out into the river. If this point of rock stayed above the water during high water, it was called a rocky point. If covered with water during the river stages, it was then called a reef. A narrow rocky passage that the river flowed through was always called a channel. Channels were often dry, though, during low water. Many times a channel would have such a swift current in it during high water no boat could either live in such water or navigate it. They were still called channels. When they spoke of the Columbia River channel, it was sometimes referred to as the channel, but more often they spoke of the river's main channel. Islands or any pinnacle of rock or mass of rock that reared up over and above the rocky shore was called an island. An island may be high and dry during low water and connected to the shore by a dry reef, or an island may be surrounded by water during high and low water. It didn't seem to make much difference whether an island was always surrounded by water or not, but islands did have a channel separating them from the main shore; but, as I have said, these channels more often than not were dry during the low water. This all

may sound confusing; there were reefs that were islands and islands that were reefs, you just had to learn
which was called what.

Fish sites or fishwheel scow sites around The
Dalles consisted of rocky points or reefs projecting out
into the river. A reef or point would direct or divert the
current toward the center of the river away from the
shore. The salmon swimming upriver nosed into this
current coming off the reef or the rocky point and followed it on the down side as they swam upriver, because the down side water was less swift.

Surprisingly enough, where the main channel current was very often along the rocky shore the flow
would actually run upriver, and when a salmon found
this current he swam upstream with very little effort.
Often there were huge bays called back eddies behind
these rocky reefs or points. Fish gathered in these to
rest. A fishwheel on the outer edge would catch the
salmon as he came around the end to continue upstream. Fishwheel No. 5 and the Big Tumwater Wheel
were situated in positions like this. Some successful
wheels had channels blasted through the rocky point
about halfway out to the end. These channels would
attract the salmon that collected in the back eddies.
Such a wheel was the Little Tumwater Wheel.

Salmon seem to follow paths along the river bank.
The trick was to simply find the paths, which you seldom ever did. Deep rocky river channels attracted lots
of salmon. A wheel on such a channel would always
do well, such as fishwheels No. 3 and No. 4. If a fishwheel had a channel that led into the heavy cross current just below the upper end of the reef, it would often
do well. Just below a reef where this heavy current was

diverted across river was an ideal place to fish a large
wheel scow, especially if you had a large water boil at
that point, which would lift those salmon up and into
the scow wheel.

From time to time we worked inside of the fishwheel itself. After the wheel had been pulled and the
wheel was well above the water, the center of the
wheel, the flange and shaft would be level with the
fishwheel deck. We selected the dip to work inside of,
and the part to work on. The wheel was then turned until the part we wanted to work on was level and the end
of one of the fishwheel arms was snubbed to the deck,
gin post or railing with a rope. We were sure to snub
the fishwheel arm directly across from the first arm for
safety's sake. For further safety, a plank was shoved
from one side of the fishwheel deck across the channel
to the other side, with the plank placed under the
wheel arms. Then we entered the dip with safety. If the
fishwheel wire was intact we walked on it, if not, several planks placed across the dip would safely hold a
workman. After completing work at that particular
place, one could return to the fishwheel deck, release
the ropes holding the arms in place and remove the
plank across her channel, blocking the fishwheel arms.
The arms could be moved to a new position, always
having the place you worked in the dip on the bottom
and level to be repaired without too much trouble.

I want to point out again that of all commercial
fishing gear, wheels were the most inefficient of all.
First, a wheel cost much more to build than any other
gear. If a fixed wheel caught no fish, the entire invest-
ment was lost. Because of location, either in isolated
areas or surrounded by swift water, or both, it was often

difficult and expensive to remove the fish from the wheels in order to deliver them to the cannery. Seufert's had a number of fishwheels that were abandoned simply for the reasons of impractical transport.

If you fished a new seine site and caught no fish, you simply moved the seine boat and gear to a new site. If your trap site caught no fish, you moved your netting and piling to a new trap site. But when you spent money building a wheel and it caught no fish, you were stuck. You couldn't move your fishwheel. There it sat, a dead loss, while the gillnetters with their fish boats went up or down the river until they found the salmon runs.

Seufert's fishwheels were all built on parts of the Columbia River where the water was extremely swift. The wheel was the only gear that could be operated in the wild, fast water of Fivemile Rapids, Eightmile Rapids, and below Celilo Falls. Along with other salmon packers on the Columbia River, Seufert's used seines where possible and purchased salmon from the gillnetters and Indians. Some years Seufert's would have fishwheels whose total salmon catch for the season was less than the total catch of one of the commercial gillnetters fishing for Seufert's.

A man operating a fishwheel might be thought of by the general public as a commercial fisherman, but no fishwheel operator would think of referring to himself that way. A commercial fisherman was a small boat operator, a gillnetter, a man using a dipnet or a setnet. Men who operated fishwheels spoke of themselves as fishwheel operators, or they said they ran a fishwheel or owned a fishwheel. A man who operated a seine spoke of himself as operating a seine or he said he had a seine. Trap operators said they had a trap or operated a trap or fished a trap, but never did fishwheel owners or men who owned and operated a seine or a man who owned a fish trap ever refer to themselves as commercial fishermen. Commercial fishermen were always small boat operators such as gillnetters. Likewise, the Indians at Celilo were never referred to as commercial fishermen; they were simply thought of as the Indians fishing at Celilo.

We never talked about the full diameter of a fishwheel itself. We never talked about a 40-foot wheel. When we talked about the wheel, we only described the wheel by the length of the arms. If the fishwheel had 20-foot arms, that was the only way the size of the wheel itself was ever described. After all, when a fishwheel was fishing it was the length of the arm that determined how deep into the water the fishwheel could fish.

In the commercial fishing business, regardless of the type of fishing gear used, the operators of that particular type of fishing gear were only concerned with the depth of water that particular gear was to be fished in.

The depth of a fishwheel channel might be 50 feet from the wheel deck to the bottom of the channel, but we always described the channel by its width. A fishwheel could have a seven-foot wide channel, but we never described the channel by the depth from the fishwheel deck to the bottom of the channel.

I will talk about No. 5 Fishwheel. I use this name simply because it is familiar to all of us. When the men talked about a particular fishwheel they almost always used a name. They spoke of No. 5 Wheel, or No. 5

Fishwheel, and always referred to it in the female gender. It was always her dips, or she did so and so. Or they might say she was fishing. They would also oftentimes say, if the wheel had been raised so she wasn't fishing on the bottom, they would then say that the wheel had went out. A fishwheel was always lifted, or she was lowered, although sometimes they would say a wheel was up, or she was down. When a fishwheel was operating they said that she was running, or if it had been raised and stopped, they simply said she was up. A fishwheel had what they called good years when she caught plenty of fish, and they said they had bad years when she caught few. Lots of salmon was always referred to by saying she caught well, so they described good years as simply lots of salmon, and poor years as no salmon. They also described a fishwheel that caught poorly as a bad wheel or simply as no good, and sometimes they would say that she was no damn good. A fishwheel that caught well was simply a good wheel.

On the Columbia River the state of Oregon was always referred to as this side of the river. The state of Washington was always referred to as the other side or the other side of the river.

The foreman or operator of a fishwheel was always said to be running the wheel. To legally operate a fishwheel the company had to buy a fishwheel license. After you bought the license you said that she could run. If there were a lot of salmon in the river during the big runs they said the river was full of fish. All legal fishing seasons or times were always referred to as seasons, a spring season or a fall season. When a fishwheel was licensed you recorded the fish that were caught and paid the state the fish tax or the poundage tax, as they called it. You always had to be sure that you identified the wheel that you were paying the tax on.

Just below the present The Dalles Bridge on the Washington shore were the Rorick Wheels. J. T. Rorick was a newspaper publisher who came out west when the Rev. Taylor promoted Grand Dalles, Washington, in 1890. J. T. Rorick later acquired the land the Rorick Wheels were built on. These fishwheels were not too successful, so Seufert's leased the fishing sites over a period of some 40 years from Mr. Rorick, operating two fishwheel scows there. The scows were known as Rorick No. 1 and Rorick No. 2. Seufert's operated these two fishwheel scows through 1934, when the fishwheels were outlawed in Washington.

In 1926, when the people of the state of Oregon voted out the fishwheels in Oregon, Seufert's of course closed its Oregon fishwheel operation down. The Company moved all of its fishwheel scows to the Washington side of the Columbia River and fished them until the voters voted fishwheels out on the Washington side of the Columbia in 1934. Then Seufert's fishwheel scows were all beached in a cove on the Oregon bank just below Phelps Fishwheel and just above the Lone Pine Tree Indian village. They were abandoned and let go to ruin. When the voters voted Seufert's out of business the fishwheels themselves were just hoisted up out of their channels and let hang in the air. After a few years the wheels on some of Seufert's wheel operations were removed from the structures and the empty fishwheel channels were used by both white and Indian fishermen for dipnetting. But none of the dipnet fishermen ever caught any salmon to speak of in these former fishwheel channels. The fishwheel structures were made overnight into pieces of worthless junk not worth salvage, so they just sat on the bank of the Columbia and fell into disrepair.

Some of Seufert's fishwheels, No. 3, China Pete, and the Little Wheel on the Washington side of the Columbia River were carried away by the flood of 1948, and the rest of Seufert's fishwheels were burned by the U.S. Army Engineers before flooding The Dalles Dam pool.

Of all the fishwheels on the Columbia River, Seufert's China Pete Wheel was the only fishwheel named after a Chinaman. China Pete's given name was Ah Fook. Seufert's hired China Pete to be watchman and operator of China Pete Fishwheel. I don't know what this wheel was called before Seufert's bought it in 1907. That wheel had the distinction of being the most isolated of Seufert's wheels. It was located on the Oregon side of Eightmile Rapids, miles from nowhere. China Pete Wheel was completely isolated, on the edge of the rapids, out on a long finger or bluff of solid rock, with no trees or grass anywhere around. In the summer the wind blew a gale and there was no shade. There was only a one-room watchman's shack on the deck of the fishwheel where the operator 'batched'. There was no running water. If the operator wanted or needed water, the river was full of it. The hot summer sun beat down all day long. The shack was hot. The shack furnished a little bit of shade, but you had to move as the sun moved from east to west, if you wanted to stay in the shade. If you stepped away from the shack, the wind nearly swept you off your feet.

At China Pete you hoisted the salmon from the fish box with a hand-operated crab. When the salmon were on the wheel deck, you put them in a little car, shoved them on a trestle nearly an eighth-of-a-mile long to get over to the railroad track. They would send you your groceries and mail on the little local passenger train. Later, once a day a fish truck would pick up your fish. Because it was so isolated it was hard to get fishwheel men to go and stay at China Pete Wheel, but China Pete (or Ah Fook) didn't mind. He took the job, and each year he came back, so after a while when the Company talked about China Pete, they were talking about the fishwheel China Pete was running for Seufert's. The name China Pete stuck, and while at the time no one gave it any thought, China Pete was the only Chinese who had a fishwheel named for him.

China Pete Wheel was a low-water wheel. It did reasonably well when the Columbia River had a low spring season.

China Pete Wheel had another distinction. It was the only fishwheel Seufert's had that was designed by a civil engineer. This man worked on the construction of The Dalles-Celilo Canal, and F. A. Seufert hired him to design the upper works of the fishwheel. He did this while he was stationed at Dillon, Oregon, during the canal construction. The engineer's design was so successful that all of Seufert's fishwheels rebuilt after that were copied from the design of the China Pete Wheel. The wheel was badly damaged in the floods of 1916 and again in 1917, but Seufert's rebuilt the wheel each time, and it survived until it was destroyed in the flood of 1948.

As for China Pete the man, well, he worked for Seufert's for years. And when he wasn't working on the wheel he ran the Chinese garden out by the railroad yard. Some said China Pete had a misunderstanding with the law, but as time went on, he simply disappeared from the picture.

During the 1920s Henry Wickman was sent up to China Pete Wheel to do some repair work. He took a couple of men and drove up to the wheel in a truck. Leaving the truck, the men crossed The Dalles-Celilo Canal and started to walk out to the wheel. They hadn't gone far when they ran into a big billy goat. This goat had a nasty disposition and considered the men intruders, and let the men know exactly how he felt about the situation. Two of the men got to the bridge and over the canal and into the truck cab ahead of the goat, but Hank Wickman climbed a willow tree instead. Hank was a big man. The tree bent over, but not too much. The goat took up his position under the tree. Since Hank and the goat had arrived at a standoff, the men in the truck drove down to the cannery and got a rifle. They drove back, and the goat was still under the tree and Hank was still up the tree, so the men did the only thing they could—they shot the goat. When the crew came back to the cannery and everybody was safe again, the men really kidded the one who had shot the goat. They would ask why he had shot the goat, when he had Hank up the tree.

If you considered the total salmon catch of the Columbia River, fishwheels took only some two percent of all the salmon caught each year. Still the seines were never such controversial subjects as fishwheels. Fishwheels always fished very well if there were salmon in the river and clear water. No fishwheel would catch in muddy water. A fishwheel did best in the very early morning and just before sunset. All of the

fishwheels that Seufert's had—that is, Nos. 1, 2, 3, 4, 5—were all high-water wheels that fished in May, June, and July. By July the river was dropping and these fishwheels were by then entirely on dry land.

The important thing in locating a fishwheel site was to find a place where there were salmon, or at least where the wheel would catch salmon. The most successful man around The Dalles, and really the only successful man to locate a fishwheel site was F. A. Seufert. I once asked my grandfather how he located the site for a wheel. He told me the only way was to simply take a dipnet, go up along the river and fish along the bank, and when you came to a place where you could dip a lot of salmon from the river, you knew the salmon were there and that was the place to put your wheel. If you couldn't catch a salmon in your dipnet, you knew it would be a waste of time and money to build a wheel there.

I would say that between The Dalles and Celilo every inch of the shore on both sides of the Columbia was fished at one time or another. But good fishing sites were few and far between. Really, what attracted the salmon to one place over another no one knew. You would think from all indications you had found a good fishing site, but you could not be sure until you fished it. These salmon followed definite paths in the river, but just where these paths went, no one ever could find out. Salmon coming up the river at Threemile Rapids hugged the Washington shore. They came around Grass Island, up past the old Blue Jay Wheel (still on the Washington shore), and fishwheel scows on all of these places did well; but from there the salmon disappeared, and crossed to the Oregon side of the river. At least, they never showed up again until a few were caught on the Oregon side at Half Bridge Scow.

The salmon appeared at the upper side of Big Eddy on both the Oregon and the Washington sides of the Columbia River, but there were never any fish caught on the lower side, the Washington side, of the entrance to Big Eddy.

In the years past there were many seals in the river. When Seufert's started its salmon operations on the Columbia River in 1880, the seals in the river were a nuisance. They would gather at the mouth of a fishwheel channel to catch salmon. Although they would only actually catch a few fish, they would drive away all the other salmon approaching the channel mouth and put a fishwheel out of business in a hurry. They were especially bad on the long channels leading from Big Eddy up to Seufert's Fishwheel No. 3. The seals would swim up the river and collect in the deep river channels around Memaloose Island and then go on up these deep river channels down below Fishwheel No. 3. The Company always had a seal rifle handy. These rifles were Winchester repeating rifles which used a .44 cartridge. While they were short range, the bullet had terrific killing power. Seals were a bother up until the 1920s, then they more or less disappeared on the river around The Dalles.

In the beginning were the wheels owned only by the Seufert family, or were there others?

As far as we know, the Seufert family built, owned and operated the first fishwheels in The Dalles area. By 1889 we knew of one other fishwheel built by a family by the name of Covington, but we don't know of any other wheel.

Fishwheels have been criticized because they were efficient. Why not be efficient? If they were inefficient, then the money was thrown away. And not only were fishwheels criticized for being efficient. As a general statement, all fishing gear is criticized if it is efficient. It just seems that the general public wants an inefficient fishing industry. Politicians cry because the Russians fish off our coast, but inefficient American boats can't or won't. Let us put it another way. Why are we as Americans so proud of our efficient American farmer, but perturbed over the development of highly efficient fishing gear?

I will talk a bit more about the fishwheels that Seufert's bought. First, there were the two Gulick Wheels, at one time called the Twin Fishwheels. Gulick settled at the Lone Pine Tree Indian village, married an Indian woman there, and made his home there. At the cannery, this village was simply referred to as down at Sam Williams', or down at Fat Charlie's, or in later years, down at Easterbrook's, and of course during Gulick's life, everybody around the cannery just referred to it as Gulick's.

In the natural channel between Threemile Reef and the mainland there was a channel generally called Gulick's Channel. This channel was dry during low water but deep and swift during high water. Today Gulick's Channel runs under The Dalles Bridge just north of the bridge toll station. In about 1890 Gulick built two fishwheels on this channel. They were identical, one on each side of the channel just opposite each other. They were referred to for this reason as the Twin Fishwheels. These wheels were only so-so as far as catching salmon was concerned. They were destroyed in the high water of 1894 and never rebuilt. Gulick later sold out to Seufert's. Gulick was a carpenter, and a good one. For years he worked off and on for Seufert's.

Covington always told the story of how he was a scout in the American Army during the Mexican War. He became separated from his detachment and wandered in the desert, and lived on grasshoppers until he could get back to his unit. After he had told his story many times, people started calling him "Grasshopper Jim" and the name stuck. He built a fishwheel out on Covington Point; this wheel was also destroyed in the 1894 flood.

On the Washington side of the Columbia River Seufert's bought out the fishwheels of The Dalles Canning and Packing Company in 1907. These people owned the old Blue Jay Wheel right across the river from Covington's Wheel. The Blue Jay got its name because jays were thick around the area where the wheel had been built. The Blue Jay was a good high-water wheel, but in those days the salmon had to be taken from the Blue Jay by boat. At that time there was just no boat around The Dalles that could approach the Blue Jay during high water, so the wheel was allowed to fall to pieces and Seufert's never fished her.

Later, Seufert's had a scow that fished the old Blue Jay Wheel site; this scow was known as the Blue Jay and was one of Seufert's best.

The Dalles Canning and Packing Co. built a fishwheel at the head of Big Eddy on the Washington shore. This wheel was constructed about 1890, ruined by the 1894 flood, and then rebuilt. It was originally known as the Cove Fishwheel. When Seufert's took over they called it the Bay Wheel. It was a good wheel, and Seufert's operated it until 1934.

Above Bay Wheel was the Little Wheel, another belonging to The Dalles Canning and Packing Co. This wheel was up Fivemile Rapids a bit, and on the Washington shore. It was called Little Wheel (but not because the wheel was small, which it wasn't) because it sat on a large rock outcropping so there was not much cribbing that could be built. This made the wheel look small, and hence its name. The Little Wheel was a good wheel, and like the Bay Wheel and the Cyclone Wheel, it was a high-water wheel. Seufert's operated them all until 1934.

Up the river above the Little Wheel was the big Cyclone Wheel, another one built by The Dalles Canning and Packing Co. The Cyclone Wheel was the furthest up Fivemile Rapids on the Washington side. Cyclone Wheel was huge. It sat on piers of reinforced concrete some fifty feet high, and her gin posts were thirty feet or more on top of the concrete piers. She was massive and made the Little Wheel look even smaller by comparison. The Cyclone Wheel got her name because the west winds of summer blew a gale there. Anyone who was ever around that wheel on a windy summer day knew this wheel was well named. At the Cyclone Wheel, Seufert's had headquarters for all of its fishwheels operating on the Washington side of the Columbia river along Fivemile Rapids. There was a mess house, a bunk house and a small fish house. This was the headquarters for all the fish buying Seufert's did with the Indians around Spedis. This was also the northern end of the fishery cable across the Columbia River. Although the Cyclone Wheel couldn't operate after 1934, because Washington outlawed fishwheels, the Cyclone fish-buying station and its operations continued to be operated by Seufert's until 1952.

Before spring floods came, the fishwheels and the superstructures were unbolted and hauled up to high ground far enough above the river bank to be above any high water. Here the wheel and its parts were just stored or laid on the rocks. When the river fell and the fishing site was above water again, the wheel and the parts were hauled back down to the site, the men bolted the wheel together, and the temporary fishwheel was ready to fish again. A wheel like this that could be put in and taken out was called a temporary wheel. A crew could put one of these temporary wheels together and have it fishing in a week.

The important thing about a fishwheel was the channel. Around The Dalles the fishwheel channels were all blasted out of solid basalt, and the various parts of the wheel—the arms, cross pieces, wire, etc.—were constantly being replaced as needed, so we can say that the lifespan would be forever. But after a number of years, probably the entire wheel had been replaced, and not a single piece was original. The shaft and flange were heavy, cast steel, so they never had to be replaced. The basalt channel never had to be repaired, and it would always withstand the Columbia River floods without sustaining any damage.

The wooden cribbing used on the original fishwheels had a life of about 25 years. The dry climate in The Dalles area, the heavy dry west winds in summer, the high summer temperatures and the hot sun beating down all summer long sapped all the utility and strength from the timbers of the wooden cribbing until it had no more life. These cribbings might appear sound, but the wood might have lost all its strength so that it would no longer hold spikes and bolts put in the timbers. Seufert's would build a concrete form around the cribbing and pour concrete to preserve and hold the cribbing in place.

The gin posts of a fishwheel also had a lifespan of some 25 years. Here again the hot dry west winds of summer, and the hot summer sun, sapped the wooden gin posts of all their strength, so that after about 25 years Seufert's rebuilt or replaced the gin posts, wooden decks, et cetera, on all their fishwheels.

The fishwheels destroyed in the flood of 1894 and rebuilt in the winter of 1894 and early 1895, had so deteriorated by 1921 from the wind and summer sun that every wooden part had to be replaced. In fact, Seufert's just tore down the fishwheels and replaced all the wooden construction by 1922. The wooden rock cribbings were replaced with concrete, and the wooden gin posts, decking, et cetera, were replaced with new timbers and planking.

When a fishwheel channel was built, for the first year either the taste or smell of fresh concrete or the lingering odor of exploded dynamite would affect the wheel's ability to fish. After the first year, when the channel had flushed out all the strange odors, the wheel would start to fish. In general it was true that none of the fishwheels were ever painted. But for some reason Phelps Wheel, the Big Tumwater Wheel, the Little Tumwater Wheel and the Cement Wheel had painted gin posts. They were painted boxcar red. The watchman's shacks on the fishwheel decks were painted a gray-white. This color was supposed to be cool in summer. Well, that shack sat out in summer sun that was 100 degrees in the shade, the sun beat down all day long, and the shack had a tarpaper roof. The gray-white paint may have had some cooling effect, but no one who ever worked on a fishwheel in the middle of summer knew it.

I would like to tell about the cable ways that Seufert's had built across the Columbia River or out to the islands in the river from time to time. Seufert's built its first cable way across the Columbia River in 1907. This was built between the Cyclone Fishwheel on the Washington side of the river and the fishery. It was built to haul fish from Seufert's Washington wheels and the salmon receiving stations at the Cyclone to the fishery; to avoid the long wagon hauls from these wheels to the cannery. In order to get these cables across the river, Seufert's first took a skyrocket to the Cyclone Wheel, attached a linen line to the rocket, and fired it across the river to the Oregon side, where they had taken their entire Chinese crew from the cannery. When the rocket was fired and landed on the Oregon side, the Chinese crew picked up the linen line and pulled it across the river. The line was attached to a rope, and the rope was attached to a steel cable. One after the other, these were pulled across the river by the Chinese crew. I suppose there were nearly 50 Chinamen in the crew at that time. When the steel cable reached the Oregon side of the river, it was permanently attached to a capstan in the cable house at the fishery. Then by working the capstan it was no job to pull the cable taut on the cable pier well above the river.

This cable way was operated by Seufert's until 1954, when it closed down its salmon canning operation on the Columbia River. It was operated out of the cable house at the fishery. It was probably a quarter of a mile between the fishery cable house and Cyclone Wheel. When you ran the cable car across the river you watched for a rag that had been tied to the cable. When it was in front of you, you stopped the cable, knowing that the cable car on the far end of the cable had reached the wheel and was in position to be load-

ed with salmon. The cable way was operated by a gasoline engine. It carried a fish box that would haul about 400 pounds of salmon per trip. When the fish box arrived on this side of the river at the fishery cable house, a hinged door forming the bottom of the box was opened, dumping the salmon out into a little four-wheel railroad car you had spotted under the fish box. If any salmon fell onto the cable house floor, you piked them from the floor into the little car. You then shoved the car on a little narrow-gauge railroad track across The Dalles-Celilo Canal. At the end of the bridge across the canal Seufert's had a short trestle. You could park a truck under this trestle and dump the salmon directly from the little railroad car into the truck. The truck was then driven to the cannery and the salmon delivered. This cable way was not used to carry people across the river. The sheave that rode the cable was attached to the fish box by hangers that hung on only one side of the cable. If a sheave jumped a cable with the hangers on only one side of the cable, there was nothing to prevent the fish box from falling into the river.

The next cable way that Seufert's built was at Tumwater in 1930. In that year, Seufert's fished two big fishwheel scows on Big Island on the Washington side of the Columbia River across from the Tumwater Wheel. This cable ran from the wheel to a pier on the island. The pier was there to hold the cable above the river even during high water. This cable way had two boxes. One, the fish box, had a hinged bottom so the fish would be dumped directly into a little, four-wheel railroad car out on Tumwater Wheel and then be hauled to the Tumwater fish house. Directly in front of the fish box, that is, closest to the Oregon shore, there was another box with a solid bottom that was used to haul Indian dipnet fishermen out to Big Island to dipnet salmon that were to be delivered to the cannery. This cable way was operated by a gasoline engine out on the Tumwater Fishwheel. This cable way was built so that the sheave riding on the cable was attached to the boxes by hangers that hung down from both sides of the sheave. If a sheave should jump the cable, the boxes could not fall off the cable into the river. The person in the box was safe as long as he stayed put. This did happen once, but no one was in the box. The man rode out the cable in a little makeshift box, and above the river, he put the sheaves holding the box back on the cable, and then of course there was no more problem.

Up around Celilo Falls Seufert's built five or six cable ways each year. They were all operated by gasoline engines. They all had their point of origin around Downes Channel. They were put in only to accommodate the Indian fishermen, to make it easier for them to reach the fishing grounds and to deliver their fish to Seufert's. Of course, if the Indian fisherman rode your cable, he would deliver his fish to you just as long as you paid the same price as the competition. These cable ways generally consisted of just a fish box. The Indian fisherman rode over in the fish box and came back in it with his fish. All of these cable ways at Downes Channel were put in during the late summer, August, to be ready for the fall fishing season in September.

After the fall fishing season was over, all of these cable ways were removed. If they weren't removed in the fall, they would have been destroyed in the spring flood.

The Gulick, Phelps, Covington, Seufert's No. 1 and No. 2 wheels were all on the Oregon side of the river between Threemile Reef and the mouth of Fifteen-mile Creek. In an average year none of these wheels caught many fish. But on the other side of the river the Grass Island and Blue Jay scows were Seufert's best scow fishing sites.

In the so-called Long Narrows, or Fivemile Rapids, the salmon followed both the Oregon side and the Washington side of the river, and Seufert's best wheels, No. 3, No. 4 and No. 5 and the Cement Wheel, were all on the Oregon side. Bay Wheel, Little Wheel and Cyclone Wheel were all on the Washington side. Above Fivemile Rapids the salmon disappeared. There were no good fishing sites between Fivemile and Eightmile rapids on either side of the Columbia River; the only exception was China Pete Wheel at Eightmile Rapids on the Oregon side. China Pete did fairly well in low water but not at all well during high water. Above China Pete the salmon again disappeared from both shores and weren't seen again until they reached Seufert's Mumpower Seine on the Oregon side. Salmon were also thick at Seufert's Seine Bar 1 on the Oregon side, and over Celilo Falls. On the Washington side of the river there were no salmon above Eightmile Rapids until you reached Seufert's Washington Seine Bar 2. From there the salmon ran thick on the Washington side over Celilo Falls.

Seufert's had a Washington seine called Clantons Bar. This was below Bar No. 2. Clantons Bar never caught enough fish to pay for her seine license. In front of Bar 2 and Bar 1 and the Mumpower Seine and Clantons Bar the gillnetters did well; but between Fivemile Rapids and Eightmile Rapids the gillnetters caught nothing. In fact this area was so poor that there was no commercial fishing at all. No one who tried it ever caught anything, and it was just written off as a fishing area.

One thing we could be sure of was that the amount of fish in any one site depended entirely on the flood stage of the river. A good fishing site on one stage of the river did well. Let the river fall six feet and you would catch no fish there. Let the river rise six or eight feet and a previously good site might do poorly. Fishwheel channels seemed to need at least eight feet of water flowing through them before they would fish. A wheel such as Phelps did well during the high water of 1894, but the flood of that year created a swift-flowing river through a channel that flowed in back of Lone Pine Tree Island. The river was never again high enough to begin to create a similar situation and Phelps Wheel never again caught enough fish to talk about. Thus a fishwheel or a scow fishing site depended entirely on the particular stage of river flood. Above or below this level the river currents were apparently so changed that a particular site would not attract salmon. This was the reason that Seufert's built high- and low-water wheels, so that at least one wheel could fish regardless of the river stage. I want to emphasize the fact that there could very easily be a difference of 50 feet between high and low water on some sections of the Columbia between The Dalles and Celilo.

It was also possible to lower a fishwheel channel. Several of Seufert's fishwheels had their channels lowered by being dug out deeper. This didn't seem to change a fishwheel's characteristics a bit, as long as you didn't change the mouth, or entrance, to the channel. By lowering the channel a wheel might have enough water to fish sooner than before, but as the river rose and the depth of the water in her channel increased, the wheel was off bottom sooner than before and couldn't fish. Apparently the height of the river itself determined where the salmon were, so that at a certain river stage if the salmon would not approach the entrance of the fishwheel channel, it did no good to have water in the channel.

Opposite Seufert's Cannery, Seufert's fished eight wheel scows between Big Eddy and Threemile Rapids. These scows were moved to their fishing sites by a salmon tender. The scows were taken to the fishing sites before the river reached flood stage, when the river would be too swift for the tender to handle the scows. What this meant was that each spring you had to have the fishwheel scows ready to operate before the spring flood. This could mean the scows had to be at their fishing sites at least two weeks earlier in some years than in others. The fishing season opened May first, but you had to have the scows in position to be ready to fish at that date, and the date on which you moved them out onto the river was always determined by the height of the river.

If the river was too swift for the salmon tender to move these scows, they had to be moved either up or downriver by using the capstan on the deck of the scow. From the capstan a steel cable was anchored to shore. By working the capstan and pulling on the cable the scows could be moved upstream. One could use the capstan to slacken the cable to allow the scow to move downstream. The line that ran from the capstan to shore was fastened to whatever might be available on shore; a round outcropping was best. The cable was run around the rock, brought back to the deck of the scow and snubbed to a snubbing post. If nothing on the shore would hold the cable, then you could always drill a hole in the rock with a rock drill and a sledge hammer, place a large eye bolt in the rock, attach the cable, and that was that. The cables could be bound together with steel clamps so they wouldn't slip. If properly tightened the steel cable clamps would never slip; the cable would break before these clamps would slip. If for some reason you felt that one clamp was not safe enough, you put on two or three or however many seemed necessary. The scow was held offshore with a spar, which was a wooden timber 6x10 or 8x12, and about 20 feet long. These were run out from the side of the scow to shore with a block-and-tackle on the scow's deck; the spar was attached and then you could move the scow out onto the river far enough to stay off the rocks. Two spars were used when the scow was stationary, one at the bow and one at the stern.

When the scow was moved you had to move the spars to a new position. This meant that every time the scow moved up or down the river a few feet, every line and spar had to reset by hand. This meant a lot of hard, physical labor. But the men could and did move a scow anywhere up and down the river bank, regardless of how swift the river was running, just as long as the scow could stay afloat in the swift water. Seufert's crews moved fishwheel scows up and down the Columbia River between Threemile Reef and Celilo Falls by capstan for years. In fact, they even took these scows over Celilo Falls, under the SP&S railroad bridge, down the main river channel on the Oregon side of the river.

Henry Wickman operated one of Seufert's scows, and fished it down below Fishwheel No. 3 at the entrance of the long channels between the islands that led up to that wheel. The channel entrance was just below Big Eddy on the main river. This scow did very well. Wickman told me many times just how well this scow did. But he was afraid to report the total daily catch to F. A. Seufert. He was afraid that if Seufert knew how well the scow was doing, he would make Wickman move the scow for fear the scow was catching No. 3's fish. So each day Wickman showed this scow as not doing well; showing most of her catch on the records of other scows fishing farther down the river. Whether Wickman fooled Seufert or not I don't know, but old man Seufert never made him move this scow out of the lower end of the channel.

Seufert's Covington Wheel on Covington Point was only fair in the amount of fish caught each season. She would always catch some fish during high water, but in 1907 the Army Engineers blew off the end of Covington Point. The point was shot away for a considerable distance inland, and down deep below the surface of the river. The Army Engineers did this to slow the fast waters that flowed past Covington Point during high water, so the sternwheel river steamers would have less trouble passing during high water, and when the steamers were coming upstream to approach the lower entrance to The Dalles-Celilo Canal. After the engineers blew the point off the fishwheel was ruined; the flow of water was so changed outside the wheel that salmon never again approached this wheel as they had before. Seufert's fished Covington Wheel as long as she required no repairs, then junked her.

Across the river from Covington Point were Seufert's old Blue Jay Wheel and later the Blue Jay fishwheel scow; Covington Point being blown up did not affect Blue Jay scow at all. In fact, it was one of the best scows Seufert's ever had. Its channel had not been changed at all, either in front or below.

By 1886 Seufert's built fishwheel Nos. 1, 2, 3, 4 and 5. In 1887 and 1888 Covington built his wheel, so by then there were six fishwheels in The Dalles area. By 1890 people had seen Seufert's fishwheels. They knew that Seufert's was making money and there was a rush by others to build fishwheels around The Dalles. There were at least eight more wheels built by 1894 by Gulick and Winans. But the floods of 1894 destroyed all the wheels around The Dalles except Seufert's Phelps Wheel. After the flood some of the fishwheels were rebuilt, but by 1900 the rush to build wheels to get rich quick proved just another illusion of The Dalles.

There were really only two good fishwheels on the Columbia River, and Seufert's had both of them: No. 5 and Big Tumwater. Seufert's No. 3 and No. 4 were dependable but nothing big. When Seufert's built the Cement Wheel it was the last one built that was any good. By 1900 the people who had invested in fishwheels had had enough and were selling out. They left The Dalles area and moved to Portland and sold out to Seufert's. Many of these fishwheels were worthless, built with high expectations but only a few days' fishing showed that these wheels had little prospect of ever repaying the investments. Offhand I can count 18 fishwheels that Seufert's bought, built or leased that were worthless.

Tumwater Fishwheel No. 3 was destroyed by ice in 1899 and never rebuilt. The second Klickitat Wheel in back of the Washington seine bar was built but seldom used. In the fall of the year when the Washington seine was doing well you didn't have time to haul the fish from this wheel down to the river for transportation. When the SP&S Celilo railroad bridge was built one of the piers went into the Klickitat Wheel's channel, completely blocking the channel, but no one cared.

As various fishwheel builders and owners wanted out of the fishwheel business, Seufert's bought them out, not because the fishwheels had any prospect of ever producing a profit, but because Seufert's wanted to own and control the shore lands above and below their fishwheels and around their salmon cannery. Nearly all of the other salmon canners and packers on the Columbia River financed and loaned money to others to build fishwheels and other types of fishing gear. These other salmon packers were just that, salmon packers and cannery operators. They were really not interested in operating any kind of fishing gear. They would loan money or finance a fisherman or a man who wanted to build a fishwheel, but these salmon packers wanted nothing to do with operating fishing gear. All they wanted to do was operate a salmon cannery and have the salmon delivered to their cannery dock by the fishermen. The Seuferts were entirely different. The Seuferts were really not cannerymen, but highly successful fixed fishing gear operators, that is, operators of fishwheels and seines. Their main interest in a salmon cannery was that they had a place to use or can all the salmon that their fishwheels and seines caught. The Seuferts' attitude was if they were going to put up the money to build a fishwheel, then they were going to take all the profit. If the wheel was no good, that was too bad, but they would take their loss and look for another fishwheel site. Then too, a partner was a nuisance; when you ran things yourself you could do everything the way you wanted to.

But getting the salmon out of the wheel and into the cannery was always a problem. Seufert's wheels on the Oregon side of the river were close to the old OR&N railroad tracks so salmon could be hauled to the cannery in boxcars. Some people who built fishwheels on the Washington side of the river between The Dalles and Spedis abandoned some of these wheels because there was no way to get the salmon out of the wheels after they were caught.

In the early days no one went up to the wheel sites on the river during high water because there were no boats capable of operating in swift water and the north banks was nothing but wagon roads. Henry Wickman used to drive his team from what was later to become Seufert's Cyclone Fishwheel and haul salmon to a cannery in The Dalles. The wagon would hold about a ton-and-a-half of salmon. He left early in the morning, drove down to The Dalles Ferry and then crossed over to The Dalles and then upriver to the cannery and then down to the ferry and back on this old wagon road to the old Cyclone Wheel. It took him all day to deliver a ton-and-a-half of fish to The Dalles (a distance of about three miles to The Dalles plus the ferry crossing and three miles back).

I want to talk a little bit about floating salmon down the river on barrels. Late in the spring fishing season after the spring salmon runs were over and the river was getting low, the Indians around Spedis had stopped fishing and gone back to the reservations and the Bay Wheel, Little Wheel and Cyclone Wheel were not doing well because of the falling river. The area I am talking about now was on the Washington side of the river between the Big Eddy and the head of Five-mile Rapids. These would be the days when you would have only five or six salmon caught by Seufert's Washington wheels. This small amount of salmon was hardly enough to send a truck and driver up the river to the fishery to pick up these few fish, so every day these five or six or so salmon were strung on a rope, the rope passing into the salmon's mouth and out the gills; the few salmon were all strung on the same rope. The rope was then fastened onto a barrel or oil drum. Then the oil barrel and salmon were all dumped into the river from the Cyclone Wheel. The barrel would keep the string of salmon from sinking and the barrel and salmon would drift downstream to the lower part of Five-mile Rapids, out into Big Eddy and down past the cannery. At the cannery, a pick-up boat would pick the fish up from the river and deliver them to the cannery—a cheap and efficient way of moving a few salmon down the river to the cannery.

In this kind of operation the important thing was timing. Of course, the crew over at the Cyclone Wheel would always call on the telephone on the days when they were going to send the fish downriver attached to a barrel. You threw the salmon and barrel into the river from the Cyclone Wheel at exactly 12 o'clock noon. It took from 30 to 45 minutes for the barrel and fish to drift downriver past the cannery. The pick-up boat crew had time to eat their noon meal at the cannery mess house, then go outside the mess house, sit on the bench in the shade and watch the river for the barrel and its salmon. When the pick-up boat crew saw the barrel floating downriver in back of the cannery, they walked down to the pick-up boat tied up at the river bank and went out in the river and caught the barrel and its salmon, and delivered them to the cannery.

After several days you had collected a number of empty barrels; you would send a truck driver with the barrels back up to the fisher, haul the empty barrels across the river on the cable way to the Cyclone Wheel and start all over again. As far as I know there were never any barrels lost.

THE RIVER

Now I want to talk about high and low water and its effect on fishing around The Dalles from Fivemile Rapids downstream. In the spring of the year the high water between Threemile Reef and the head of Fivemile Rapids would rise some 50 feet between high and low water. The spring flood would start in April and generally crest in the first week of June, and then start to fall. By July the river was down, and we would say the water in this area was low. This was the area where most of the fishwheels were. The fishwheels used in this area were high-water wheels, except for the Cement Wheel. The river had to be in flood before any of these wheels had enough water to fish, and when the river was low again, all except the Cement Wheel were high and dry, with their channels many feet above the river level.

Through and down Fivemile Rapids the river when high or in flood was wild, with whirlpools as much as 20 feet across constantly to be seen. I have stood on the deck of No. 5 Wheel and seen huge bridge timbers used in railroad trestles come floating down the river, enter Fivemile Rapids and be sucked into one of these whirlpools. The whirlpool would stand the timber on end, and then suck it down and out of sight.

Then these huge whirlpools would break and a huge boil would rise from the center of the pool and the water would boil up and above the flooding river. Sometimes the boiling river was *five or more* feet higher than the surrounding water. Huge back eddies would form along the shore, and would actually rush upstream. In this kind of water, no boat could survive even for a minute; a man just didn't have a chance. Anyone who fell into this wild stretch of river was dead. The current must have been rushing downstream at least 20-miles-an-hour. In back of the cannery the river was wider and deeper, but here too it was full of whirlpools, boils and rushing water, although I would say in back of the cannery the river had a current of at least 10-miles-an-hour.

The big pick-up boats that Seufert's had could operate in the flood waters of the Columbia in back of the cannery, but they could only operate alone. It took all the power their engines could produce just to move upriver. At Covington Point during high water, even with full power, these boats could only go upriver at a snail's pace. In fact the river was so fast that they would make scarcely any headway upstream at all. It would take some ten or fifteen minutes just to cover the few hundred feet; they had to move upstream through the river channel opposite Covington Point. Trees, logs, driftwood of all sizes would be seized by the river and tossed around like corks. The whole river channel from Threemile Reef to the head of Fivemile Rapids was deep and narrow. When the spring floods came, this channel filled with water racing down the river, after the water had risen some 30 feet or more. This fast water just spilled over the rocks, out of the channel along the sides, and filled every channel and crevass it could find with fast-running water. In spring floods the Columbia just filled this bottleneck and rushed wildly downriver to Big Eddy. It was here also at Fivemile Rapids, on the Washington side of the Columbia, that the Indians came from the reservations to fish for salmon in the spring. In September when the river was low, I have many-a-time gone up or down the Columbia in back of Seufert's Cannery in a rowboat, with the river nearly as still and quiet as a lake. In Fivemile Rapids, when the river was down in the fall, the narrow channel produced some current, but any boat with an engine could pass up the rapids without much trouble.

All of this area was high-water fishing grounds. When the river was low there was no commercial salmon fishing by either whites or Indians.

I will now talk about high and low water from Fivemile Rapids upstream to Celilo Falls. The Columbia River above Fivemile Rapids to Celilo Falls was the area that most commercial fishing was carried on in during the fall season; spring floods nearly put a stop to most commercial fishing here. The extreme end of Fivemile Rapids, opposite No. 5 Fishwheel, acted as a huge block or bottleneck in the flow of the Columbia downstream. In spring the river backed up very rapidly behind this bottleneck, the upper end of Fivemile Rapids. The river would spread out and over the gravel bars and flood, the shorelands of the Columbia River between Fivemile and Eightmile rapids.

At Eightmile Rapids there was another bottleneck in the flow of the Columbia downstream during the spring floods. On the Oregon side of the river there was a huge, high basalt plateau or reef that extended out to the river channel; this plateau broke off on a sheer bluff down to the river and low water. Across the river channel on the Washington side was Rabbit Island. Its south bank was also a high, sheer basalt bluff. In low water the Columbia flowed between these two bluffs forming Eightmile Rapids. On the north side of Rabbit Island there was a wide rocky channel, which extended to the Washington shore. When the river backed up in the spring flood at the head of Fivemile Rapids, it filled the channel at Eightmile Rapids very quickly, and when these rapids also filled, the Columbia backed up to Celilo Falls. When both Fivemile and Eightmile rapids filled from the spring flood, the river would then spread out and flow in back of Rabbit Island, and fill this channel with flood waters. This backwater soon put Celilo Falls under water. From the head of Fivemile Rapids up past the submerged Celilo Falls you had a wide, fast-flowing river. The river here was fast, but not wicked. Past and through the Eightmile Rapids channel the current was swift, but on the north side of Rabbit Island the current was fast but not too swift for a boat to navigate. It was during this flood time that the river steamers in the 1890s were taken over Celilo Falls down the river.

They would go in back of Rabbit Island at Eightmile Rapids, and then would tie up above Fivemile Rapids to wait for the river to fall so they could continue downstream through those rapids—this would be in late July.

There was little commercial fishing in any of this area during the spring flood. When Celilo Falls was drowned out, the Indians had no place to fish. There were only two exceptions, Seufert's China Pete Fishwheel at Eightmile Rapids, and Seufert's Big Tumwater Fishwheel at Tumwater. Both were low-water fishwheels. China Pete would do fairly well during a low-water spring season, but did not do much during high water. Big Tumwater was also a low spring wheel. If the spring flood was low, then Tumwater Fishwheel would do very well. In fact, during a low-water spring flood, Tumwater would do as well as No. 5 would do in a high spring flood. So here we have the two best fishwheels ever built: Seufert's No. 5 fishing at the head of Fivemile Rapids during high water in the spring season, and Tumwater fishing during a low water spring season at Tumwater. I must emphasize that the high water in the spring would back up at Fivemile Rapids and drown out Celilo Falls, and this would put an end to any prospect of the Big Tumwater Wheel catching any salmon to speak of. And in a low-water spring, No. 5 would not have any water in her channel, so she could not fish. Later in the summer and in the fall, when the Columbia was low, the gravel bars below the SP&S railroad bridge, below Celilo Falls, and downriver to Eightmile Rapids were uncovered, and it was there that Seufert's had their seines, and there that the gillnetters did their fishing.

The river here was fast, but the seine boats and gillnet boats were built for fast water; they had no trouble navigating, although there were whirlpools. Generally they weren't too big in this stretch. But even so you tried to avoid them if you could.

Celilo Falls was above the SP&S railroad bridge, and the narrow, deep, swift, vicious channels of fast water were fished only by the Indian dipnet fishermen from their wooden scaffolds. No man, no boat, could survive more than a few seconds in this swift water. The Celilo Falls that we see nowadays in photographs carried only half of the waters of the Columbia. The other half was flowing into two deep treacherous channels on the Washington side of the river; it came out below the SP&S bridge some distance above Seufert's Washington seining bar. In the fall the Columbia was cold and clear and had no driftwood of any kind. Driftwood and debris were found only during the spring floods. In this fishing area below the railroad bridge whirlpools were wicked, but most of the time we never gave them any thought, just avoided them if we could.

One fall, Guy Whipple, later our cannery superintendent until his death, was working on the Washington seine, and for some reason he wanted to cross the Columbia to the landing on the Oregon side. He took an empty ferry boat, one of the large rowboats used to ferry fish across the river. These ferry boats were about twenty-five feet long and at least five feet wide. Guy Whipple got in the boat and took one of the men working on the seine with him and shoved off. Whipple had a pair of oars and the other man also took a pair, and they started rowing. It was just a routine crossing Whipple had probably made dozens of times each fall fishing season. But when they reached the middle of the river a large whirlpool opened up alongside them. The ferry boat fell stern-first into the whirlpool and went down. Whipple grabbed the painter at the end of the bow and hung on. The whirlpool broke and formed a huge boil, which tossed both men and the boat back up to the surface. The boat was upside down. Whipple and his companion managed to climb on top of the ferry boat, and waved their arms and shouted to the gillnetters fishing nearby. The men came alongside in their gillnet boats and picked up both men. Guy Whipple found that he still had his hat on his head, and that his hat was dry. I asked Guy what he had thought when the boat went down. He said he thought that if he was going to drown they should find his body, so he grabbed the painter as the boat was going over and hung on for dear life. He knew that the wooden ferry boat would come to the surface; by locking his hands onto the painter his body would come up too, and be found.

The ferry boats used to carry fish across the river from the seine bar to the Oregon landing were open and rowed by two oarsmen. You put fish into the boat until they were four to six inches below the seat, but no more, because you didn't want to get the seat of your pants wet when you were rowing. These boats would hold at least a couple of tons of salmon. They were sturdy, built entirely of wood, and lasted for years. They had no rudder; one used oars to guide the boat.

Out on the river death was ever-present. Around the many river channels you could stand at the top of the channel and look down into the raging current below and know that if you slipped you were dead. There was absolutely no chance of survival if you fell in. And any number of men who worked on the boats were proud of the fact they didn't know how to swim. Their philosophy was simple: if you fell in the river you didn't have a chance, so why try to swim and struggle? If you couldn't swim, death was quicker; and since you were going to drown anyway, the quicker the better. Of course some men did fall into the river and survive, but they were exceptions. All accepted death as something that could happen to anyone at any time. When death did happen on the river it was a sobering experience to the survivors, but, after all, things couldn't come to a standstill. Fishing had to go on. Everyone felt sorry and the men felt it was too bad; but of course their feelings in the matter were tempered by just how well they knew the person. If they didn't really know the man they just felt it was too bad; if for some reason they hadn't liked the person who died, they were somewhat indifferent.

Drowning among the Indians was common, for they were often pulled off their fishing scaffolding into the river when the big salmon hit their dipnets. These big salmon would actually sometimes pull a man into the river. In the mid 1930s the Department of Indian Affairs made all the Indian fishermen tie themselves securely with a rope around their waists, fastened to shore, so they couldn't be pulled into the river from the fishing scaffolds. Surprisingly enough, this was a simple solution to a bad situation, and you might think anyone would have thought of this solution; but no Indian would ever think of tying himself to shore when fishing. I suppose it might have been thought of as kid stuff. But when the Indian Department ruled that the Indians must do it, and furthermore stated that no Indian could fish unless he was roped to shore, all the Indians quietly accepted this ruling without any question of their manhood.

CELILO FALLS CABLE WAYS

Celilo Falls was perhaps the richest fishing grounds in the world for the area involved. This entire fishing area was made possible by the development of Seufert's cable ways. Prior to about 1936, Celilo Falls had an Indian population in the fishing season of some 30 or 40 families that lived there permanently or came from the reservations to fish.

Most of the fishing spots around Celilo Falls were inaccessible because of swift waters. In some places the Indians could get to the fishing grounds by rowing a boat through the swift water. In others a few of the Indian men swam through the swift currents.

The salmon caught was packed out in gunny sacks to a rowboat where they were strung together by ropes passed through their mouths and gills. The rope was then tied to the back of the rowboat with the salmon floating in the water behind and towed to a landing just above the Tumwater Fishwheel. Here the salmon were dragged over the rocks to a buying station at the base of Tumwater Fishwheel and purchased by Seufert's fish buyers. In the early thirties salmon were cheap, bringing 1½ to 2 cents a pound for prime fall Chinook.

In 1930 Seufert's put two fishwheel scows on Big Island directly across from Tumwater Fishwheel. These two fishwheel scows caught a lot of salmon. The problem was how to get the salmon out economically. To solve the problem Seufert's built the first cable way at Celilo Falls from Tumwater Fishwheel to Big Island. Then the salmon could be moved from the fishwheel scows to the Oregon shore economically.

The Indian dipnet fishermen wanted to ride the cable way instead of rowing the fast current outside of Tumwater Fishwheel. The Indians carried their salmon to the cable way on Big Island and rode with their fish to the buying station. It was all so simple and easy and efficient that in about 1936 Seufert's put a cable way from Downes Channel over to Chief Island. Now it was easy to get Indian fishermen out to where the salmon could be caught and easy for the Indians to deliver their salmon to Seufert's buying station at Downes Channel where they were to be purchased. From then on it was a matter of deciding where the next cable way should be built to what good fishing area.

In less than ten years Celilo had developed from a few Indian fishermen to an estimated 1,000 Indians coming there to fish in the fall salmon season.

INDIANS

As earlier noted, at Celilo Falls all the Seufert's cable ways were centered around Downes Channel. These cable ways were run out to the islands by Celilo Falls where the Indians fished. You always put in the cable ways for the convenience of the Indian fisherman and his fishing site. These cable ways had an operator on duty from early morning to take the Indians out to their fishing sites and to bring them and their salmon catch home at night.

When Seufert's had their seines operating in the fall and the cannery was busy just canning seine fish, Seufert's would rent all of these cable ways at Celilo to the Columbia River Packers Association. They would then operate the cable ways and purchase all the salmon the Indians would deliver at the union price. Seufert's and the CRPA had an agreement that when the seine catch dropped off Seufert's could can all their seine fish plus all the Indian fish delivered at the cable way. Then Seufert's would again take over and operate the cable ways at Celilo. During the big fall salmon run, at least while the Company owned all the lands around Celilo Falls and could keep competitors off the property, the competition for salmon was heavy. Fish buyers would go to the Indian village and along the highway and offer the fishermen two cents or so above the union price for the fishermen to deliver their fish to them. These outside buyers had no expenses. They didn't own the land or pay property taxes, or annually pay to put in the cable ways and operate them for the fishermen. At times these fish buyers up in the Indian village and along the highway would make it expensive for us to keep our fishermen. The easy way for you to keep your fishermen was just to raise the price you were paying the fishermen up to the same as the buyers along the highway were paying.

The Astoria canneries would all send fish buyers to The Dalles during the fall salmon runs. Oftentimes they would rent land for a week or so in The Dalles and just set up a fish buying station there, paying the union price and in addition paying the fishermen so much per pound bonus for hauling the fish to The Dalles. McGowan from Chinook also bought salmon at The Dalles, but McGowan had a pick-up boat that always bought fish from the Indians down on the beach in front of town. Buying salmon from both the gillnetters and Indian fishermen around The Dalles-Celilo area was a highly competitive business.

The one big problem with the Indian fishermen at Celilo was liquor. In those days the Indians could not purchase liquor legally, but of course around The Dalles there were always white men willing to see that the Indians got all the liquor they wanted just as long as they had money to pay for it. I never knew of one Indian exploiting another, but there were plenty of white men around The Dalles who exploited the Indians every chance they got. One of the tragedies of the Indians drinking was, of course, their drinking to excess, and at Celilo, Indians looking for a place to sleep off a binge would often decide that either the main line of the Union Pacific or the SP&S was a good place to sleep. Sleeping on a railroad track was fatal if a train came along. A surprising number of Indian fishermen at Celilo met their death sleeping on the railroad tracks. They would have the whole countryside to lie down in but for some reason they often insisted on sleeping on the railroad tracks.

Some of the Indian fishermen at Celilo in the fall fishing season would take their fish money, drive to The Dalles and spend it with the white men in The Dalles who bootlegged liquor to the Indians. When an Indian fisherman in The Dalles got badly intoxicated the only thing the local police could do was to arrest the Indian and put him in The Dalles city jail. The next day the Indian would appear before a local judge, be fined for drunkenness and be sent back to Celilo to fish. Some of the Indian fishermen would just repeat the entire episode over again and by the weekend would be back in The Dalles city jail. After the same Indians had been in jail three or four times one weekend after another, the chief of police would get tired of booking these same Indians over and over.

This is how the police chief would handle the situation. When this particular Indian was brought in again for drunkenness, the Indian was put in the jail cell to sleep his drunk off, but the police were careful not to lock his cell door. In the morning when the Indian woke up and started to move around he would find the cell door unlocked. The Indian would push the cell door open, look out in the jail corridor and no one would be in sight. When he went to the jail door leading to the alley alongside of the police station, this door would be unlocked too. Now the Indian would open this door and look out and down the alley; not a cop in sight. So he would just walk out of jail and down the alley and disappear.

About an hour later the police chief would start to look for the Indian in all the wrong places, but where the police chief was sure to find some of the Indian's friends. The chief would ask these Indian friends if they had seen this particular Indian, and of course they had not seen him for weeks. But the Indian friends would like to know just what the chief of police wanted to see this Indian for. Then the police chief would tell the Indian's friends that the Indian had broken jail and that was a very serious crime and the police chief was sure looking for that Indian so the chief could lock him up for breaking jail. "You know," the police chief would say when he had finished telling me the story, "that poor Indian would be afraid to come back to The Dalles for months, afraid he was going to be locked up

42

for a long time for breaking jail." And the chief would laugh and add, "I would not be bothered by that Indian getting drunk in town for a long time."

You may wonder why didn't the city police arrest the white bootleggers for selling liquor to the Indians. Well, it was impossible to catch the white bootleggers selling booze to the Indians. The way it worked was this. The white bootlegger would have a room in a cheap dump. The Indian would come to the hall outside the room and pay the white bootlegger for a bottle of liquor. Now the money has changed hands but no liquor has changed hands. The Indian would go stand at the head of the alley in back of the cheap rooming house. The white bootlegger went out the back door into the alley, put a bottle of liquor on the outside windowsill in back of the flop house. The white bootlegger went back into his room, and the Indian, making sure no one was in the dark alley, walked by and picked his bottle of liquor off the windowsill. He had his liquor, the white bootlegger had his money, but no one had seen him actually sell the Indian any liquor. This stunt was worked in the east end of The Dalles for years. The cops knew it and regularly patrolled that alley, but never were the police able to get the evidence for an arrest and a conviction.

Our local Indians would invariably carry their pint of whiskey in a hip pocket. When the police would meet one of the Indians, they would whack him across the backside with a billy club. This would break the bottle of liquor. Not having time to drink more than a few gulps, and all that whiskey running down his pant legs and the broken bottle to boot, would make anyone most unhappy.

This is as good a place as any to point out that when the U.S. government built The Dalles Dam and flooded out Celilo Falls and the Indians fishing there, the U.S. government paid the Indians for destroying the Indians' fishing sites, but in no way did the government either purchase or pay for the Indians' treaty rights. The Indians' treaty rights (as set forth in the Indian Treaty of 1855) for the right of the Indians to fish in their usual and accustomed places, were in no way affected when the U.S. government paid the treaty Indians for destroying the fishing sites. The Indians' treaty rights are still in full force and have in no way lessened. The government, in paying the Indians for destroying their fishing sites at Celilo, was doing no more for the Indians than the United States government did for Seufert's when they bought Seufert's shore lands that were flooded out by The Dalles Dam pool.

I have mentioned the land that Seufert's owned along the Columbia River shore. But I want to point out that on all the land that Seufert's owned along the Columbia River, an Indian who was a treaty Indian could cross the Company land to reach the shore of the Columbia River to fish in his usual and accustomed places. This was a right guaranteed the local treaty Indians under the Treaty of 1855, and since a treaty is the supreme law of a land, the Indian treaty rights were superior to any rights conveyed to the Company by land deed.

At the end of World War II all the Seufert fish buyers paid cash to the Celilo Falls fishermen. This meant that we would have to get $7,000 to $8,000 in cash each day from the local banks during the fall fishing season. The Company office force would write out how

43

many rolls of each denomination of coins would be needed, how many dollar bills, fives, tens and twenties. A twenty-dollar bill was the largest denomination a fish buyer wanted. Each night they would tell the office force if they needed more or less of any particular coin or currency. You knew how many fish your fish buyers were getting each night and how much the Company was paying per pound for salmon, so there was no problem in determining the total amount of cash you would need. In those days the banks in The Dalles closed at three o'clock in the afternoon. I would take a Company check payable to the bank, drive my car into town, and the bank would give me the required money in one or two money sacks. I generally went to the bank alone and always unarmed. The Company was insured, and we had definite instructions if anyone tried to rob us, give up the money and no heroics. After all, the money could be replaced, but if you resisted and the robber shot you, no one could replace your life.

When I got the money from the bank I took it to the Company office, had it counted and placed it in the Company office vault. When the fish buyers came into the office for their fish buying funds, each was given what he needed. Again, you knew how many salmon each fish buyer was buying each night, and to figure his needs was no problem. He was given a sack of money. The office force counted out the sack of money in the fish buyer's presence. He took the money and signed a receipt for it. When the buyer returned from Celilo just after dark, he turned in his unspent cash to the office and at the same time, his fish tickets for salmon purchased. The total amount of the fish tickets, plus the

unspent cash, would be the total of the cash the fish buyer had picked up earlier. I don't remember any fish buyer returning to the office in the evenings with his fish tickets and cash ever either being short of cash or the necessary fish tickets to cover the amount of money spent for salmon.

In those days I collected silver dollars for my coin collection. Each afternoon when I went to the bank to get the salmon purchasing money I always got five rolls of silver dollars, for the Indian fishermen wanted them. I would open these rolls of silver dollars, go through them and pick out the silver dollars I wanted for my collection. Any silver dollars I took from the fish money I replaced with paper dollars from my pocket. It was an easy way for me to get a nice coin collection.

In all the years that Seufert's bought salmon from the Indians at Celilo for cash, none of Seufert's fish buyers were ever robbed or in any way threatened by anyone trying to steal cash from them. Seufert's big buyer station at Celilo was at Downes Channel. There were always whites and Indians around, and I suppose that so many people around the fish buyer protected him from robbery.

Old Seufert's records go back to about 1883, and they show that the records of the catch were very accurate, both for the intake of the fishwheels and for the Indian catch; both were recorded every day. One thing that these men did in the early days on these records was to be absolutely accurate. There was no deviation from anything, from one day to the next. Everything was put down each day exactly as it happened.

If one of the Indian fishermen fell into the river and was swept to his death, then immediately all of the

Indian fishermen would stop fishing for the day and would not return to the river until the following day. There were no exceptions, when an Indian fisherman lost his life fishing all the Indians stopped fishing regardless of how thick the salmon were in the river. I remember being down at Tumwater and looking up at Celilo Falls. Unknown to me an Indian had lost his life in the river and the word had swiftly spread to all the fishermen. They quit en masse, every Indian fisherman on the rocks simply walked off the fishing site together. It was a sight you could never forget.

One of our problems with our Indian fishermen was their love of being in a parade, riding horses in full regalia. The Indians were paid $2.50 a day to appear in parades, and regardless of how thick the salmon were at Celilo, or how many fish were being caught or how much money the Indians were making, whenever there was a parade around the countryside some of our best fishermen would leave their fishing and go to ride. The Pendleton Roundup was a particular headache, especially if the Roundup was during the open fishing season at Celilo, which it generally was.

These Indian fishermen loved cars. When the fall fishing season was on at Celilo, The Dalles was a prime used-car market in the state of Oregon. Of course these cars were just a means of transportation to an Indian, as the horse had been before. The car just took the Indian to where he wanted to go, and of course there was no better way to transport salmon from one place to another than by car. So if the Indian had a sack of salmon that he wanted to sell in town, into the back seat went the sack of salmon and that was that.

I remember very well one time an Indian came into the cannery. He had bought a brand new Buick, and that was in the days when a Buick was a big, expensive automobile. He had two squaws with him. They stopped at the cannery door, went over to the Chinamen and bartered or brought some four or five sacks of salmon heads from the Chinese butchers. These two squaws picked them up and carried them out to that brand new Buick, opened the back door, put the sacks of bloody salmon heads on the back seat; and then the Indian and the two squaws walked around to the front of the car, got in and drove away.

I always regretted that I never learned Chinook jargon. Around the cannery and Celilo some of the old Indians spoke only Chinook jargon. Around the cannery when an old Indian would come up to me and start talking Chinook I would tell them to wait a minute. I would look up Guy Whipple, who spoke Chinook jargon as well as he spoke English, tell Guy that an old Indian wanted something, that he was speaking Chinook, and would he find out what the Indian wanted. Well, I never learned Chinook jargon simply because it was so simple to ask Guy. When Guy Whipple died there was no one left who spoke Chinook jargon around amongst the whites. As for the poor old Indians who only spoke Chinook jargon, well, they were real old too, and somehow by sign language you would find out that they usually wanted salmon heads.

The Indians got salmon from the river, sold them to Seufert's, then when the salmon were butchered the Indians caught the salmon heads from the gut box and dried them for their own use in winter back at the reservation. This last summer I met an old Indian woman at an Indian gathering out at the old cannery grounds and she was reminiscing to me about the good old days before the dams were built on the Columbia River, how she and her family used to set up camp in back of Seufert's Cannery and dry salmon heads from the gut box for the coming winter. To her, those were the old, old days.

All of the Indian fishermen were extremely fond of watermelons. In the fall of the year the farmers around Hermiston would bring a load of watermelons down to The Dalles and sell them. Later in the season when the stores had had all the watermelons they could sell, these Hermiston farmers would have part of a load of watermelons unsold and rather than haul them back home and dump them, these farmers would come to the office and offer the rest of the load of watermelons to the Company for a few dollars. The Company would pay the farmer for his watermelons and have him deliver the melons to the fish house at Tumwater. He would pile the watermelons in the shade on the fish house deck and every Indian who delivered fish, in addition to his fish ticket, got to go over to the pile of watermelons and pick one for himself. If the Indian fisherman had two or three or four fishing partners, then each one got a watermelon. Now whether these free watermelons ever got us any more fish I don't know, but it sure didn't make us any enemies amongst the Indian fishermen.

Indians were always referred to by the men as just Indians, or if they were speaking about a particular Indian, they would say that McKinley Wesley is doing so and so. Indians always lived in a camp, and they always referred to it as up at the camp, or up at the village, or up at Celilo.

Seufert's always bought some fish from the natives in the area, even from the time the cannery was started. I would say that after the operation started in 1889 or 1890 at Celilo, where the Indians were fishing, they began to buy many more fish from the Indians in the fall of the year simply because the Indian fishery was available.

The Indians fishing at Celilo were a decent people. I never heard of a Celilo Indian ever being involved in a serious crime. I am talking about armed burglary or a violent crime against property.

Time after time in the winter when it was cold and these Indians needed fuel to keep their shacks warm, they would come down to the cannery and ask permission to pick up waste lumber to use for fuel. Any white man would have taken the scrap lumber, and the Company could have gone and jumped into the Columbia River. Still, when these Indians needed food in the winter, such as flour, sugar and salt, they would come to the Company office and ask for credit, or an advance on the fish they expected to catch the next summer. Instead of giving the Indian cash, the Company would call a local grocery store, tell the store that a certain Indian was coming in for groceries, and to give him the goods and charge them to the Company. You expected the Indian to pay you back by bringing you his fish the next summer, but the Indian would seldom do this. He seemed to enjoy making a game out of delivering the fish to you, but under someone else's name, so he wouldn't have to have his advanced grocery money deducted. Of course you found out whose name he was delivering his fish under and took the money out of that ticket. You got your money, the Indians settled the withheld cash from the partner's receipts among themselves. Now everybody had his money and the Indian's credit was good and next winter he would come to the office, borrow money, and start the whole little episode all over again.

When my grandmother lived out at the cannery she collected Indian arrowheads and artifacts for years. Many of the items from her collection are now in the Smithsonian Institution at Washington, D.C. Indian arrowheads and artifacts were so common around Seufert's Cannery that in the 1920s, in front of the cannery in the yard, we put Indian stone bowls beneath the water faucets to catch the water that leaked out; in the office they used Indian artifacts for door stops; the upstairs attic of the old Seufert home at the cannery was full of Indian artifacts.

In the 1920s a retired U.S. Army major was collecting artifacts for the Smithsonian. He asked F. A. Seufert to give some, and this was readily done. This retired major took out two automobile-loads in one afternoon. I helped carry them out of the old house and the major paid me fifty cents for my work. I was one surprised boy, since I was just helping for fun and not expecting to be paid. The next day, just to show his appreciation to F. A. Seufert, the same major went down in the dry channel just above the Lone Pine Tree Indian village and sifted the sand and collected enough Indian stone beads to make two necklaces over two feet long, which he brought up to the office and gave to my grandfather.

Indian artifacts were especially plentiful in front of the government houses at Big Eddy alongside The Dalles-Celilo Canal, and any day when we had nothing to do and wanted to kill time, we would go across the creek in back of the cannery and hunt arrowheads in the orchards, the best days being just after the wind had blown a gale. Arrowheads were so common that in an hour or so you would find eight or ten, all good ones in perfect shape, and broken ones you didn't even bother to pick up.

Seufert's lands between Big Eddy and No. 5 Fishwheel on the Oregon side of the Columbia River were fished by both white and Indian dipnetters. The Indians fished all along Fivemile Rapids, and the whites around No. 3 Fishwheel. These were generally white men who worked for the railroad, but had been on the extra board and had been laid off. They would dipnet to earn some money until they were called back to work. Seufert's would send a fish buyer with a truck twice a day to visit all these dipnet fishermen in the area. There was only fishing here during high water in the spring. It was simply a case of the fish buyer going to the fishermen to get the fish. After all, a fisherman was not going to pack his fish any father than he had to in order to sell them, so if your buyer was there, then you got the fish. In this area owned by Seufert's, competitors' fish buyers could not buy fish on Company land. If they did, they were trespassing and you could have them arrested; a competitor's fish buyer could buy salmon along the public highway, but he had to pay considerably more than the union price to get the fishermen to pack fish up to the highway.

You always had a few Indians who would take their fish into The Dalles when they wanted to go to town, so Seufert's always bought a fish-buying license for a butcher shop in The Dalles, and the shop could then legally buy salmon for Seufert's from any Indian who came to that particular butcher shop. The shop got a commission for any salmon it purchased from the Indians and delivered to Seufert's.

On the Washington side of Fivemile Rapids the Indians fished in the spring. Seufert's owned most of the Washington shore along these rapids, but the Indian village at the head of the rapids was a place where any of your competitors could buy all the salmon the Indians would sell them. Seufert's had the Cyclone Wheel fish house in this area, and had a fish buyer take his truck there twice a day to visit all the Indians dip-netting along Fivemile Rapids and he alwo went to the Indian village.

The legal limit applied to white fish buyers when they were purchasing fish from the Indians. An Indian could fish under his treaty rights for his own use above the legal commercial fishing line on the Columbia River and its tributaries. But the white commercial fresh salmon buyers and packers could only buy salmon fron the Indians that had been caught during the legal fish season below the mouth of the Deschutes River. Any salmon caught above the legal line by an Indian was illegal if it was sold, and a white buyer was subject to both a fine and a jail sentence for buying illegally-caught salmon from the Indian. Now when an Indian brought you fish, if there was any doubt in your mind about the Indian selling illegal salmon, you would ask the Indian where he had caught the fish. He would always say Celilo, even in the spring when Celilo Falls was under the floodwaters of the Columbia. But then, if the Indian said he caught the salmon at Celilo, who was about to insult him by calling him a liar? You took the Indian's word for it, and bought his salmon.

On April 27, 1945, the reservation Indians and a colonel of the U.S. Army Engineers held a meeting in The Dalles, the Indians to protest the building of The Dalles Dam that would destroy the Indians' old and accustomed fishing sites at and around Celilo Falls. An attorney for the Indians who knew me asked if I would like to attend, since this might be the last meeting between the old Indian chiefs and the U.S. Army. I was glad to have the chance to be present at the meeting. It took palce that afternoon upstairs in The Dalles city hall in a room on the northeast side of the building. It was a hot day and it was soon apparent that many of the Indian fishermen from Celilo were present. The colonel was there in his full uniform and also present were the old Indian chiefs from the reservation.

The Indian chiefs were all old men, very dignified. Each of the old chiefs came forward, one at a time, shook the colonel's hand and talked through an interpreter giving the Indians' story of their dependence on Columbia River salmon, and the serious effect that the building of the dam at The Dalles would have on the Indians' livelihood. The old chiefs made many references to the Indian Treaty of 1855, the terms of the treaty and the obligations of the U.S. government to uphold the sacredness of the treaty and not build The Dalles Dam.

The elegance and dignity of the old Indian chiefs in stating the Indians' case, their choice of words, the beautifully put phrases, excellent prose, their poetic way of using picturesque and yet descriptive speech, was something that no one present would ever forget. The simplicity of the old chiefs' speech was a moving

48

thing to hear. I was impressed with the respect the old chiefs were held in by the younger Indians. I had never seen anything like it before. After all the old chiefs had spoken, a number of the old women also addressed the colonel, these old Indian women telling the Indians' side of the story of previous promises, and only receiving broken promises and excuses from the U.S. government. These old Indian women pleaded with the colonel not to let that history from the Indian standpoint repeat itself again.

After the old chiefs and the old Indian women had all had their say, the good colonel expressed extreme sympathy for the Indians, and wanted them to know that the Army Engineers would have nothing to do with the decision to build a dam at The Dalles, only Congress could do that.

As I left the meeting and walked down the stairs, I couldn't help feeling I had witnessed another bit of history in our government's dealing with the American Indian, and I was sure of one thing at the time: if local merchants saw a chance to make money through the building of a dam at The Dalles, then nothing as simple as an Indian treaty signed some 90 years before was going to stand in their way.

I have talked about fishwheel scows that were operated by Seufert's and by other white fishwheel scow operators, but I only know of two cases where an Indian ever owned and operated a fishwheel scow. It took a lot of hard work and responsibility to operate a scow. You had to be on the job all the time. You had to visit your scows at least twice a day, once in the morning and again at night. The scow had to be bailed each morning and night. You had to adjust your lines holding the scow to shore, you had to check your spars, and always when the weekend closures to commercial fishing began at 6:00 P.M. Saturday night you had to be there to pull your wheel. If you let the fishwheel scow run over the weekend, the fish warden would put you in jail; and if you pulled your scow over the weekend, then you had to be back and put your scow in on Sunday night at 6:00 P.M. or miss that much legal fishing. You just couldn't leave a fishwheel scow unattended for any length of time or your scow would sink and you would be out of business.

This constant necessity of looking after your fishwheel scow just ruined an Indian's way of life. He just could not pick up at any time he chose and go back to the reservation to visit his relatives and friends; and anyhow, an Indian could catch all the salmon he needed with a dipnet, so why tie himself down by having to operate and be responsible for a fishwheel scow. The only exception I ever heard of was an old Indian named Oscar Charlie who lived in Spedis, or Spearfish as we sometimes called it. Somehow in the late 1920s he had gotten hold of a fishwheel scow that he fished at the head of Fivemile Rapids on the Washington side of the Columbia River. He fished this scow until 1934 when fishwheels were voted out by the state of Washington. While Oscar Charlie operated his scow he never caught many fish, although he caught more salmon with the wheel than he ever would have caught with a dipnet; but even at that, Oscar Charlie's fishwheel scow had her wheel in the air over half the time.

Sam Williams was an Indian who lived down on Lone Pine Tree Island Indian village. A couple of whites in The Dalles had been peddling liquor to the local Indians around The Dalles. They had been on Seufert property, and F. A. Seufert told these two white bootleggers that if he ever caught them selling liquor to the Indians around the cannery he would turn them over to the federal authorities. To get even with Seufert, these two white bootleggers somehow got possession of a dilapidated, old fishwheel scow and gave it to Sam Williams, and then moved the scow out to the end of Threemile Reef for Sam Williams to operate. Seufert's had operated a fishwheel scow on the end of that reef for years, and when F. A. Seufert found this broken down old scow on the end of the reef right at his own fishwheel site, he took a crew from the cannery, moved Sam Williams' scow downriver and carefully tied it up at the bank, and moved Seufert's fishwheel scow into its usual fishing site at the end of Threemile Reef.

Sam Williams took his troubles to the U.S. Indian Department, who turned the case over to the U.S. attorney's office in Portland. Seufert's was brought into federal court and charged with interfering with an Indian's fishing rights under the 1855 treaty. Seufert admitted he was familiar with this treaty, and with the treaty Indian rights to fish in their usual and accustomed places along the Columbia River at The Dalles; but he argued that, although the treaty guaranteed the Indians' rights to fish in their usual and accustomed places, at the time the treaty was signed the Indians were using spears and dipnets, not fishwheels, and that he would let an Indian cross Seufert land to the Columbia River to fish with a spear and a dipnet but not with a fishwheel scow.

However the U.S. federal judge saw things differently. He ruled that Sam Williams had a right to fish a fishwheel scow at the end of Threemile Reef under the Indian treaty. He ruled the Indian had the same right to advance and become civilized as a white man, and it was unreasonable to hold an Indian to fishing at all times by the same methods used by his forefathers at the time the treaty was signed. I mention this case because of its importance, for it established the Indians' civil rights to become civilized and advance along with the white man and other citizens in the United States.

After the case was settled in 1917, Sam Williams' scow sat for years in one of the channels below Threemile Reef and just slowly fell to pieces. To my knowledge after the federal court ruled in Sam Williams' favor, he made little effort to fish his scow wheel again.

SEINES

Seufert's had two seines. These were said to be at Celilo but in fact they were about a mile below the SP&S railroad bridge. The one on the Oregon side was called just the Oregon Seine, or sometimes the Company and the men called it Bar One. On the other side of the river the seine was called the Washington Seine, or just Bar Two.

Year after year in the thirty-day fall fishing season, Bar One and Bar Two caught as many or more fish than all of Seufert's fishwheels would catch in the two-and-a-half month spring season. But still the seines were never the political football the fishwheels were. The seines were highly efficient, but not spectacular. The seines used horses, boats and crews, and perhaps for this reason people felt less prejudiced against them.

When the men talked about the Company's seines down at the cannery or upriver at one of the fish houses, the bulging seine itself was simply called the seine or the net. Down at the cannery you referred to the seining operation as up at the seine, or up at Bar One. Actually the proper term was a drag seine.

After making a sweep out into the river, the net was dragged up on the beach, hence its name. The up-per end of the seine was attached to the shore, and the rest was laid out from the stern of a seine boat. The seine boat moved downstream. The salmon were corralled or encircled in the seine. The encirclement was complete when the lower end of the seine was landed on the beach downstream. Then the seine was pulled up on the beach and the salmon were removed from it. While the salmon were being encircled, they would back away from the net, which was slowly moving toward them. Also these alarmed salmon would dive deeper into the water, only to find they were unable to get under the lead line that dragged on the bottom. This made the salmon either back away from the net or race about in the water. Actually the salmon only had to surface and jump a few inches over the cork line to be safe, but that would not have been a natural way for the salmon to react, so they rarely escaped that way.

When you were on a seining bar and wanted to attach a line or cable to something secure, but there was nothing suitable on the beach or bar, you could dig a pit or hole and put a timber in it. Then you would attach the cable to the timber and fill up the hole. If the timber was buried deep enough, you didn't have to worry about the cable pulling out. The seining crew would refer to this operation by saying they had buried a dead man. The first time you heard the expression it was a shocker, but you soon learned that when the crew buried a dead man you didn't call the sheriff.

The upper end of a drag seine was anchored to the shore by the dead man; or more often the upper end of the seine would be held by a team of horses — the anchor team. When the lower end of the seine landed it was taken on shore and pulled up on the beach by another team of horses — the running team; the team raced up the beach pulling the seine ashore as fast as possible, which was why it was called the running team. As long as the lower end of the net remained open, any salmon could race through the opening and escape from the seine. The seine itself was carried on the back of a seine boat. As the seine boat made its fishing circle in the river, the men were said to be laying the net, or making the lay, or you could say the crew had started fishing.

The crew members on a seine boat were never sailors. They were just called the seine crew. All of the men on the seine crew, regardless of what job they performed, received the same wages. One job was just as important as another. The only exception was the seine boss, and he received more than any other man in the crew. He was never called captain, but he was said to be running the seine.

When the season opened a seine would not fish well the first day. The net was dry and had to make several lays before it became wet so it could sink down into the water rapidly as it should. The seine boat was either pulled by a power boat or, years ago, rowed by oarsmen. As the net slid off the back of the seine boat

into the river you said the net was being laid. After the seine was on the beach and was loaded back onto the stern of the seine boat, you said the net was picked up. The act of the men placing the net on the stern of the boat, and the seine being laid back and forth in large folds, was called swiping the net. When a seine came ashore after making a lay, and was pulled up on the beach, it was said to have landed, or beached, and the men said they had completed a haul. If you asked the seine foreman how the seine was doing, he would say that in the last haul he had caught so many fish. A haul was the complete operation of laying the seine out in the river and then landing it on the beach.

A seine had a cork line that floated on top of the water. It also had a lead line, which was a heavy piece of lead attached to a line at the bottom of the seine. This was to hold the lower end of the net on the bottom. The seine always had to be on the bottom. If the lead line ever came off the river bottom, the salmon could duck under the seine and escape.

After a seine landed on the beach the salmon were removed by tossing them on the beach. If they were left in the water or in the net they might get away. The person who removed the salmon wore a pair of cotton gloves and grasped the salmon firmly under the gills and tossed them up onto shore. The boat that collected the salmon from the seine bar was called the pick-up boat. If it had a gasoline motor it was called a launch by the oldtimers, or sometimes even a gasoline launch. If it had no motor and was operated by oarsmen, it was called a ferry boat.

The seine was woven by the net manufacturer to the Company's specifications. The length of a seinewas stated in feet, but the depth, that is the distance between the cork line and lead line, was stated as so many meshes deep. When you ordered the seine you always specified the size of the mesh (the diamond shape of the net between knots pulled taut), which was measured in inches. The mesh (or diamond shape) was measured between the extreme length of the diamond from top to bottom. Both ends of a seine were tapered so that when it was laid out in the river the taper would be the same as the slant of the river bottom from the shore outward. If a seine web was torn, it was said to have a hole in it; this was repaired by putting in a new piece. The seine was laid out and fished every hour on the hour during daylight. This hourly basis of fishing gave the salmon time to collect on the seine bar. This was called giving the salmon time to come back. The biggest haul was always at sunset. As night approached, the salmon seemed to drop back downriver to gather on the seine bars for the night. Perhaps they did not want to be caught in the swift waters of the river after dark.

All heavy rope used in construction of a seine or in fishing a seine was called line. The men always referred to rope as manila rope. A steel cable was just called a cable. The corks that held the net afloat were made of cedar. The seine net was mended with twine. The net was the seine itself, but the diamond-shaped forms of fitted twine were called web or seine web. The twine holding the seine net to the cork line was called hanging twine. The men who drove the anchor and running teams on the beach were called either teamsters or skinners.

The seine crew always had its own cook and its own mess house and bunk house. These were large tents erected on 2x4 frames with a wooden floor.

When the seine bar was closed down the tent was removed but generally the floor and frames were left on the beach and were carried away in the floodwaters the next spring. The seine crews were hired for so much a day, plus board and room, plus a bonus of so much per ton of salmon caught per man. You took the total tonnage of salmon caught by a seine and divided that by the number of men on the seine, and that way you figured out how much tonnage was due each man on the bonus system. Under this system the more salmon a seine caught, the bigger the earnings of the men.

The seine boss, or foreman, was the key man; he really had to know his business. He rode the boat every time it made a lay, and directed it out into the river. He decided when the boat should turn to head downriver, how far out into the river the boat should go, how far downriver, and when to make the turn for a run to the beach. He made the decisions on every lay, over and over, all day long. If he knew his business, the seine caught fish; if he didn't, there were no fish caught and it was just too bad for both Company and crew. Men had to work for years on a seine crew before becoming a boss. The Company knew them all, and well. And every man on the crew knew the boss well. These men had worked on the river for so many years that they had established their reputations as good seine men long before they were entrusted with being bosses. They were a breed apart, and I don't know why. During my time on the river Seufert's had only two seine bosses, and each of these men had been on the river for some 40 years.

A seine foreman's most important tools were his pocket knife and a needle, which he used to mendnets. He used the knife to cut out pieces of net that were torn or had to be replaced. Of course the needle was used to repair breaks in the net. This was a never-ending job. The seine foreman always checked the seine web after each lay, and breaks had to be repaired before the next. Salmon would find any hole in the seine and escape through it into the open river.

A man repairing a seine net was said to be working on it. A hole in the seine was a tear. The seine itself was a very heavy cotton twine. A new seine net was treated in a solution of water and tanning bark at the cannery before it went out to the seining bar to fish. The tanning bark solution preserved the net so it would not rot quickly when fishing. At the end of the season a seine net was worn out. The net itself would become weak and rotten, and the web would pull apart if you gave it a hard yank. Old seine web was often put into a pile and burned, because there was really no further use for it.

From time to time you would have to break in a new horse for one of the seine teams. Horses that had been broken in to pull a wagon would not pull on a rope until they had been especially broken to it. The simple method used by the men on the seine bar was to make up a three-horse team, with two older seine horses on the outside and the new horse in between. This team would pull on a rope that was usually attached to a sled weighted down with gravel. Once the team started, the unbroken horse had to go along. He could balk, and some would even fall over and lie on the ground, but the two seine horses would drag him along.

If the new horse refused to pull on the rope, the men would hitch up the two older horses and make a two-horse team, and run a line back to the unbroken horse. This horse was now hitched up alone, and a line ran from his harness back to the rock sled. The first team would be started up and of course the new horse, hitched up single, had to go along. Some of these horses, however, would just lie down on the gravel, and the two-horse team would drag them over the gravel bar. If the new horse just let himself be dragged and made no effort to get up and pull, the seine crew would generally just turn him loose and give up and break in another horse. As a general rule when a new horse was first hitched between the two seine horses he might balk, but then he would usually settle down and pull. The other alternative was considered drastic.

The seine men who waited on the beach between lays always talked in very low voices. A man did not shout or raise his voice except in an emergency. A loud shout was a warning or a cry for help. Horse teams stood nearby resting. Everyone on the seine crew wore gum boots so even when a man stood up and walked on the gravel bar there was no noise except that caused by his feet making the gravel crunch. Loud talking was thought to scare the fish away from the seining bar. These men were paid a bonus of so much per ton of salmon caught and of course they would not needlessly raise their voices and scare the salmon off the bar. It would mean that much less money in the bonus at the end of the fishing season. Even the teamsters wore rubber boots. The men were also all furnished with rubber aprons, and of course, that old standby for handling salmon, cotton gloves. The men generally wore plain white cotton caps, although once in a while a man might wear a hat, but it would be old and battered.

When oarsmen rowed the seine boats while they

were making a lay, there was no noise except for the gentle slap of the water against the side of the seine boat, the muffled sound of the oars working in the oarlocks, the seine itself spilling off the back of the boat into the water made no noise at all. The boats were often rowed by six oarsmen facing the stern of the seine, sitting two to a seat, and each man handling one oar.

The foreman stood up near the stern, directly in front of the seine, which was piled on the stern. The foreman faced forward. These seine boats had no rudder. The seine foreman had two oars, one on each side of the boat. As he stood up he rowed and maneuvered the boat just by using these two oars. No one spoke in the boat. There was no need to. Every man in the boat knew his business, what to do and what was expected of him. There was no reason for the seine boss to give any orders. When the seine boat was far enough out on the river on the lay, and the foreman was ready to turn the boat to head downriver, he turned it himself.

When the boat had completed the lay and came ashore, the boss took the end of the seine in the boat. It had a loop in the end of the line. He jumped overboard in the shallow water and waded ashore. The running team was waiting for him. The foreman threw the loop in the line over a hook on the end of a chain that was attached to double-trees of the running team. This was the only time when anyone hollered. When the loop was on the hook, the foreman hollered and the running team took off across the beach as tight as they could go, the teamster running hard to keep up. Running over gravel after the team took real skill in order to stay on your feet.

After the end of the seine was ashore the currents in the river would help bring the seine into the beach. As the lead line came in it was stretched out so tight it would lift a few inches off the gravel bar. The men would place their gum-booted feet on it to hold it flat so no salmon could get underneath the lead line and escape into the river. Then the men walked into the water and took the cork line and held it up with their hands, say a foot above the water, so the salmon couldn't jump over it and get away. With the running team pulling the seine up on the beach, the seine was ashore in a very short time; but all the while no one spoke, in fact no one had time to talk. Only after the seine was landed would anyone have anything to say; and then it was generally just whether they had had a good run and caught a lot of fish.

But the business of catching salmon was silent. There was no noise on the river. You could hear the water lapping on the gravel on the beach, or the water running over the rocks, or the swells in the river piling up on the rocks, and then the quiet noise the water made when it drained back into the river. There were the birds, the seagulls and ravens, and of course you could hear their cries as they flew over the river. The only man-made noise was a person talking, or a motorboat engine; but when the person stopped talking, or the engine was shut off, then everything was silent again except for the natural sounds made by the flowing river.

The only unpleasant sound was the wind howling on a bad day, but then this sound was just part of the river and fishing, too. It belonged, and really didn't seem out of place. Although the wind blowing sand was unpleasant, it was not so much the noise as the fact that the sand got into everything. During the daytime the river was never lonely; the little noise the river made was comforting, and was especially pleasant on days in the middle of the fall, during Indian summer, when there was no wind, and the weather was pleasantly warm. I think yet of those pleasant days around the river, days when it was a joy just to be there.

Now I'll talk a little about the horses that were used on the seines. After the seine had been landed on the bar, and the salmon had been picked up by the boats, the horses would still be in the harness. The teamster would ride one of the horses, and all the animals would be driven knee-deep into the river and allowed to drink their fill. After they had satisfied their thirst, the team returned to shore and was allowed to rest standing on the beach. The teamster would sit on the bar and hold the reins in his hands. The Company built a makeshift barn on the bar for the horses to use during the seining season, just some corner posts with 2x12s nailed to them to form the sides of a pen; no roof, really, just a corral, with hay and grain. When the seining season was over the Company just left this on the bar. The spring floods would carry away the timbers. When fall came the place was clean, and you could just put up another temporary barn.

After the season in the fall the horses were driven down to the cannery and put into the horse barn, which was across the railroad tracks from the cannery. Wagon Bridge, owned by Seufert's, spanned Fifteenmile Creek at the barn. The land just across the creek opposite the barn was used as horse pasture. In spring and fall the horses were used around the cannery for plowing if they were needed. They were used in the

orchards, since the men thought the only way to plow around fruit trees was with a team of horses.

The men on the seine were hired only for the seine fishing season. In the days when the boats were rowed by oarsmen, most of these men were Finns who had at one time been seamen on the windjammers carrying grain out of Portland. Seufert's used these Finns until there were none of the old sailors left. Surprisingly this continued on into the 1930s; and after that Seufert's seine boats were pulled by gasoline engine tenders.

A man's age was never considered in hiring for Seufert's Cannery fishing operations. In fact, most of the men working for Seufert's were middle aged. A man was hired for his ability to perform the job, and for no other reason. Middle-aged men were highly skilled; they knew their jobs and that was all that counted.

Seufert's had a third seine down below Bar One on the Oregon shore. This was operated by a man named Mumpower, who was a good man and knew his business. The Company furnished the seining bar and the boat, and Mumpower furnished the men and operated the seine on a share basis; Seufert's received one-third of the fish, and Mumpower the rest. Seufert's was not concerned with what he paid his men; they only cared that the operation caught fish. Once the salmon were caught and landed on the beach, Seufert's picked them up and hauled them to the cannery.

A great many of the men who worked all of these seines had steady jobs in The Dalles, but in the fall they would take their vacations and spend the next two weeks or so on the seining operations. They would not only get their vacations but would also pick up a nice piece of money from wages and the bonus from the successful seine fishing season.

The seine boats and ferry boats used on Seufert's seines were all painted boxcar red. The pick-up boats were usually gray-white, and all the fishwheel scows were red. The mess and bunk houses were all yellow. The China bunkhouse and China cookhouse were also painted yellow. The big fish houses were all painted boxcar red. I know of no reason that any of these colors were used at a particular place; probably they were available and cheap.

I would like to mention the effect of the seines and gillnetters on Indian fishing. Up at Celilo Falls in the fall of the year, when the Indians were fishing for their own use, it would be in the first week of September before the commercial fishing season opened, the Indians would do well, catch lots of fish. Then on September 10th the commercial fishing season would open. This would mean that Seufert's seines and the gillnetters would all start fishing below the SP&S railroad bridge. No matter how many fish Seufert's seines caught, or how many fish the gillnetters caught, it made no difference at all in the size of the Indians' catch at Celilo Falls. The Indians would go right on catching just as many fish as before the seines and the gillnetters started to fish.

GILLNETTERS & DIPNETTERS

I want to talk now a little about the gillnetters. They and their union were always agitating against Seufert's and their fishwheels, claiming the wheels took too many fish.

In 1931 Seufert's had some 50 gillnet boats fishing for them on the Columbia River below the SP&S railroad bridge. These gillnet boats would average 1,800 pounds a night per boat. They caught so many spring salmon for Seufert's that the cannery could not begin to can them; so the surplus, some 20 tons a day, was sold to downriver canneries in Astoria, to the Columbia River Packing Association (CRPA), and to the Pillar Rock Packing Company.

The net fishermen who fished for Seufert's generally fell into two groups: white gillnetters, and the dipnet fishermen who were usually Indians from the reservations. The gillnet area around The Dalles was divided into two parts: the gillnet fishery above The Dalles, and the one below Celilo Falls, starting just below the railroad bridge and continuing downstream for several miles; it ended just above Rabbit Island. I assume this was about a mile-and-a-half of fishing area. The gillnetters were generally spoken of as coming

from Oregon City, because a number of them used either an Oregon City address or had fished the Willamette River below the falls at Oregon City at some time or other. This salmon gillnet fishery was swift water, and the gillnet boats were especially designed to fish there. They were a dory design, and had an inboard gasoline engine. The bow of the boat rode high out of the water; the sides had plenty of flare. These gillnetters, even in the early 1930s, hauled their boats to the fishing grounds on trailers pulled behind their cars. These same fishermen also fished the many Oregon coastal streams for salmon.

The gillnet fishing from The Dalles downriver to Mosier was fished by the big gillnet boats from Astoria. These boats had a round bottom, were designed to fish in front of Astoria in the rough Columbia River. The river below The Dalles was considered quiet water, not swift water. But this part of the river was as nasty a stretch of water as any on the entire Columbia, especially when the west wind was blowing a gale up the river. This created a nasty chop with big swells, and the waves were close together, that is, the crests were close together. You couldn't ride them; you had to plow right through them. If you weren't careful, they would swamp your boat. When the west winds blew, these heavy Astoria boats just tied up in a harbor and waited for the winds to die down so they could fish again. The area here was largely fished for the CRPA and for McGowan's, although Seufert's had a buying station on the Oregon side at the Lyle-Rowena Ferry. This station was operated for Seufert's by the operator of the ferry. This buyer was paid so much a pound for each salmon he bought from the gillnetters and delivered to the cannery.

The Indian dipnetters, who came down from the reservations to fish for Seufert's, fished at Celilo Falls in the autumn, and on the Washington side of the river between Spearfish and Spedis and Big Eddy in the spring. These Indians owned their fishing sites at both areas, acquired either through inheritance, passing from father to son, or by marriage. As a rule the Indians who owned, or at least claimed, a particular fishing site would form what they called a company. An Indian and a number of his friends, generally four or five other Indians, would form this group or company and they would fish that particular site together, dividing the salmon caught or the money earned from the sale of fish equally. When these companies were formed, each Indian took his turn fishing from the fishing site for a short time. Then he would turn the site over to another member of the group. In this way the Indians fished the site all day long, but no one had to fish continually and become tired. Some would fish for about ten minutes and then rest for the next half hour.

The Indians' wives also figured in the picture. After the Indian fisherman caught the salmon, his wife would come down, put the salmon in a sack and pack it over the rocks to the weighing station. All he had to do then was to collect his fish ticket. I would say that these squaws could easily pack 100 pounds of salmon in a sack on their backs and walk over those rough rocks with no apparent effort. Surprisingly enough there were not too many Indians fishing at Celilo Falls during the Depression. Of course the Indians then took all the salmon they needed for their own use. The ones they kept were usually dried. The surplus salmon would be sold to Seufert's for cash. At the outbreak of World War II, with the big increase in the price of raw salmon to the fisherman, a large number of Indian fishermen from all the reservations around The Dalles area flocked to Celilo Falls to fish. The price of salmon for the fishermen was high, the profits were good, and the Indians, like white men, recognized a good thing when they saw it.

In 1931 the gillnetters fishing for Seufert's caught more fish in one day than any fishwheel ever caught in a single day, more in fact than *all* of Seufert's fishwheels ever caught in one day: this was over 50 tons caught by the Indian gillnetters in one day in May of 1931.

Neither the Company nor the men working for it ever broke any fishing laws. If there was any doubt in a matter, you always gave the law the benefit of the doubt. Between the gillnetters on the river and the politicians in Salem, who constantly played politics against Seufert's and the fishwheels, you never, and I repeat never, gave these gillnetters or the politicians the vaguest reason to charge you with any fish law violations. There was nothing these politicians and the fishermen's unions would have loved better than to have Seufert's convicted in court for a salmon-fishing violation. They would have used the case in the state legislature.

We were on friendly terms with all gillnetters. When we met there was always a friendly exchange of information about the salmon runs in the river, how much fish the gillnetters had caught, where they were fishing, and when they would be in with their fish for us; but when the gillnetters were gone and out of sight, you never really trusted them.

The gillnetters were a clannish group and didn't care what a man did as long as they were left alone. Some lived on their boats, but most made camp on shore wherever it was convenient. When the gillnetters were not fishing they were ashore mending their nets or repairing their boats. As a group, they were not quarrelsome and didn't cause anyone trouble. When they were not working on their boats or nets they would sit around and talk or lie on the rocks, just resting as they said, or go to their camps for meals and rest. Some of the gillnetters had their wives along, and one unwritten rule was to let another man's woman alone.

The gillnetters never saw a fish law broken by another gillnetter, and you were never supposed to see them break a fish law either. The gillnetters and the law were always on opposite sides. The gillnetters just never had much use for a law enforcement officer. After all, the law was always trying to get something on the gillnetters. The gillnetters were just trying to make an honest living, and if things sometimes seemed to be a little farfetched, the gillnetters could explain everything. The only trouble was that sometimes the dumb cops didn't seem to be able to understand, but as far as the Company was concerned, any problems the fish warden had with the gillnetters was the fish warden's problem. The Company wasn't hired to police the river. Once in a while you might tell these gillnetters that you could see a couple of them out on the river when they weren't supposed to be there, and you didn't know which one it was, but they had better watch it or the fish warden some night would grab him for sure. Of course, if a state policeman should show up down at the landing during legal fishing, it was surprising how much intense interest everyone would show in whatever job he was doing at that moment. I would say, however, that it never entered anyone's head to hate a policeman. The police had a job to do, but everyone wished he would do it somewhere else. If a fisherman was picked up by a warden no one was particularly angry with the warden. Everyone thought that the man who got pinched should have been more careful, and anyway, any damn fool who would operate like that fisherman did should know that sooner or later the cop was going to get him. So, what-the-hell, pay your fine and next time be more careful; and as one of the local judges once summed it up, how can they pay their fines if you don't let them fish? After all, you didn't want a fisherman in jail all winter, because that would cost the taxpayers money.

There was a death from time to time among the gillnetters, mostly caused by heart attacks; a man might fall into the river from his boat, and the shock of his body hitting the cold water would cause the attack.

Seufert's gillnetters were white professional fishermen. The Indian dipnet fishermen were all professionals, too. They came each year from the reservations to dipnet salmon, and they were fine fishermen. No one else could use a dipnet with the proficiency of an Indian. We always had some white men who used a dipnet, but they were always men who had another job.

When a man's regular job was closed down during the Great Depression, he would take a dipnet out and fish for a living while he waited for his regular job to call him back. White men usually fished around No. 3 and No. 4 fishwheels. No whites fished at Celilo Falls. The Indians would not permit it, and of course the Indians had the full backing of the United States government because of the Indian treaties.

The big area where there was stiff competition for salmon was in the gillnet fishing area above the upper end of Rabbit Island and just below the SP&S railroad bridge. It was important here to own a boat harbor or gravel bar where the gillnetters could land their boats, and also launch their boats at the beginning of the fishing season and remove their boats from the river at the close. Seufert's owned all the land on the Oregon side of the Columbia River. Just below the railroad bridge was an incline down to the river, so it was easy to launch or remove a boat. There was also a good harbor here, protected from any wind on the river. Seufert's called this place The Landing, and here were unloaded all the ferry boats carrying fish from the seines, unloaded into fish trucks to be hauled to the cannery. I would say half of the gillnetters used The Landing and fished for Seufert's.

On the Washington side of the river below Clantons Bar, a long gravel bar ran down the Washington shore. This was where the gillnet operations of the CRPA were carried out. The bar was convenient for the fishermen, and the CRPA had built a row of cabins for its gillnetters along the riverbank well above the high water. Seufert's never built cabins for its gillnetters. The gillnetters who fished for Seufert's either pitched a tent or had a camper or trailer with their car. Down the river at the head of Eightmile Rapids, and on the Washington shore, there was a good protected harbor. This property was leased by Barbey, and the gillnetters fishing for these people worked out of this harbor. When you owned the shorelands this had nothing to do with fish buyers using pick-up boats in the river. Out on the river the boats could go anywhere they wished, as long as they didn't touch shore. All the islands in the Columbia River from Celilo Falls to The Dalles were the property of the United States government, so any pick-up boats could visit the islands as often as they wished to pick up fish. By 1950 the engines of these boats were so powerful they could actually take their boats through the rapids right up to the foot of Celilo Falls.

PICK-UP BOATS

Getting the salmon from the fishwheels to the cannery was a problem. Seufert's wheels on the Oregon side of the river were close to the old OR&N railroad tracks so salmon could be hauled to the cannery in boxcars. Some people who built fishwheels on the Washington side of the river between The Dalles and Spedis abandoned some of these wheels because there was no way to get the salmon from the wheels after they were caught. In the early days no one went up to the wheel sites on the river during high water because there were no boats capable of operating in swift water and the north bank was nothing but wagon roads.

All the salmon pick-up boats operated by Seufert's were eventually run by gasoline engines. In this area of rocky shores and swift water there were no docks. If the shore was rocky the boat might be tied to a rock, or held offshore by spars, or tied up to either a crib filled with rock or a float. Of course some areas had gravel bars. The pick-up boats had no deck houses. Spars on scows for holding gillnet boats off the rocky shores would have knocked the deck house off. If you ran the boat you sat right out in the wind, rain and spray. You were tough enough to take it, and you dressed for it. I

nearly forgot, there was a coaming covering the engine to keep it dry. That was not pampering the engine more than the men; a wet engine meant a stopped engine, and in that fast water it could mean a man's life.

Because of the kind of water the boats operated in they had high-speed gasoline engines. If the river current was running 10-miles-an-hour, the propeller of the boat must turn at a greater speed to bite into the water; hence the need for the high-speed gasoline engines. The boats had flat bottoms. If you had to nose the boat up to a gravel bar to pick up fish, you wanted a flat bottom so you could sit on the beach without capsizing. The boats were broad of beam. This gave the vessel good carrying capacity. The broad bottom also meant that even when the vessel was fully loaded it drew little water. This was important, especially when working swift channels and rocky shores. The less water the vessel drew, the less chance of putting a hole in the bottom. I would say that these salmon pick-up boats only drew a foot of water when loaded. They were about thirty feet long and at least seven feet wide. In swift water, huge boils would come up alongside of you. Your vessel had a good freeboard, and you needed the length so that if a whirlpool opened up under you you didn't fall into the opening, and this is no joke. Whirlpools five to ten feet across, and more, were common. You slid across them. Your vessel had enough momentum to get across them especially if the whirlpool opened under your propeller and you lost control and lost power. You generally slid across and no harm done. These boats had a blunt bow. They plowed through the water like a scow, but the high-speed engine generally gave them enough speed to lift the bow up so there was no problem. Downriver below the seining bar the river was not so swift, and on windy days these boats simply plowed through the waves. Then the dry spot, and the only dry spot, was way forward up near the bow and below deck. All the spray then passed over you and you stayed dry.

These were good boats. They operated for years. They had few problems, were cheap to operate, and surprisingly cheap to keep in repair. They probably couldn't carry over a couple of tons of fish at a time but they could get around the compact fishing grounds; and after they had picked up all the gillnet fish, the Indian fish and seine fish, they landed them all at one place. This place was just called The Landing. So these boats served their purpose, and there never was a time they could not handle all the fish that there were for them to haul in any day. And in some days in the fall this might amount to some 40 or more tons of salmon.

FISH BUYING

Fish buyers were terribly important to our organization. If your buyers weren't successful you simply didn't get any fish. They meant as much to the success of the operation of the Company as any employee you had. First of all, a fish buyer was a breed apart. These men were nearly always white, but once in a while they were Indian. They were good talkers, good listeners, always well-liked by the fishermen, and above all else, they were honest; honest in dealing with the Company and honest in dealing with the fishermen. The fish buyers who operated the fish-buying boats were highly skilled swift-water boatmen. They prided themselves on their ability to maneuver a boat in swift water, and on how far up a channel they could go.

They were proud of the fact that wherever an Indian fished they could go to him with their boat; if the swift river prevented them from going to the actual Indian fishing site, they went as near as they could maneuver the boat so the fishermen would not have so far to pack their fish down to him. Of course where Seufert's operated cables to the Indian fishing grounds, the men who operated the cables and bought the Indians' salmon had all the same requirements as the fish buyers who operated the fish pick-up boats. The main difference was that one man was skilled at swift-water boat operation, and the other was skillful in operating a cable way in a manner that anyone riding on the cable had complete confidence in him. And of course the man who operated the cable way was always an accommodating person. Any time an Indian wanted to ride the cable way to the Indian fishing grounds the buyer was glad to accommodate him by taking him out or bringing him back.

These fish buyers bought fish by weight, and paid so much per pound to the fisherman. The price was set by the fishermen's union in Astoria. White fishermen—gillnetters—all had their salmon catches weighed either on the deck of the pick-up boat, or if the gillnetter delivered his catch to a shore station, the salmon were weighed on the scale when the gillnetter unloaded his boat. The gillnetter was given a signed receipt for his fish. The receipt was payable in cash on demand at the Company office. When you bought fish from the fisherman he was given a receipt. This was referred to as a ticket. When he came down to cash in his fish tickets, he was said to collect his money.

Indians at Celilo were paid cash as soon as the fish were weighed. It was common for a fish buyer to have a sack of money with $7,000 or so in it. By the time the Indians had delivered their fish the money sack would be empty. Nearly all the money used by the fish buyers at Celilo who bought Indian fish was currency or paper, but the buyers did use some silver dollars every night, often two or three rolls. The Indians liked silver dollars because after dark when they played games and gambled on the rocks, the wind could not blow them away.

Always during the salmon run on the Columbia River any salmon the other packers managed to get from your fishermen were lost to you forever. You had no way of getting the fish back. During the big fall salmon runs around Celilo Falls a fresh-fish buyer would show up, generally with a pickup truck and some cash in his pocket. He would want to buy a thousand pounds of salmon or more. These fresh-fish buyers would offer the fishermen three to five cents above the union price, get a load of salmon, and take off to peddle them in the interior. These fresh-fish buyers were a nuisance, but they handled very little of the salmon tonnage caught at Celilo.

Now, if outside salmon packers came in and raised the price of salmon to your fishermen, you immediately met the price and your fishermen would continue to sell to you. This way, by meeting the price of outside packers, you ran the other buyers out. When an outside salmon packer came to Celilo to buy fish and didn't get any, he would leave and not come back. We got rid of them. Once you raised the price of salmon to the fishermen you were stuck with it. Under no circumstance could you cut the price back for the rest of that season. If you tried to cut the price you paid your fishermen, the other salmon packers would hold to the higher price, and then you would get no salmon.

One thing in the Columbia River salmon business, you never fully trusted what a fisherman told you about fish prices, and you distrusted competing fish packers even more.

When you were buying fish you wanted to be sure the salmon were fresh, and so you looked at the gills. If the gills were dark, blood red then you knew the salmon were fresh. If the gills had lost their dark red color and had turned pale red or gray, then the salmon were not in prime condition. Once in a while an Indian fisherman would pack an old salmon that had laid around too long on the river bank in ice, freeze the salmon and tell you that he had just caught it. "See how nice and firm he is." Well, the salmon was firm until he thawed out, and then you knew you had been taken. If you didn't know what to look for, then your nose would tell you.

When buying salmon from a fisherman, you always used a scale or a box with a steel bottom. Indians would once in a while shove a piece of gravel down the throat of a salmon, or a railroad spike, to increase the weight of the fish; but the iron bottom of the scale would ring when you dumped anything such as gravel or iron on it. When you heard the ring you inspected the salmon and removed anything which had been shoved down his throat. After all, you were paying for salmon, not gravel or railroad scrap. If a salmon arrived on the cannery floor with a railroad spike still down his throat, and the Chinese butcher in the cannery cut that particular salmon and hit this spike, it would ruin both his knife and his disposition. If the Indian fooled you,

65

and you bought and paid for the railroad scrap iron along with the salmon, the uproar in the cannery when the Chinaman ruined his knife on that fish had repercussions right through the cannery office and up the river to all the Company fish buyers.

Salmon of course were sold to the buyers and to the buying public by color, but when you bought salmon from a fisherman you insisted that any salmon that was supposed to be a fancy Chinook must have the color you would expect. If there was any question in your mind about the color, you took a pocket knife and with the blade made a slit on the side of the salmon about an inch in front of the tail to show just what the color of the meat was. When a salmon started to lose color, he always lost it at the tail first.

The fishermen's union on the Columbia River was an old-time union formed before 1900. The Columbia River salmon packers met with the union heads in April to settle the price to be paid for salmon for the coming fishing season. No salmon cannery on the Columbia River could pay less than the union price, because the fishermen would not deliver salmon to anyone for less than the union price; competing salmon canneries would gladly buy all the salmon at the union price that they could get. You could pay more than the union price—nothing the fishermen liked better—but immediately the other salmon packers would meet your price so again you got no more fish. You just raised everyone's price. But once in a while a salmon packer would do exactly that, because he was mad at one of the other salmon packers.

None of the Indian fishermen belonged to any union, but every Indian expected to be paid the union price, and that was what he got. Some of the white fishermen around The Dalles-Celilo area belonged to the union. All of these upper-river fishermen expected and received the union fresh-fish price, but they refused to join or have anything to do with the Astoria Fishermen's Union, felling that it was continually agitating to close the upper river to commercial fishing and destroy the upper-river fishermen's livelihoods.

One headache in buying salmon from the fishermen, both white and Indian, was that the fishermen would tell your fish buyers that your competitors were paying more for fish than you were. If you didn't raise your price, then the fishermen would have to deliver their fish someplace else. You would ask the fishermen to show you a fish ticket from the other packer so that you could be sure the price had been raised. As a general rule the fishermen couldn't produce such a ticket. It was just a gimmick to try to get you to raise your price. The gimmick seldom worked, but it cost the fishermen nothing to try it. If the other packers raised the price of fish, you soon knew it because the price would immediately be paid by all the other salmon packers, and you got no fish until you raised your price, too.

Generally when Seufert's and the CRPA were working closely together at Celilo, if the CRPA was forced to raise the price they would tell you, so you could raise your prices together. You would have some packer raise his price to your fishermen, and then you would call him, and he would admit it but say that so-and-so, working for him, had forgotten to tell you. He would come right back and say that someone else had raised *his* price, and he had had to raise his price too. Or maybe you would get hold of a noble packer who was pious and prissy who just thought the fishermen deserved more money. This type really made you sick to your stomach, the hypocrite.

Terminology: Around the river and on the boats the men never used the title captain. The captain of a pick-up boat·was simply referred to as so-and-so running such-and-such a boat, or buying fish, or taking care of the scows. The seines were run by seine bosses, never a seine captain. The fishwheel did have a foreman, but usually you said so-and-so is running No. 5, or is up at the fishery. The buying stations were the charge of a boss, but when talking about the buying stations, or the pick-up boats you had out on the river to receive fish, you would simply ask, "Did so-and-so get any fish this morning?" A receiving station was simply a place where fish were delivered for purchase from the fishermen. When the fish buyer was out picking up salmon from fishermen you said he was looking for fish. When you bought salmon from the fishermen you said you were picking them up; and one who regularly sold the Company his fish was referred to as a good man or a good fisherman. You always said so-and-so brought you fish, or you might say he brings his fish to us. Any fisherman who fished for the other companies was referred to as no good, or if he was the kind of person who only brought you fish once in a while, then they referred to him as that. Or you might ask the buyer about this man and he would reply, "He brought you a few fish and never showed up again." There were good and bad fishermen. Good fishermen always delivered to us. Poor fishermen, or ones you had a poor opinion of, were referred to as, "He always delivers his fish to the CRPA," or some other company who was your competitor. If he fished for one of your competitors, the fish buyer would often refer to him by saying, "He fished for the CRPA." If he fished for the competition, in other words, he was just a son-of-a-bitch.

All of these men on the river almost always used the word no instead of any. Among these men long, detailed explanations were not well received. Of such a person they would say, "He talks too much." The men's conversations were always short and to the point while they were on the job. When something was ordered from the cannery to be sent up by truck, and when the driver arrived the conversation would go something like this: "Did you bring up the rope I ordered?" "No." "What the hell is wrong with that bunch down at the cannery?" End of conversation.

As a rule when two men talked about a third, or the office gave orders to one man and these orders were for a man who was not present, he was always referred to by his full name, such as, "Tell Jack Johnson to . . ." or "When you call Henry Wickman, tell him . . . ." Men were absolutely never referred to as Mr., and they were never, repeat never, referred to by last name alone—it was considered insulting.

Years ago, between about 1900 and 1910, above Fivemile Rapids and below Rabbit Island on the Washington side of the Columbia River, there were several fishwheel scows operated by people who sold their fish to Seufert's. There were no wagon roads in this area at all, so these people brought their fish to Seufert's by rowboats. These rowboats were landed in a cove on the Oregon side of the river just above No. 5 Fishwheel. These boats had a sail, and on windy days you could hoist the sail and go upriver. If there was no wind you had to row. But going upstream had one advantage: the rowboats were empty because they had unloaded their salmon and sold them to Seufert's. Coming downriver with a rowboat full of salmon, you let the current carry you; and of course you rowed also, and used the oars to steer, since these boats, like the rowboats and seine boats that operated above The Dalles, had no rudders.

CANNERIES

Our cannery was located at Seuferts, Oregon. When Seufert first bought the land where the cannery was eventually built, the place was called Rockfield. In 1884 the OR&N Company changed the name to Seufert. In 1896 F.A. Seufert had the railroad station name changed to Seuferts, with no apostrophe. This was probably done because people were by then accustomed to going into the station and saying they wanted to go to Seuferts; so because of general usage the railroad changed the spelling of the name in that year.

At one time there were four salmon canneries and two salmon saltries operating around The Dalles. Seufert's eventually bought all. The owners had operated for a number of years but finally decided to sell out because they felt there wasn't enough profit in salmon canneries at The Dalles. Seufert's also bought a saltry along with the Phelps Fishwheel, but never operated the saltry.

Seufert's bought their first salmon cannery at the fishery in 1895-96, but never operated it. It was closed down in 1896 and the salmon packing operation was moved down to Seuferts. The fishery salmon cannery was destroyed by fire in 1905. The fishery was always the center of Seufert's fishwheel operation; there was always a fish house, mess house and bunk house, and it was from the fishery that fishwheels Nos. 3, 4 and 5, and the Cement Wheel were supervised and operated. The cable house for the cable across the Columbia to the Cyclone Wheel in Washington was operated from the fishery. The cable was operated until the 1950s.

Seufert's also bought The Dalles Cannery and Packing Company's salmon cannery in 1907, but tore the old building down to retrieve the lumber. Seufert's owned this property until The Dalles bought the land in the 1950s to build the city sewer plant on it.

Taffe operated a salmon cannery at Celilo for years, but it had long been closed when Seufert's bought it to use as a warehouse.

In 1886 Everding and Farrell built a big salmon cannery on Seufert land at Seuferts, Oregon, with a ten-year lease. When the lease expired in 1896 Seufert's wanted to take over the cannery, but couldn't agree on a price with Everding and Farrell. An outside arbitrator was called in to appraise the cannery; he set what he considered a fair price of $2,500, and both parties agreed to this. Seufert's paid this price for the cannery building fully equipped and ready to operate. By comparison, Seufert's built a new fishery salmon cannery, with the same capacity as the one at Seuferts, and equipped it, for $5,000. The original land that Seufert's bought took in the land at Seuferts and extended up to the head of Fivemile Rapids. The water in Fifteenmile Creek was of prime importance in making this a desirable purchase. Seufert's paid $12,000 for the property, put a three-year mortgage on the land, and paid twelve percent interest a year. Seufert's was able to retire the mortgage and meet the interest payments because the arrangement was profitable, thanks to the building of the fishwheels and the fact that Everding and Farrell built the salmon cannery at Seuferts and agreed to purchase Seufert's salmon from the fishwheels. This property had originally been a land grant to The Dalles Military Road Company. F.A. Seufert and his family lived out at the cannery in their own private home until about 1900, when they moved to The Dalles, on West Fourth Street. In 1915 F.A. Seufert moved to Portland and bought a home, where he lived until he died in 1929.

The front of Seufert's Cannery building was at ground level on the south side. At this level the floor extended the full length of the building, and here all cannery operations were conducted. The warehousing was done on the east side overlooking the creek. On this latter side there was a second story on the north half of the building where empty tin cans were stored to be used in the canning process. The back of the cannery was two stories above ground level. The retorts were on the main floor, and the company boilers and steam engine were on the basement floor on the east side of the retorts. The steam engines were directly under the retorts. The machinery shop was on the main floor in back of the cannery, on the west side of the building. It was almost precisely across from the Blue Jay fishwheel scow. When this was fishing well you could stand at the window of the machine shop and watch the scow catch salmon. It was so close that if you watched carefully you could tell the species of salmon before it slid down the fish chutes into the fish box.

The last good blueback run in the Columbia River at The Dalles was 1934, which was also the last year that fishwheels operated in Washington. Blue Jay did very well on bluebacks that year. The bluebacks were running so well that we had to work on the Fourth of July. We finished work early in the afternoon, and since we had not had dinner we were really hungry. We went to the mess house for lunch and found that because it was a holiday the cook had left. Our lunch was on the table in the mess house dining room: a huge bowl of string beans, cold, covered with cheesecloth to keep the flies off. I had never cared for string beans, but I was so hungry I can still remember how good those cold beans tasted that afternoon. The funny thing is that I have liked string beans ever since.

There was a small room at the back of the machine shop; the door was unlocked, and the wall was simply an enclosure made of fishwheel wire. There were many little cubbyholes and partitioned shelves lining the walls of this room; we kept an assortment of nuts, bolts, screws, washers, et cetera in these individual compartments. This room was always called the snake room, but I have no idea how that came about.

The label room was on the north end of the main floor; this was always locked. All the Company and buyers' labels were kept here, as well as gum boots, rubber aprons, knives, books of fish tickets, et cetera. All the things the Company had to keep track of were kept here. You had to unlock it every time someone wanted a rubber apron or something; but at least you could keep track of what was handed out to the crew that way.

I must mention the big steam whistle on top of the cannery, and what a nice tone it had, deep and mellow. On clear, still days at noon the whistle would echo and re-echo off the rock bluffs around the cannery. My grandmother told me that when the family lived on West Fourth Street in The Dalles, some three miles from the cannery, she could clearly hear the cannery whistle at noon when the atmosphere was right.

The old label room, or upstairs label room, was on the second floor over the warehouse. It had not been used for years as a label room, but the name was kept. This room had shelves on all four walls and was used to store Company records no longer needed in the office. Every three or four years all the Company records in the cannery office were cleaned out. They were put into wooden salmon cases and taken upstairs to be stored in the old label room. (All the old Seufert Cannery records that are now in the archives of the Oregon Historical Society were once put into just such a box, stored in this room and forgotten.) Between 1896 and 1902 my father, Arthur Seufert, took many photographs of the railroad, steamboats, fishwheels, and other things of interest around the cannery. For years the glass negatives had been stored in empty salmon cases on the floor of the old label room. (This collection is now the property of the Oregon Historical Society.)

As the years went by we installed new machinery in the cannery and around the seines and fish houses, but I don't recall that we ever put in a new piece of machinery to replace men. The idea was to use the machines to make the work easier for the men. If the machine speeded up the work, then you were able to do more work with the same number of men.

In the 1920s, during the spring and fall when the cannery was very busy, it was Company practice to stop work each morning at 9:30 to give the crew, both white and Chinamen, a coffee break with doughnuts and cinnamon rolls. The Chinamen had tea and the white crew had coffee. The Company had a big ten-gallon coffee percolator back by the retorts. At 9:00 the steam engineer would load it with coffee, which would be ready by 9:30. The Company had a local bakery send its truck out to the cannery at 9:30 to deliver the doughnuts and cinnamon rolls. There was another break in the afternoon, but this was just long enough for hot coffee for the white crew and tea for the Chinese; no rolls this time. Once a day was enough for that, and furthermore the bakery did not want to make an afternoon delivery. By the 1940s things had changed. Coffee breaks were still continued, and the Company furnished the coffee or tea, but by then coke machines had been put in, and men and women were bringing their own lunches, so the Company no longer furnished pastry during the breaks. The employees could smoke, have a cup of coffee, and if they wished, could have a snack from their lunches.

Up until about 1905 the usual practice in the canning industry for obtaining a vacuum in the cans was to place the canned salmon in a retort for 30 minutes and process it. At the end of 30 minutes you blew down your retort, removed the cans, and punched a hole in the top of each can to let the pressure out. The China-men re-soldered the hole in the can. The cans were returned to the retort and processed. This way you removed all the hot air in the can, then by re-soldering and processing again, a vacuum was created. The cans had to be vacuum packed when they were shipped by rail across the country, otherwise when the salmon were hauled across the Continental Divide, and the rarified air pressure, the top and bottom of the can would bulge, and no one would buy it.

F.A. Seufert was for a long time concerned with the expense of creating a vacuum in this way. He designed the double-ring top for his salmon cans. When the can tops were stamped out of tin plate, Seufert's new die produced a top which had two raised rings inside, with each ring encircling the top and a little round ring in the center of the top, which we called the button. These tops were so strong that you could process salmon without venting the cans; and when the train took the salmon over the Divide the tops would not bulge, so the salmon would arrive in New York City with both ends of every can flat. This top was used on all salmon and fruit Seufert's processed up until about 1932. At that time the Company started code marking each can, but the button was so small it would not take a four-letter code, so at that time Seufert's began to use conventional can tops. By that time the Company was using vacuum closing machines for salmon, so there was no problem.

Before the Depression the big wholesale houses in New York used a wraparound label on 6/10 fruit cans; during the Depression, in order to cut expenses, the wholesale houses would have the Company cut these labels in half. Both halves were the same. These were called spot labels, and within a few years all canned goods packed in 6/10 cans used spot labels, and still do.

The retort seems to be the one piece of equipment in a salmon cannery most confusing to the layman. The retort was the large tank in which canned goods were placed, the doors of the retort were closed and bolted, live steam was admitted, and the cans were then sterilized, or as we said in the cannery, cooked. Once they were thoroughly sterilized, the cans were removed, and because they were tightly sealed, they would keep safely for several years without fear of spoiling. A retort was either square or round; some were horizontal, others were upright. Modern retorts are built of steel. Seufert's original retorts were made of iron and lasted for 50 years before being replaced by steel. Retorts were covered with asbestos to help hold the heat. I was told that long ago Seufert's had two retorts built of wood. Retorts could sometimes be opened at both ends for placing and removing cans.

The steam pressure in the retort was ten pounds of pressure, or 240 degrees of heat. The cans of salmon were cooked 60 minutes at ten pounds of pressure for half-pound cans, and 90 minutes for one-pound tall cans. Once the steam was admitted to the retort the steam pressure was automatically controlled by a system operated by compressed air. The pressure was set by the engineer and would not vary one degree, regardless of the length of the cook. When the cook was completed, the engineer turned off the steam and the pressure was then released; the retort was opened, and the cans were removed. In many salmon canneries the retorts had a little railroad track in the bottom where you could run small four-wheel, two-axle cars loaded with baskets or trays filled with cans; these trays were called coolers.

Seufert's Cannery had four steam retorts for cooking salmon. Each held four little cars. A retort always had a steam gauge to show the pressure in the retort; there was a safety valve, too. Along the top of the retort were three or more small valves that were barely open, or as we said, cracked. They let a small amount of steam escape at all times, so that any hot air pockets that might have collected could escape so the steam could be uniformly distributed around all the cans in the retort; this assured that the heat in the retort was constant. Since this was at ten pounds of pressure, the retorts were always noisy when they were operating. There was a recording instrument attached to the steam valve that made a permanent chart recording the heat in the retort and the amount of time the heat was used. Thus we had a record of the time and temperature. Retorts were used in the salmon cannery because they were cheap in regard to original cost, simple to install, and inexpensive to operate.

The retort operator, who was always the steam engineer, had one of the most responsible jobs in the cannery, since he was in charge of the safe sterilizing or cooking of the salmon.

Up until about 1900 the old-timers spoke of a salmon cannery as a so-many retort cannery, but later retorts were varied in size so this was no longer an accurate measure. Retorts at Seufert's held four cars, but many of the retorts in the big Alaskan canneries would hold eight.

The original cannery at Seufert's was a two-retort cannery. The cannery at the fishery was also a two-retort; this one was closed in 1896. Actually, I do not believe it was ever operated, but rather that the two retorts from the Fishery Cannery were moved down to Seufert's, so that from 1896 on, that cannery was a four-retort.

Within the industry the size of a salmon cannery was described by saying how many lines it had. One line meant a one-pound tall salmon can-closing machine. A half-pound machine was referred to as a half-line; if you had two half-pound can-closing machines, you were said to have two half-lines, although the capacity was actually that of a one line cannery. Seufert's Cannery at The Dalles had a half-pound closing machine and a one-pound tall closing machine, thus it was a line-and-a-half cannery. These closing machines, used to seal the lids on the cans, were all built to operate at the same speed to seal the same number of cans per minute, so the canning lines were an accurate way of describing capacity.

The closing machine puts the lid on a can. Seufert's installed their first ones in about 1904. This machine rolled the lid on; before that tops were soldered on. Cans with soldered lids were just cans, but cans with rolled lids were always called sanitary cans. The first of these latter machines were called Johnson machines. They could close 30 cans a minute. By World War I Seufert's was using a closing machine put out by the American Can Company. This was called the CanCo 00, and could close 60 cans per minute. By 1929 or 1930 this company had a machine called the NR closing machine, which could close 120 cans per minute.

Seufert's used this machine for about two years. In 1932 or 1933 Seufert's bought a vacuum-closing machine from the American Can Company. By the time of

73

World War II this high-speed machine could close 240 cans per minute. Of course when you were closing 240 cans per minute all the operation in the cannery had become mechanized, because it was impossible for a human being to handle that many cans.

Water for the boilers came from Fifteenmile Creek. The water used in the cannery operation and for drinking came from deep wells that the Company had drilled for that purpose. Seufert's also had a water generating electric plant just below the mess house and down near the bed of Fifteenmile Creek. This had a Pelton wheel, and ran from water piped to it from the creek. The electricity generated was all direct current. The lights powered by this water wheel were very dim. The lights were used outside the cannery around the various buildings. The main purpose of these dim lights was to illuminate the area around the cannery at night for safety. The highway bridge (which the highway department called Seuferts Viaduct) across Fifteenmile Creek on the old Columbia River Highway was also lighted from this same generator. There were probably eight lights, four on each side. They were very dim, but they did show the outline of the bridge at night for approaching cars. When a light on this bridge burned out you had to stand on the railing with one arm around the light post and use the other hand to change the bulb. It was a good 50-foot drop from the railing to the bed of the creek.

After the cannery had closed down for the day, all machinery and floors were washed down with fresh water under heavy pressure from fire hoses. Then all the machinery was washed again with a steam hose, operating on steam from the cannery boilers. Next,

wooden chopping blocks were washed with high pressure fresh water, and then were liberally covered with rock salt to keep them clean. All the floors were concrete for ease in cleaning. They were also washed down every day with fresh water from fire hoses, and then they too were heavily sprinkled with rock salt to preserve their cleanliness. Under no circumstances was any scrap of fish ever left on the floor or in any crevice in either the machinery or the packing table. The high pressure water and the steam would clean out even the smallest crack. Rock salt was the old standby to help keep the cannery fresh and clean. When concrete floors were wet they could be slippery and dangerous, but a generous handful of rock salt would take care of that problem.

The cannery had four boilers. One was a horizontal fire-tube boiler of about 80 horsepower; the second was a horizontal fire-tube boiler of about 100 hp; there was a big water-tube boiler of some 250 hp; and a little donkey boiler that probably had 15 or 20 hp. Originally the boilers burned slab wood, shipped to the cannery from the sawmills by rail and boxcar, first from Portland and later from Dee, Oregon. This was always fir. The Company preferred to get the slab wood from the tie mills because you would often get wood in which one railroad tie had just been taken out of the heart of a tree. The slab would be so big a man could not lift it. He would have to stand it on one end and roll it or work it back and forth toward the fire box door. Even the firemen couldn't lift them; they had to lean them against the fire box door, and then they would pick up the other end and shove the whole thing into the fire box. The firemen liked them, because although they were heavy and awkward, they were so huge that once they got into the fire box they would burn for a long time. These old steam boilers were hot. Many a time I watched a fireman put a fire into the boiler and actually watch his wool shirt smoke from the heat. If the men kept their arms bare the heat from the open fire box door would singe and curl the hair.

By the early 1930s the cannery boilers were converted to burn fuel oil, called Bunker C boiler fuel. The reason for changing to oil was simply that slab wood was no longer available from the sawmills; they were starting to reclaim the big slabs by re-sawing, and in order to be used for boiler fuel, the slabs had to be big and heavy. If they were small it was impossible to raise a head of steam. When you were firing oil you had to have steam pressure to start the oil fires. The boilers would stay hot overnight so that they would still have 50 or 60 pounds of steam in the morning, and this was enough to start the oil heaters and oil pumps and to light the fires. But if the boilers were down over a weekend, then they would be cold and there would be no pressure. In such a case the Company used the little upright steam donkey boiler, firing it with wood, generally about the size one would use in a stove. When you had raised 60 or 70 pounds of steam on this little donkey you could start the pumps and heaters on the big boiler, until you had 50 or 60 pounds, then the big boiler would cut in and from then on would furnish all the steam needed to continue to raise the pressure. Then the little donkey boiler was cut out and allowed to cool down. It was then said to be dead, and was not used until needed the next time.

After about 1940, or the start of World War II, the oil burners on the boilers were changed from steam to electricity. Then of course it made no difference if the boiler was dead when you wanted steam, you could just flip a switch and the oil would come on.

Salmon cannery boilers, after operating all day long, had to be blown down each night. There was a valve called the blow-off valve; it was at the lowest point of a steam boiler, and in the cannery boilers it was at the point farthest from the fire box. This valve was connected to a steam pipe that led outside the boiler room and carried the steam and water harmlessly outside where no one could get injured. To blow a boiler down, you kept a good head of steam, maybe 100 pounds, filled the boiler full of water so the water stood at the top of the water glass, then opened the blow-off valve; then the high steam pressure would flush water out of the bottom of the boiler and carry away any mud or scale that might have collected during the day. This operation kept your boiler clean and prevented a buildup of mud, making the boiler shell dry and lead to a boiler explosion. You generally blew the boiler down until there was only about an inch of water left in the water glass. Then you would close your blow-off valve, and then the boiler was clean and ready to operate another day. Blowing down a boiler was the noisiest operation you could imagine.

The boilers at Seufert's had a tendency to collect boiler scale from the hard water. Every day we pumped about 50 gallons of scale remover into the boilers. At the cannery we used a tanning bark. A sack of tanning bark left in the sack was soaked in a 50-gallon drum or barrel. When the water in the barrel was thoroughly saturated with the tanning bark solution, the mixture was pumped into the boiler. The best time to do this was just after you blew the boiler down at night. This solution kept the boiler surprisingly clean and free from scale.

By the beginning of World War II the Company started to buy commercial boiler compounds that were already made up. These were just diluted in water, pumped into the boiler, and they took care of keeping the boiler free of scale. All boilers, steam retorts and compressed air tanks in the cannery were inspected by both the state boiler inspector and the insurance company once a year. The inspectors checked to see that boilers and retorts were in safe operating condition. Inspection took place just before the cannery opened for operation in the spring.

Garbage was always a problem around the cannery and the mess house. Seufert's Cannery sat on the edge of Fifteenmile Creek, about a quarter of a mile from where it emptied into the Columbia River. The creek was at the bottom of a sheer bluff some 50 to 75 feet high and several hundred feet across. The sides were perpendicular and sheer right down to the water. For safety, the Company had erected a fence along the bluff opposite the cannery. All garbage from the mess house was tossed over the fence into the creek. This included all the dented cans, wooden boxes, paper boxes, buckets, odds and ends of all kinds that would accumulate around a salmon cannery. If anyone asked what to do with any kind of debris, he was told to just throw it into the creek. Twice a year the creek in flood or high water from the Columbia River would sweep away all the debris. Paper was generally burned in an oil drum.

Garbage was collected once a day from the mess houses up the river and thrown in the river. Down at the China house in back of the cannery, the Chinamen just tossed garbage and things like empty liquor bottles or medicine bottles over the bluff into the river. Anything that didn't sink eventually floated away.

There was the gut box in back of the cannery. After the Chinamen had butchered the salmon in the cannery, all the waste was carried away from the cannery in a water flume. The flume was built of rock and concrete and had been constructed in the early 1900s by Italians working for Seufert's. The flume carried the salmon waste to the top of the bluff overlooking the Columbia River. This is where the gut box was. It was just a big concrete box, four to six feet wide, ten to twelve feet long, and about four feet deep. The flume with the salmon waste emptied into the gut box. In the floor of the box there was a hole that could be covered if you wanted to collect the waste, or uncovered so the waste would flow down into another flume that carried it down the face of the cliff into the Columbia River. At such times the river would be alive with carp and suckers consuming this salmon waste. Several hundred feet below the point where the flume entered the river there would not be a single sign of the waste, for it had all been cleaned up immediately by these scavengers.

At the lower side of the end of the gut box there was a little trap door and a chute. The original idea had been to collect this salmon waste and haul it down to the orchard to use for fertilizer. To haul the waste, there was the gut wagon, just an ordinary farm wagon drawn by a two-horse team. The team and gut wagon were driven by an old Indian hired for the job; his name was

Fat Charlie. He was about five feet tall and weighed about 300 pounds. He was as wide as he was tall. I can still remember him driving that gut wagon. He was proud of his job, and when he drove the wagon he sat ramrod straight, and of course it made quite a sight to see the gut wagon dripping blood and water from every crack in the wagon bed, and there would be salmon entrails hanging down and swaying with the motion of the wagon. Fat Charlie certainly handled his job with dignity. The first year this waste was used in the orchard for fertilizer the waste was just spread on top of the ground; the plan was to then take a team and turn over the ground. But the crows knew a good thing. They came from miles around to enjoy the feast. Some three or four days later up at the cannery they began to realize this was not such a good idea after all. When the west wind blew, everyone realized it was a mistake.

The next year the Company was still determined to use the salmon waste as fertilizer, but certainly did not wish to repeat the last year's mistake. This time they dug a trench between the trees in the orchard. The trench was about three feet deep and probably six or eight feet long. Then Fat Charlie just backed the gut wagon up to the trench, opened the little trap door in the rear of the wagon, and dumped everything out. The Company took several men along to fill in the trench. Everything seemed to be working out beautifully. At first the fruit trees thrived on this, but a year or so later the trees were not doing well. They dug down into the soil and found that the salmon waste had decomposed, but the salmon oil had combined with the sandy soil to form sandstone, all through the orchard. No water

could penetrate, nor could the root systems of the trees penetrate; the trees looked as if they were dying. To save the situation the Company had a powder monkey place a stick of dynamite into each block of sandstone and shoot. The blast would shatter the sandstone blocks so both water and roots could penetrate and the trees would become healthy again. From then on they only used the gut box in spring or fall. The Indians would set up camp by the gut box, plug the drainhole in the floor, and collect the salmon heads as they floated down the flume from the cannery.

Ice was a necessity around the cannery, but the Company never iced the salmon before canning it if they could avoid it. It took time and work to ice it, so if it was at all possible they preferred to can the fish as they arrived at the cannery. If you had to ice the fish, you had to be certain they had good drainage. If the salmon were iced on a wooden floor, the water from the melting ice could of course just drain right through the floor out onto the ground or into the water; but at Seufert's the cannery floors were concrete, so we had to put down a duck walk, which was just a series of thin boards nailed together crosswise. This formed a lattice work so the salmon could be put on it and covered with crushed ice; the walk allowed the water to drain off and also allowed the air to circulate under the fish. Salmon could be put on a duck walk, iced, and kept for three or four days with no trouble. Then the salmon were removed from the ice and canned. If there was not enough room to ice the salmon in the cannery, Seufert's would order several refrigerator cars from the railroad, put the salmon in fish boxes, cover them with ice, and put the boxes into the refrigerator cars. This

77

was an excellent way to keep the fish, but of course it was expensive. In a few days, after the height of the salmon run had passed and the cannery had time to catch up on canning, you could unload the refrigerator cars and can the salmon you had stored in them. As a general rule, you canned all the Chinooks every day, and separated out the steelhead, which kept better than any other kind of salmon when iced.

Seufert's never manufactured their own ice. The Company had an ice dam up Fifteenmile Creek about a quarter of a mile from the cannery. In winter, if the weather was cold enough, you could cut and put up your own ice from this ice dam. In later years, after The Dalles-Celilo Canal had been built, the Company cut ice there. This ice was cut in the turning basin of the canal at the fishery; it was hauled by truck to the cannery and put into the ice house. In the years when you had a warm winter and could not put up ice, the Company would order it from the Union Pacific Railroad, from the ice plant at North Powder, Oregon. I believe this plant was operated by the Pacific Fruit Express Company.

All during winter Seufert's would watch the temperature at The Dalles, and when a cold spell set in, they would wire North Powder to ship down a car of ice. The ice was just put into an ordinary box car, and you hoped the weather would stay below freezing during the trip down to The Dalles. At the cannery the ice was unloaded and put in the Company ice house, which was built of tile and was three-stories high. You had to keep the ice completely covered with sawdust to keep it from melting; and if this was done, the ice would keep for years. When you needed ice you opened the door of the ice house, went inside, took a

scoop shovel, and shovelled the sawdust away from the ice. Then you took tongs and pulled out a cake of ice. You had to fill in the hole you had made with sawdust so the ice cakes would not be exposed to air. Then you just closed up the ice house and went about your business.

The Company also had an ice house at the fish house at Tumwater. This was built of wood, but also used sawdust to cover and preserve the ice. The one thing about this ice I always remember was how the wet sawdust froze to the ice. When you took a cake of ice to the cook house, the cook would chip off a piece of ice with sawdust still frozen to it, and put it in our pitcher of drinking water. When you poured a glass of water you had to take a spoon and skim the sawdust off the water before you could drink.

In the cannery all communication between the China boss and the closing machine operators and the steam engineers in the engine room was done by steam whistle, which was above the retorts. A long whistle wire ran from this whistle the entire length of the cannery well overhead, and above the cannery machinery. By the closing machines and salmon-gang knives there was a drop cord from the long whistle wire. This drop cord was a rope with a knot tied in the end. When you wanted the steam engineer to start the steam engines that ran the cannery machinery, you reached up and pulled the whistle cord twice—two toots—which was the sign to start the engines and operate the cannery steam engines at full speed. If you blew three toots, this was a signal to operate the steam engines dead slow. You had to have the cannery machinery turning over dead slow if you wanted to put on leather or rubber belts between a piece of machinery and an overhead pulley. At a dead slow speed these belts could be put on without too much effort; you just shoved the belt with the flat of your hand on the edge of the pulley, and the belt would climb right on and around the pulley. After the belt was on, you signalled the engineer with two toots, and he then opened the valve on his engine and the machinery would operate at full speed.

Closing machines were the worst for throwing a belt, especially when they were started up. If you threw in the clutch too fast you would throw the drive belt off, and then you had to signal the engineer for dead slow so you could put the drive belt back on the pulley. The drive belts were tight so they wouldn't slip while the machinery was running, so it was impossible to put a drive belt on a pulley unless the pulley was turning over very slow.

If the drive belt was slipping between the pulley and the closing machine or one of the other machines, an easy way to tighten the belt was to turn some water on it from a hose. The water would tighten the belt in no time. If the belt was tight but still slipped, then we used some crushed resin from a can we kept on hand. A little sprinkle of resin on the drive belt would give it plenty of grip.

When you wanted to stop the cannery, you gave one toot.

When I was a kid we had an old China boss who was almost blind. Just before he was ready to start the cannery by signalling the steam engineer, I would reach up, grab the whistle drop cord and give it a quick yank. This was not enough to blow the whistle, but it would make the cord bounce up in the air and land on the whistle wire, which was probably ten feet above the cannery floor. This old China boss could not see the cord even when it was hanging in place, so he would stand there with his hand over his head reaching for the cord so he could blow the steam whistle. After he had waved his hand around in the air for a while, trying to find the cord, someone in the cannery crew would take a long stick and knock the cord off the wire so the poor old man could find it. I should have been spanked.

There was a big steam whistle outside on top of the cannery. This had a nice tone (I never heard another whistle that sounded like that one); the tone was deep but mellow. This whistle was only blown at noon when the cannery was operating, and at 5:00 P.M. if there was steam up. There was a third steam whistle directly over the retorts, but it was loud and shrill and had a very unpleasant sound. This whistle was given two toots when you called the China retort crew to empty a retort.

The engineer's desk was right across the walkway in back of the retorts against the cannery wall. He did all his paper work there. He had a swivel chair at his desk, and beyond the chair there was a wash basin and a mirror, and plenty of hot water. The hot water, in fact, came directly from the boilers' feed pumps. On Saturday nights the regular men would gather there to wash and shave just before quitting time. Henry Wickman would stop to shave after work, and he always used a straightedge razor. Gus Bansch had been Seufert's steam engineer for years, and nothing pleased him more than to see that a retort had finished cooking and had to be unloaded so he could blow the whistle while Henry was shaving with that straightedge razor. Gus would give two loud shrieking toots on the retort whistle to call the China retort crew, just as Henry was scraping away at his face. This always brought the expected result from Henry, who would shout, "What are you trying to do? Make me cut my throat?" Gus was always unconcerned; after all, it wasn't his fault that the whistle made Hank jump. I must add that Henry never cut his throat, but the fact he did not, could never be credited to the steam engineer.

Gus Bansch had a habit of sending away for gadgets that would keep his safety razor blade sharpened for months of shaving. He would see ads in the pulp magazines that the night watchman bought, and then he would send his 25 cents or 50 cents for the patented-guaranteed perpetual razor blade sharpener. When the gadget arrived, Gus would sharpen all our blades so we could get a good clean shave from a used blade. None of the gadgets ever worked, but Gus certainly tried to keep us in sharp blades for years.

Canned salmon labels were always kept in the label room, and the room was locked all the time. Only the white foreman or someone from the office had the key. When we had a car of canned salmon to label, the cannery foreman would take the required number of labels from the room and give them to the China boss. Labels came in bundles of 1,000; usually there were 10 bundles to a case, so there would be 10,000 labels in a box. The warehouse foreman would tell the China boss how many cases of salmon to take down out of a pile of unlabeled cans of salmon cases.

When the number of cases on the warehouse floor had been checked and found correct, the China boss would have his China crews start labeling the salmon cans. Each man would sit down on a box while he put on the labels. He would take a bundle of 1,000 labels and put them into a hand labeling machine face down. The machine sat on an empty canning case. This contraption consisted of a small three-sided metal container, with the fourth side open. The top was about an inch higher than a bundle of labels and the fourth end, a slide, sat on top of the labels. It was a little wider than a label. Three sides were fixed, and the fourth slid down in a groove. The container held paste. As the Chinaman pulled the top label out and under, the slide had just enough paste left on the face of the label so that the overlapping ends of the label would stick together. The labeler sat between a case of unlabeled cans and an empty case. He would pick up the unlabeled can, put a label on it, and pack it into the case. In the Chinese crew these men were generally the older workers, men who were too old to be capable of heavy physical labor in the warehouse.

Up until the late 1920s all canned salmon was shipped in wooden boxes. The first job the China crew had when they arrived before the opening of the spring salmon canning season was to make the wooden boxes. They would nail together thousands of cases for both half-pound and one-pound flats. With a crew of some 50 men all making boxes at the same time, this operation was noisy to say the least. By the late 1920s the paper cases replaced the wooden ones. The main advantage was that paper was much lighter and thus cheaper to ship. Paper cases were shipped to the cannery knocked down into flat bundles. A case was taken from the bundle and stitched on a machine operated by the China crew. Stitched cartons were stacked, empty, in the upper floor of the warehouse until needed.

Filled cases were carried out to the middle of the warehouse floor where a Chinaman with a glue pot and brush painted the flaps of the case and closed them. A second case was put on top of the first, which held the flaps of the first case while the glue set, which took about five minutes. This process was repeated for an entire stack of cases. The top case was turned upside-down so the weight would hold the flaps closed until the glue hardened.

Half-pound cans were stacked five cases high. One-pound flats and one-pound talls were stacked four high. One thing you needed in the warehouse was plenty of room, especially plenty of floor space. All cases had to be end marked. The mark showed the can size, number of cans, brand name, species of salmon, and the name of the packer or wholesaler. All this was required by law. If the cases were marked by hand they were put on the floor up on one end, and as many as 50 cases might be put in a row. You might use a brass stencil which had been cut for you in Portland [see endpapers for example of brass stencil label]. A Chinaman stenciling would use a stencil brush and ink made of oil and lamp black. He would place the stencil on the end of the case and brush ink on. The ink had to set for a couple of days to penetrate the paper and become permanent. Neither time nor water would remove such a stencil mark from the case. This was always a dirty job, and your hands would be absolutely black. Many a time I have done this. It was not a hard job, though your back got tired until you were used to it. After you had stenciled several hundred cases, your back would feel as if you could never again stand up straight.

Sometimes a buyer would instruct you to put a paper label on the end of each case, in which case of course the stencil would not be necessary. Labels were soaked in a pan of water, each at right angles to the one below it so they could easily be picked up out of the water by their edges. A wet label was placed face down on a flat surface, brushed with paste, put on the end of the case, and brushed with a dry brush to smooth it.

In the middle 1930s the Company bought a printing machine to print the ends of the cases. Rubber type was used, and any number of words could be set into type holders, which were put into a frame. The frame went into the machine. The end of the cases was put into the machine, you stepped on a pedal, and the machine printed the case. Any error in spelling was just too bad. The men who made up the type soon learned to proof their type on a piece of paper before trying it on a case, which was expensive and had to be thrown away if you made a mistake.

The China boss had his crew handle as many cases as you instructed him, but the white foreman always counted too, so there would be no error. It was not that the China boss couldn't count, but there was always the problem of the language barrier, and the chance of a misunderstanding.

Up until World War I, fancy Columbia River Chinook salmon cans were not only labeled, but also wrapped in tissue paper which was about three times as wide as the salmon can was high. It was very thin, thinner than the tissue paper used to wrap apples, thin enough so you could easily see and read the label underneath. It was a slow process to label salmon cans by hand and wrap them in paper. It took three times longer to add the tissue paper, but the cans did look very nice and were especially attractive on the shelves of the grocery stores. But after the war the wholesale grocers decided the extra expense of the paper was too much. The last time I remember this being done was 1929 or 1930; at that time only the old-time China boss, out of all the Chinamen in the crew, knew how to wrap the tissue paper around the can and tuck in the ends properly.

The stacks of cases, either four or five high, would just fit onto a hand truck. The Chinamen trucked the cases into a freight car, stacked the cases, and when the car was sealed the salmon was all ready for shipment. When a freight car was to be loaded you figured the number of cases, so many rows wide and so many long and so many high. You used two empty cannery cases to figure with: put one down, then the other, then pick up the first and move it beyond the second, across the width of the car. The process was repeated for the length and height. If you had figured correctly, the last case loaded in the car should fit right into the last opening in a row of cases. The entire loading crew would gather around to see if this was the case, or if you had several cases left over which had to be thrown on top of the load in the car. It was not too difficult to figure if all the cases were the same size, but when you shipped half-pound salmon cases, one-pound salmon cases, two-and-a-half-pound cases of Royal Anne cherries and 6/10 cases of cherries, then it took some figuring. Usually you miscalculated, and then the China crew would have a good laugh. But we did have a China boss who could figure these loads right down to the last case, and when he figured a car, the last case went into the last opening. I don't remember that he ever miscalculated. We all used to gather around to watch. When the last case fit right in, he would smile and turn his back on us and walk off. All we could do was shake our heads and admit that that old China boss was good. The China bosses were well educated in their native China. This particular man worked for Seufert's for years. His name was Sid Fong, and as a young man he

had been secretary to the Chinese consul in Portland.

In the early days salmon packers had a problem with the cans rusting. If you used a white label the rust spots would show through. Thus packers started using red labels, and soon nearly everyone was using red labels on canned salmon. Soon the public expected salmon cans to have red labels. Today nearly all cheap canned salmon, both chums and pinks, are still sold with a red label. The only exception was on the Columbia River, where the fancy spring Chinook salmon always had a white label, which I suppose designated purity and superior quality.

In order to overcome the problem of rust, the industry started to lacquer the salmon cans after they had been processed. Lacquer came in 50-gallon drums. It was a very dark brownish red, about the consistency of cold molasses, and was mixed with gasoline to thin it. The cans were dipped in this thinned lacquer, then allowed to stand long enough for the gasoline to evaporate. This left a thin coat of lacquer on the cans. The gasoline used in the 1920s was aviation gasoline, and everyone was quite impressed that the Company used the same gasoline to dilute lacquer that was used to fly airplanes. I scarcely need to add that the no smoking rule was strictly enforced. Lacquering was discontinued at Seufert's by the middle of the 1920s, when the process of coating tin plate had advanced so that rusting was no longer a problem. We still see lacquered tops and bottoms on cans today, but that is for show. Some packers think there is more appeal to a can treated in this fashion.

The process of lacquering prior to the 1920s was rather complex. This was done during a time the cannery was not busy. Filled cans were taken from the stacks on the warehouse floor and placed in a cooler or tray. The cooler was on a wheeled dolly. The cans were laid on their sides in a row all across the cooler, until the cooler was filled. The second layer was staggered on top of the first. This was continued for about twelve layers. The cooler was then wheeled to the lacquer house about 25 feet from the cannery across the railroad siding, and here a Chinaman unloaded one row of cans at a time onto a wooden rack with a V-shaped bottom. The cans went onto a little track formed by two iron rods about 2½ inches apart. The rods directed the cans into the lacquer house as you pushed them. The lacquer machine inside had two moving chains, with a rod between. The machine lifted the cans from the iron guides and placed them on the rods, and the chains carried the cans down into a tank of lacquer diluted with gasoline where they were submerged for a few moments. When the cans emerged from the tank they were carried over a drip tank so the excess could drain off. The cans would still ride the rods, on their sides, as they emerged from the lacquer house, to be removed by a Chinaman who used the wooden rack to place the cans in the cooler as before. The cans were left in the coolers in the warehouse for 24 hours to dry. The following day the cans were taken from the cooler and restacked on the cannery warehouse floor until shipment.

Seufert's started to code mark their cans in about 1933. Earlier, the Chinamen just tied a string or wire to one corner of the cooler to designate a particular grade of salmon. Each grade was kept separate in the warehouse to avoid confusion in labeling. Then the Company began to use a code mark on top of each can to identify the contents and packing date. Codes had four marks: for example, S for salmon, 1 for fancy Chinooks, A for May, 1934, and A for the first day of the month; this code would be S1AA. The packing season of six months would take six consecutive letters of the alphabet, so it would take four years to use all 26 letters of the alphabet. On the fifth year you would start over again using A for May, 1938. For marking days of the month, Z was the 26th, so 1 through 5 was used for the 27th to the 31st. Code marks and the code records were always kept in the fireproof vault in the office.

Generally salmon were cooked according to prescribed time for the various can sizes; but if the salmon were running very large, 30 pounds and over, special tests were made. After the cook you would open a can of salmon and test chew the bones to be certain the backbone was soft. Sometimes fish with very large backbones had to be cooked a little longer than usual, and this simple test was an easy method of determining this. Generally an extra ten minutes would do the trick.

By 1946 the cost of hand packing one-pound flat cans had become so prohibitive that the market had all but disappeared.

When there was a labor shortage during World War II, Seufert's put in automatic can-filling machines for packing choice Columbia River Chinooks, in both the half-pound cans and the one-pound talls. This machine cut costs so much that the price was well under hand-packed salmon. The appearance of the salmon was not as nice, but since the price was so much lower, the public did not object. Seufert's never installed the machines for one-pound flat cans, because such machines had not been successful in other canneries; so as long as the cannery was in operation, this size can was packed by hand.

When cans were needed at The Dalles, one called long distance to the American Can Company in Portland to order a car of empty cans. A boxcar would hold enough cans to fill about 3,000 cases. The car might carry just one size can, five or six sizes, but you had to order a full carload. Cans were shipped to Seufert's in paper bags; tops were in a standard cannery case. Until the mid 1940s the canner had to sign a seven-year contract with the American Can Company agreeing to buy cans only from them. Empty cans were shipped by rail because it was both cheaper and safer than truck. One could use old boxcars to haul empty cans. The smallest car I remember was an old Southern Pacific car that had been set aside during the war just for the empty can run; its total capacity was only 20,000 pounds.

Cans had to be ordered according to what they were to hold. Different products required a different weight tin plate, and for some products the inside of the can had to be lacquered. Originally, Seufert's made their own cans at the cannery, but this practice stopped when the tops were rolled on instead of being soldered. The can company would allow you to rent a closing machine very inexpensively as an inducement to buy cans from it. When I worked in the cannery the only bit of can-making machinery left was an old stamping machine that had stamped out tops from sheets of tin plate. It was used to punch holes in strips of soft steel.

Paper labels were purchased from several different companies. Ridgway Lithograph in Portland printed some of the labels; Simpson Doellar in Baltimore printed others; still others came from San Francisco. Labels printed in Portland were shipped by truck to the cannery; those from San Francisco came by rail or steamer to Portland; the ones from Baltimore were shipped via freight forwarders to Portland by rail, and then shipped on to The Dalles by LCL freight on Union Pacific. Ordinarily minimum orders were for 25,000 labels; after World War II minimum orders were 60,000. Until 1930 labels were shipped in heavy wooden boxes; during the war they came in paper cartons bound with heavy wire. Until about 1930 most labels used on fancy canned goods were embossed; but after then many canneries were using automatic labeling machines that would not work on embossed labels. Also, until then the fancy labels were sprinkled with what we called "gold" but was really powdered bronze; by the time of the war rising costs stopped this practice, too. If you still wanted a gold border you had to have the label printed with yellow around the edge.

Until the 1930s the label vignettes were engraved, but after that photoengraving was used, and I must admit these were more attractive and appetizing.

The paper boxes Seufert's used came from Fibreboard Products, Inc., at Sumner, Washington, and were usually shipped by truck. The boxes were knocked down, and came in bundles. A box stitching machine at the cannery was used to make up the boxes as they were needed. Labels and paper boxes were always ordered by letter; when you ordered paper boxes you always specified the thickness or strength, whether the cartons were to be made of corrugated paper or solid paper, and whether the cartons would be used for export.

Seufert's bought their first automatic labeling machine in 1918; it really needed an experienced man to operate it; we had none, and so we had to use four or five inexperienced men and women. The early machines were slow and would only label one can size, so it was necessary to have a separate machine for each size. The machines were used when the cannery was so busy it was impossible to use the China crew to do the labeling by hand. The 1930s' machines were faster, but could still only label one size can. Usually the Company had three machines, one for half-pound cans, one for the one-pound flat, and one for the 2½ fruit can. After the machines had been used, the paste pot had to be cleaned and washed out, and the entire machine had to be cleaned. This took a great deal of time, so when you weren't pressed for time (including the winter, when there was nothing outside for some of the regular white crew to do), you still had the men label by hand. By the 1940s there were machines that could be reset to label different sized cans, from half-pounds right on up to the 6/10 fruit can. From then on the Company ceased hand labeling.

Canned goods that were to be exported to England could not have labels using the word "royal," because of the connotations of the royal family. Thus you could not label a fancy Columbia River Chinook as a Royal Chinook. Seufert's never worked the export trade, but the big grocery warehouses in New York City did, and Seufert's sold to some of these and so we would often label and case canned goods for export markets.

Until the 1920s the American Can Company in Portland shipped empty tin cans to Seufert's in wooden crates about three feet square. These crates were shipped in boxcars. At the cannery the cans were removed, and the empty crates were loaded back into boxcars and shipped back to Portland to be refilled. These crates were filled, emptied and refilled many, many times. The crates were heavier than paper can

packages, so it was expensive to ship them back to the American Can Company, and as soon as paper cartons were introduced, this wasteful practice was stopped. In the 1920s some of the empty tin cans were stored upstairs on the second floor of the warehouse, and made-up cannery cases were also stored there, to be out of the way. Sacks of sugar and other bulky, heavy items could be stored on top of the cases. Such items were hoisted off the warehouse floor by a block-and-tackle. The rope was long, so you could get eight or ten Chinamen pulling on the rope, and it was no problem to lift anything to the second floor. In the next decade a truck was hooked up to the hoist rope, and by driving the truck forward or backward you could do the hoisting, although the truck cab could get surprisingly hot, and the gasoline fumes were a nuisance too. The smell was unpleasant even with the doors open, but then, in those days no one had heard of air pollution.

By 1940 the Company put in a roller conveyor between the floors of the warehouse. You could just push a button and a motor would move the conveyor up and down, and then the only work was to unload the supplies from a hand truck onto the belt.

That old cannery building could be spooky at night. The cannery was dimly lighted, so you could just barely see to walk around. There were cats in the building, and wharf rats, and hot cans of salmon would pop all night long as they cooled, and the building itself would creak and groan. One night after dark I was walking through the cannery warehouse alone. One of the big air vents on top of the building groaned in the wind. I nearly jumped out of my skin.

Down in the cannery boiler room the Company had two boilers. You always put in two, so if you had a big run of salmon and one of the boilers quit, you were never out of business. Neither the engineer nor the fireman ever left the engine or boiler room for any reason whatsoever. They were hired to tend the boilers and engines and operate the retorts, and that is where they stayed. If they started to wander around the cannery when it was operating, you immediately wanted to know why. I don't remember that ever happening. In the days when boilers were fired with slab wood, it was understood that a fireman was not expected to buck in wood to fire the boilers. The slab wood was always stacked directly in front of the boilers, so the fireman had all the fuel he needed, right in front of the boilers. Bucking in the wood was a job for the night watchman. He usually bucked in two cords of wood at night, and if this wasn't enough to fire the boilers all the next day, then you hired a wood buck to keep plenty of wood available for the steam fireman.

There were not many special terms used in reference to the cannery operating. It was either closed or open or getting ready or busy. If it was operating but there was not much fish to can each day, you might say, "Hardly enough fish to get steam up for." If the cannery had more salmon than you could handle, you were swamped.

Other terms were in use in the cannery. Salmon brought to the cannery by truck or boat was hauled. If the fishermen brought the salmon to the cannery, it was delivered. All salmon brought into the cannery was weighed on scales. When it was unloaded on the cannery floor, it was dumped. Men who removed slime from the salmon in sliming tanks were called slimers. Men who filled cans by hand were called fillers. If the cans did not weigh enough, a small square chunk of

salmon was added to the top of the cans. The men who performed this operation were patchers, and a man was said to be patching a can, or more likely, watching the weight. The machine that put the lids on the cans was a clincher. The machine that sealed the lid was a closing machine. Later machines were vacuum closing machines. Sealed cans went from the closing machine into a large tray made of steel strips called a cooler.

The cannery always used to keep cats to keep the wharf rats down. The cats were fed fresh salmon hearts, which the Chinese butchers saved for them. The cats would line up in a row by the butchering tables, and the Chinese butchers would toss each cat a salmon heart, seeing to it that each got his share. The cats waited patiently and there was no scrambling. Wharf rats were always a problem; they were big and tough, and when cornered, a rat would stand up and face a cat. More than one cat had second thoughts about rats. It was eyeball to eyeball, and often the cat would think things over and quietly walk off. But the cats did help control the rats and were worth every salmon heart they ate. In winter the cannery crews fed the cats canned salmon.

Flies were a nuisance but not a problem. Salmon on the cannery floor were kept moist by a fine spray of water that misted them constantly. After the Company stopped using horses the fly nuisance just about disappeared; this was about 1940 when gasoline engines replaced horses.

In the middle 1920s F.A. Seufert went to Reedsport on the Oregon coast and bought three carloads of coast salmon, silversides from the Umpqua River. The fish were packed in boxes down on the coast, iced, and loaded in refrigerator cars and shipped by rail to Seufert's. At the cannery the fall salmon runs had dropped off, so they had time to pack these coast silvers in half-pound cans. The silvers had nice color, but did not have the oil the Columbia River salmon had. The Company felt they were dry, and never packed coast salmon again.

At about the same time Seufert's started to pack fancy Chinooks in the spring in oval cans, both halves and one-pound cans. This pack of ovals was referred to as fancy Columbia River salmon steak. Each oval can had just one slice of salmon in it. When the salmon was run through the gang knives it was sliced to fit a regular can; you just picked out the center slices which just fit the oval can, took them to the salmon packing table, packed them in oval cans, sealed them and processed them in the retort. These ovals always brought a premium price; they were a beautiful pack. But when there was a lot of salmon to can in the spring there was not enough time to fool around with ovals; when you did have time, because there was not too much salmon to can each day, then there was not enough salmon to take just one or two slices from each to pack into ovals. Of course when you packed ovals, the rest of the salmon was packed at the same time in the regular fashion. After a couple of years the Company stopped packing ovals.

When canning salmon, the grade determined the size can. In spring, fancy spring Chinooks all went into half-pound or one-pound flat cans. In the fall, fall Chinooks, steelhead and silversides would also be packed into half-pound and one-pound flat cans, but the No. 3 Chinook, those of poor color which the fishermen often called tules, were often put into one-pound talls. Both the tall and flat held one pound, but the trade insisted on both fancy and choice salmon being put in one-pound flats. And the trade demanded that No. 3 Chinooks or standard Chinooks go in one-pound talls. The talls could be packed by machine, but all fancy and choice Columbia River salmon had to be packed by hand.

Bluebacks at The Dalles were small fish, so they all went into half-pound cans. These salmon ran in July. Because of their fine color and rich oil, bluebacks brought the same price as fancy Columbia River Chinook salmon. A slice of blueback would just fill a half-pound can. If you put blueback into one-pound flats it would take several pieces of salmon.

When you ordered empty cans, you ordered cans for the half-pound line, and you specified that you wanted a Columbia River half-pound salmon can. This was just a trifle shorter in height because they were used for hand packing; in Alaska the can was taller because it would be filled by machine. For statistical purposes within the salmon industry all salmon cases are counted as being 48 one-pound cans. It takes two 48 half-pound cases to make one case. When you counted cases of 48 talls or one-pound cans per case, or two 48 half-pound cases, you said you were using full cases. If you were counting 48 talls per case and 48 half-pounds per case, then you were recording them as they ran.

Prices were always quoted per dozen cans FOB Astoria, Oregon. When quoting prices you gave first the species of salmon offered, then the can size, then price per dozen FOB your shipping point. There was a two percent cash discount, payment in ten days. Years ago, in 1866, the price of canned salmon carried a one-quarter of one percent swell allowance. The buyer expected that one quarter of one percent of the net value of his purchase would spoil, and so he received an allowance, which was given on all canned salmon purchased until January, 1964, when all packers discontinued it. It had been just a gimmick used by buyers to cut costs. In fact, since the sanitary cans were first used around 1905, cans were safely sealed, and from then on there was no problem of spoiling. Of course prices would vary from time to time and from packer to packer, but prices were always quoted in the same manner. The price to the buyer meant that the packer would label the salmon for shipment, load it in the truck or railroad car or deliver it to the ship dockside at no cost to the buyer. If the salmon was to be hand packed, there was a higher price for it, but in general the public would not pay a premium for hand packing, and would accept the lower priced machine packed salmon. Columbia River salmon was always premium pack, the finest canned salmon produced anywhere in the world. It had the finest flavor, the best color and the richest oil; it was all hand packed for an exclusive group of customers who were willing to pay for the best and who expected and got the very best.

CANNING CREWS

The men who worked for Seufert's for years did whatever job needed doing inside or outside the cannery. This gave the men a variety of jobs, and kept the jobs from becoming monotonous, and the men were never bored. These jobs varied from day to day and week to week. And when a man was on an unpleasant job, he could see the end a few days away. These men were satisfied and felt they were doing something worthwhile. The men might leave Seufert's to work for other people because they could make more money, but they never left Seufert's because a job was not interesting or satisfying.

The men who worked for Seufert's were a number of nationalities and races—American, German, Italian, Finnish, Swedish, Chinese and Indian. Nearly all were bachelors and had come from a farm home. Most had done farm work. All had at some time or other worked in the woods, and a surprising number had also worked on railroads. Nearly all had some knowledge of steam for it was common to have been a steam fireman. The crews would also often have a man who had served an enlistment in the peacetime U.S. Army. Most of them were poorly educated, with about a fourth- or fifth-grade education. A few had gone through the eighth grade, and I remember one who was a high school graduate. As a group they were intelligent men; they had character and were honest and hard-working. Today I would say that many would be going to college or would be college material. These men were just born too early, when a high school education was a rarity. By 1930 things had changed and young men were going to school and working only during the summer season. Of course there was always an element who were part-time workers, both young and old, who today would be on the relief rolls. This type of man was never on the payroll long.

The Company had no facilities for married men. The Company provided facilities for unmarried men only—a bunk house and a mess house. At the cannery the Company had several houses for married men, but these were only for the steam engineer and the plant superintendent. The entire operation at the cannery and all the fishing facilities were set up to be operated by unmarried men only. The only other exception, often the cook would be a woman married to a man who worked on one of the crews.

In the early 1930s things began to change. Working men were buying autos and starting to drive to and from work at the cannery. Whether a man was married or not made no difference, for when they were through work the men drove into The Dalles. The cannery was only three miles from The Dalles city limits. They brought their lunches with them to work.

The pay scale started to change. Men were no longer hired plus room and board. Even the mess house at Tumwater was closed. Men who needed to be fed were done so on contract. A local restaurant took the contract at so much per meal per man. Others brought their lunches along to work, and in a few years even feeding the men on a contract with the local restaurant at Tumwater stopped. This had not been at all satisfactory. The food contract was by the meal, and of course the more hamburger and beans the restaurant served, the more profit; and with any crew that included meals as part of its pay, good meals were a necessity and this arrangement was soon stopped. The only exception, until 1949 the Company still furnished a mess house and a bunkhouse to the men on the seine crews.

If the crew members who worked for Seufert's were efficient, they were called good men. If some of the men were not efficient, or didn't know their job, you said the crew was no damn good. The foreman said, "He can't do anything or he'll kill himself," or, "I have to watch him all the time or he'll get hurt." If you had a troublemaker or an agitator in the crew you simply referred to him as that son-of-a-bitch. When the men were out on the job and something wasn't completed on time, it was always referred to as just too late. As for the men cursing on the job, it generally consisted of only three expressions, hell, damn, and son-of-a-

bitch. Of course the various combinations were endless. As a general rule the men were never vulgar in their language. One of the big conversations in the bunk house or at the table in the mess house was always what a good job they had had last year or ten years ago, or on that job how many fish they caught. Another general conversation piece was always speculation on how big the year's salmon run would be. This was always delivered with authority.

The men who worked for the Company were bachelors. They lived in a bunk house and ate in a mess house. They had few or no relatives or friends at The Dalles. They only associated with each other, and their whole world revolved around the Company. This led to a very close relationship between the men and Seufert's. No one would think of firing one of these men because of his conduct over the weekend in town, just as long as he showed up on Monday morning and was able to perform his work. Management didn't consider it any business of theirs how the men spent their time or money in town over the weekend.

The mess house was operated by the Company, whether it was at the cannery or farther up the river. The cooks were always Chinamen or white women. I don't remember the Company ever having a white man cook, except one; one cook on a construction job over at the old Cyclone Wheel. This man wasn't much of a cook because one day for lunch he served them carrot pie. That was more than they could stand and that was the end of that particular cook. One of the things that the Company always did was to feed well. Good food was a must, and of course in the mornings for breakfast there were always fried eggs, bacon and ham, and pie and cake. Often the men had to have a lunch, and if there were any eggs left over from breakfast the cook would make them up into egg sandwiches. Dinner was the main meal of the day and almost invariably was roast beef. Cold roast beef could always be made into sandwiches and sent out with the men. For some reason at supper the men were always served fried meat. Cubed steaks were popular with the cooks; they were fried on top of the stove, which had a huge cast-iron top. When the cooks were through they had an old towel that I don't believe had been washed for Lord only knows how long (it was about the color of a chocolate bar), and the top of the stove was always wiped off with that.

The Company had its own mess houses for the fishwheels, seines and fish houses. I will talk now just for a short bit about how the food was sent up to the different fishing sites. First of all, the Company had its own private telephone lines to all the fishwheels, fish houses, seines and camps. Cooks at each operation called into the cannery office their food order for the next day. The cannery office called the various meat markets and grocery stores in The Dalles, and placed the orders. Around 9:00 in the morning a Company truck picked up all the groceries and meat orders from the markets in The Dalles. Each package had the name of the camp it was to go to. The groceries were then brought to the cannery, and sent up the river on the first fish truck going to that particular camp.

Before the days of the highway, the food orders were phoned to The Dalles in the same manner from the Company office, but all food orders were sent up-river by express on the local passenger train. The groceries were then sent by wagon to the various camps not situated on the railroad. At a camp like the Wash-

ington seining bar, where there was no telephone, the cook wrote out the grocery orders on tablet paper. This was given to a crew member on one of the Company boats, who delivered it to the Oregon side of the river. It was then given to a truck driver and brought to the cannery office. From then on, this order was handled like all the rest.

In all the years I was around the cannery I don't recall a single instance when a grocery order was lost, either the list coming down, or the groceries going back up.

Sunday was a day the men didn't work. They were given breakfast and then there was a cold lunch put on the table. The men could go in and help themselves and of course dinner or supper was always the same; it too was cold and the men helped themselves. Sunday was always the cooks' day off; after they had prepared breakfast, they were not expected to prepare a lunch or supper.

When the men were getting ready for a meal, they generally quit the job about five minutes before meal time. This gave them time to walk over to the mess house, wash and get cleaned up for dinner. Sometimes there would be 20 or more men. They all washed in the same two tin washpans and used the same roller towel. Needless to say, the last man who dried on that towel certainly got a wet towel.

After the men had washed and were ready for dinner, they sat on a long bench outside on a porch. When dinner was on the table, the cook came out and rang the dinner bell. The dinner bell consisted of an old crowbar bent to form a triangle that was struck by a piece of iron. After the cook rang the bell, the men all entered and sat down and ate at the same time. When the men were through eating, each man got up and packed his dishes off the table and into the kitchen. Once the table was cleared off and a man came in late there was no food, and that was all there was to it.

One problem you always had in a salmon cannery was when the cannery was closed down during the noon hour, the retorts were still full of cooking salmon, and someone had to take care of them. And of course that was the engineer's job. But these steam engineers cooking salmon in the retorts couldn't leave to eat, so a machinist (or someone with knowledge of steam) would hurry with his meal, and rush down to the engine room so the engineer could then go up to the mess house for his meal.

In the Company mess house the crockery was white, heavy, and of a quality used in a cheap restaurant. All tableware, that is the knives, forks, spoons, et cetera, were tin with cocobolo handles. It was nothing fancy, but was cheap and durable.

After dishes were washed they were stacked on the drainboard, and the cook poured boiling water over them. This helped to take off the soap film and sterilized the dishes and tableware.

Now in those days, when the Company was operating mostly with unmarried men, the Company provided no bathing facilities whatsoever. After all, both the men and the Company felt that the river was there and if you wanted a bath it was convenient. The common practice of the men was to go to town on Saturday night. They all went to the barber shop and bought a bath and cleaned up and changed into fresh clothes. Then they returned to the cannery some time that night or the next morning according to their desires.

In the bunk houses, the Company furnished iron cots and mattresses. The men furnished their own blankets, no sheets—a working man would never dream of using such a thing. How the men cleaned their blankets, if they ever did, was each man's own problem. These men were given a single room just wide enough for the cot and that was all, but it was their own room. A man kept it locked and no one was ever permitted to enter without his permission; anyone who did was considered a thief. Whether a man kept his room clean or never bothered to sweep it out was his own business. Just as long as the room didn't smell and disturb others, the man's room was truly his castle.

Bedbugs were a problem. In fact they would get so bad a person just couldn't sleep in a room. You could sprinkle coal oil around the room and this was considered one way to control the bedbugs. Of course for a while there was no smoking, but these bedbugs did seem to go away in the fall or at least not to be so bad.

At least once every spring all the men's mattresses and blankets were put into one of the steam retorts at the cannery. The steam was turned on and the bedding was sterilized, at least when it first came out of the retort it was free of bedbugs. This condition didn't last long, though, once the bedding went back into the bunk house. Also, I might add that any bedding that was sterilized in a salmon cannery retort had a tendency to pick up a slight fishy smell—one of fish oil. Each mattress returned to the cannery from any seine operation in the fall was always sterilized in the retorts, and stored away to await another season.

My first encounter with bedbugs was one evening when I called on a married man who worked for the Company and lived in a Company house. The man had two sons, one about six and the other seven. One of the boys was named Norman. During the course of conversation with this man I mentioned I had never seen a bedbug. This man couldn't believe it. He called out, "Norman, go in the bedroom and catch Francis a bedbug." The little boy disappeared and in a minute or so he was back pleased as punch. In his little fingers he held a bedbug to show Francis. It was alive and kicking, too.

The men who worked on the river for Seufert's were not heavy drinkers as a rule. The Italians in the crew would make their own grape wine because, like so many Italian people, they liked a glass of wine. A few of the men made home brew. I suppose this was more because it was the thing to do, not because of any great fondness for it. After prohibition I don't remember any of the men making any kind of liquor at home. They went to town over the weekends, had a few glasses of beer, and that seemed to take care of the matter. In fact the men generally met either in a cardroom or poolroom when they were in The Dalles over the weekend. They saw their acquaintances, talked about their jobs, gossiped, and that seemed to be the extent of their weekend.

These men didn't gamble either at the bunk houses or at the cardrooms in town. In fact, most of them didn't play cards at all. Once in a while a few of us would play a game of pinochle in the evening for fun. One thing I must emphasize, these men were not quarrelsome, and I never heard of any of them ever becoming involved in an incident in town that required the attention of the police.

As far as money was concerned, the men were paid by check once a month. Most had some small savings, in either postal savings or the local banks. One or two had enough money to buy a few bonds. The men who were married and lived in town owned their own homes, although the houses were often mortgaged. As a rule these men paid cash for anything they bought, and had a good financial reputation with local merchants.

While they often had very little schooling, they could express themselves. They were not like so many uneducated people who cannot express themselves. These men could and did talk, in fact I would say that talking or visiting was one of their main pastimes. Perhaps I should say they gossiped, but again this was just plain talk about what was going on and what was of interest to them, mainly fishing or who had been doing what. These men were not petty or vicious in their gossiping. They looked down on an individual who never said anything as something of an oddball. I must emphasize that these men were decent and honorable; they did not lie or cheat, nor were they the kind of men to run to the boss with gossip about other men on the job. The Company took a dim view of the man who was always bearing tales. This is not to say that there was not personal tragedy in some of these men's lives, divorce, loss of loved ones, use of liquor at some time that had cost a man his job. This sort of thing in a man's past was nobody's business but his own. As long as a man did his job well, tended to his own business, no one cared about his past, and under no circumstances did any man try to be vicious and dig up a man's past to embarrass him.

These men were tough (mentally and physically), hard workers, fair and decent with others, but they had little gentleness in their nature. They would try to be kind and gentle in such acts as petting a dog or a cat or taking care of a horse perhaps, but they simply could not express themselves in a gentle manner. Any rebuff, either real or imagined, would make them get their backs up. To my knowledge they seldom had read a book, seldom if ever a magazine, maybe once in a while a newspaper. Generally when the day's work was done they had a smoke, talked among themselves a bit and went to bed. I would say it was years since any of them had seen the inside of a church.

Whether working in the cannery or on the river, all of the men wore long underwear, wool pants and shirts. In the winter or on a cold windy day one pair of pants and one wool shirt was not enough. The men then put on another pair of wool pants and shirt over the ones they were wearing. For coats the men always wore short wool coats, or mackinaws as we called them. And most wore caps. Caps didn't blow off in the wind. On cold days they had caps with an inside rim that could be turned down and used as earmuffs. In cold weather the men wore either gloves or heavy mittens. Their shoes were always heavy work shoes, and if there was snow on the ground or the ground was frozen, some of the men wore galoshes. All of the men wore wool socks. The colder it was, the more clothes they put on, one pair over another. When it warmed up they just took off some. Bib overalls were common. The men wore these if they were working on a job where the front of their bodies would rub against something. The steam firemen and engineers always wore bib overalls. Most of the fishwheel men wore bib overalls to keep their work clothes clean. Around the fish houses we generally wore bib overalls. Some truck drivers would wear them, but some didn't. On the seine the men usually wore long underwear, wool pants and wool shirts (If the day was windy and cold you just put on more clothes). Dressing in general was done according to the taste of each man. His clothes were his own, and how he protected them or took care of them was his own business.

One time I worked in the Tumwater fish house with a horse thief. He stole a horse some place out in central Oregon and the sheriff down there threw him in jail. While awaiting trial his cell partner managed to get out through the window. He asked the horse thief to come along. The thief thought he might as well. Somehow the thief made good his escape and ended up working in the Tumwater fish house. I asked him what happened after he got out of jail and he said he didn't know because he never went back to find out. My point in telling this story was that when you had a lot of salmon to handle at Tumwater and the Company needed men, if a man wanted a job, stayed sober, did his job and bothered no one, the Company couldn't have cared less about his past. Believe me, you got all kinds.

Guy Whipple was cannery superintendent for years. Around the cannery and the mess houses, all the plumbing was generally done by Guy Whipple. When Guy put in hot and cold water faucets around the sink or wash bowl, he always insisted on putting the hot water faucet on the right hand side, not on the left, as is done in homes. A new man who wanted a glass of cold water would turn on the right hand faucet and get quite a surprise; and the longer he let the water run, the hotter it got.

Guy and his wife lived in The Dalles, but Guy had never driven a car, although he was probably 65 years old or so. On Saturday night I always waited for him and then drove him home. He would always buy me a cigar on Sunday and then on Monday when I would see him again he would always tell me that my cigar was down in the label room inside the door on a shelf in a tin can. This was where Guy left my cigar.

I took Guy home one Saturday night as usual. He came to work on Monday but went home, and the next morning his family called and said he had died during the night. It was probably a week after his death when I was down in the label room and happened to wonder if Guy had left a cigar there for me. I opened the door, went in, and on the shelf in the tin can my cigar was waiting for me.

There were three Wickman brothers. At some time they all worked for Seufert's. The Wickmans were farmers, and the family lived a short way up Fifteenmile Creek above the cannery. Henry Wickman went to work for Seufert's in 1896 as a watchman on No. 5 Fishwheel. Bill Wickman, his brother, worked for Seufert's in the 1890s and early 1900s on the Celilo seines, on the fishwheels and in the fish houses. Later, in the 1920s, Bill Wickman was a steam fireman for Libby, McNeil and Libby in their fruit cannery at The Dalles. After Libbys closed their cannery in 1927, Bill Wickman worked for Seufert's as a steam fireman for years. When Gus Bansch had to retire as engineer because of poor health, Bill Wickman took over and worked as steam engineer until after World War II. After he took his pension, Bill would come back to the engine room and work as a steam fireman for a couple of weeks or so when the cannery was real busy. He was always available so long as the length of his employment each year didn't interfere with his pension rights. To have a competent man like him on call to fill in for short periods was a great convenience for the Company.

The third brother, Fred, worked for Seufert's for years on the fishwheels and on the seines. Fred was also night watchman for Seufert's Cannery for a number of years. Fred had only one hand. As a child he had found a dynamite cap and played with it. The cap exploded, blowing off his left hand at the wrist. But Fred Wickman with one hand was a better man than most with two hands. When he was night watchman he would buck in two cords of slab wood into the boiler-room every evening before dark. When he did this he had to take the slab wood from the woodpile, pile it on a hand truck, truck the load to the engine room, unload the hand truck and stack the wood in front of the boilers so it would be handy for the fireman when he came to work in the morning.

I can well remember Fred Wickman with a shovel. He could hold his own digging a ditch with the best of them; and the same was true when he pitched salmon on a fish house floor.

Slab wood was shipped to Seufert's Cannery from the sawmill usually in late winter. There would not be too much to do at this time of year and unloading wood would be something to keep the regular crew busy. The back of the cannery was some 15 feet lower than the front. The railroad siding was on the east side of the cannery between it and Fifteenmile Creek. In back of the cannery the siding ran out on a railroad trestle some 15 feet or so above the ground. This trestle would hold about four standard size boxcars. After a car of slab wood was spotted on the railroad trestle the car would often be too high above the ground to reach, so you would have to put a long ladder against the side of the car, climb the ladder and open the boxcar door; and on some old boxcars it could be a real job to open the door, especially if some of the slab wood in the cars had fallen against the door. After the men got into the car they tossed the wood out through the open door onto the woodpile. The wood was never stacked in the pile, and when the pile got as high as the boxcar door, the men had to lay planks on top of the pile and truck the wood on a hand truck to the end of the pile and dump it. If you unloaded green slab wood in February, by the time the cannery started to operate in May the wood would be dry and burn readily. The big gripe the men had in unloading a car of slab wood was that the boxcar door used for unloading was on the west side, and on a day when the west wind was blowing, it would blow sawdust and pieces of bark back into your face every time you heaved a piece of wood through the open car door.

It was common for chipmunks to get in the car of slab wood when it was loaded at the sawmill. When the men unloaded a car of wood, they would catch these chipmunks if they could and take them up in front of the cannery office where the Company had a big wire cage for them. The animals were put into the cage and everyone fed them and made pets of them. Sometimes there would be five to ten chipmunks in the cage at one time, and some of the chipmunks lived in captivity for several years. Those that the men didn't catch didn't have a chance of survival around the cannery because of the open country and lack of both food and protection.

Out in front of the cannery office there was a flower garden, and a concrete pool in it about six or eight feet across, and some three feet deep. We used to put fish in the pool, not much as fish go, generally some kind of goldfish. The pool had water running into it all the time and the goldfish had no enemies in the pool, so I suppose this was a goldfish's idea of heaven. Anyway my Dad would feed these fish every afternoon. When he went to feed them he would call to them and the darned goldfish would swim over to him every time.

I would like to mention W.O. "Bill" Hadley. In the 1920s Bill Hadley was an old man. Sometime around the time of World War II my wife and I went to the Hadley's 60th wedding anniversary in The Dalles. Mr. Hadley had been an officer in the U.S. Army back in the 1880s, had served in the Indian campaigns in Arizona and New Mexico territories. Later he retired on pension and came to Oregon. He was very much interested in salmon, and in their preservation by means of fish hatcheries and fish ladders built on streams so the fish could easily pass upstream. At one time he was game warden for the old Fish and Game Commission; he lived at The Dalles then. He was a constant visitor at the cannery. Hadley built the fish ladder in Fifteenmile Creek at the cannery over the falls and under the railroad bridge. This fish ladder must have been put in some time around World War I, and it is still in use today. Since he was convinced of the value of hatcheries, Bill Hadley wanted the state of Oregon to buy land for a hatchery at Oak Springs on the Deschutes River between Maupin and Sherars Bridge. He wanted the state to build a trout and salmon hatchery there, but the state was not interested, and so he bought the property with money out of his own pocket and built a small hatchery. To operate the hatchery he had to live there, so he had a one-room cabin. Of course his wife lived in their home in The Dalles. I remember one time, about 1932 or so, Guy Whipple and I drove out to visit Bill Hadley. He knew we were coming. For lunch he cooked fried pork sausage for us on his woodstove. I don't remember what else we had for lunch, but I still remember how good his pork sausage was.

In later years the state of Oregon bought Mr. Hadley's land and his hatchery. The state paid him $6,000 for the property. The state got a real bargain, and the sportsmen in Oregon all owe Mr. Hadley a vote of thanks for buying the site with his own money and thus keeping for Oregon one of the best fish hatchery sites in the state.

Mr. Hadley often came out to the cannery when there was a big salmon run. He would come over to talk and offer me a cigar. His cigars were not expensive, but they were strong. He would always insist that I light the cigar that he gave me, and then he would proceed to stand there and talk to me until the cigar was completely smoked. I can still remember standing there talking to Mr. Hadley and smoking one of his cigars and wondering just how much longer that cigar was going to last.

In operating a salmon cannery or fishing gear out on the Columbia River you had to have a foreman. In the cannery and fishing operation there were always some men who were highly intelligent and competent, but so many times these men would just refuse to be advanced to foreman. Money made no difference. Some men just didn't want to have the responsibility, and others just wanted to remain one of the boys. Eventually you would find a good man to be foreman, but I was always surprised to find how hard it was to find men in the crew who really wanted to advance.

In later years, during the fall salmon run, I was running the cannery and we were really busy. A young white man working in the cannery down by the retorts put engine oil in the Chinamen's teapot. This created quite an uproar. The cannery foreman came to me immediately and told me about it and said that it was causing trouble with the China crew. The foreman asked me what he was to do. I asked him if he knew for sure which white man had done this. The foreman said he did. I told the foreman to fire the man and send him immediately to the office for his time. We couldn't have this kind of monkey business in the cannery when we were busy and I wouldn't put up with anybody who caused trouble with the China crew. Nothing that had ever happened around the cannery before brought home to me more quickly than that the simple fact that I was no longer a young buck working in the cannery and having fun—now I was boss.

I want to mention a few things about the white women who worked in our cannery. Now to a man, women are always interesting; but when you have to handle and supervise, say 50 women, then all I can say is, Good God! It comes as a shock. Someone always has her claws out.

I remember an old lady who worked for Seufert's for years. She must have been in her seventies. She lived a block from my house. When our son was small, my wife and I would hire this old lady to babysit for us. In the morning when I went into the cannery I would always smile and say "good morning" to this nice old lady who had probably sat with our son the weekend before. That was all that was needed to start tongues wagging. So after a while you just treated all the women in the cannery, regardless of how well you knew them, as strangers. Women were hired to work, but let two or three women get together and the first thing you know they are talking like they were attending a sewing bee. The main thing was to keep these women busy. A busy woman hasn't time to talk. A good worker, man or woman, will stand up when he or she works. The person who sits down on the job is drawing pay but is not producing much.

You had to run the cannery and that included handling the women; but it really was not much of a job if you handled it right. What you did was pick one woman for your floor lady or your lady boss, middle aged, intelligent, one who knew cannery work and was tough enough to handle the other women; and she couldn't be prissy. You wanted a woman you could talk to as an equal, who knew what the score was; after all, aspects of sex—pregnancies and so on—were bound to come up among some of the women in your crew. You and your floor lady had to discuss the situation cold turkey and you finally had to decide what to do. When the floor lady brought you a problem, you had to have faith in her opinion and judgment; and if you didn't, you had no business hiring her for a floor lady. You discussed the problem in plain language, nothing for either of you to be embarrassed about. When you had talked the matter over and listened to her advice and discussed the situation, you decided what had to be done. Then you backed the floor lady to the hilt as she carried out your decision.

You didn't discuss the situations with any of the men working in the cannery. It was your problem and

the floor lady's, and no one else's business. You never talked to any of the other women in the cannery, just the floor lady. On second thought, I guess you handled the women crews through the floor lady just as you handled the China crews through the China boss.

Now, what kind of women did you get to work in the cannery? Well, you could say, all kinds; but as a general rule they were a very decent group. Educational backgrounds ranged from women who had only completed eight grades to college graduates. Some were widows supporting a family, others were helping their husbands to support a family, and some worked because they wanted to earn a little extra money. Some of the young girls were in high school, so during summer vacations they worked to make some spending money. We always had school teachers working during the summer when school was out. Of course, in any group there are always a few bad apples. You would always have a few women who were really tough cookies, and I mean tough. Still, these nice girls as a group could really keep a man hopping.

I remember one time we had a man working in the cannery, a not overly intelligent bachelor. At quitting time this man hurried out of the cannery, got in his car and took off for town. Some of the women in the cannery got off work at the same time and drove to town in their car behind him. The man drove straight to town, parked his car right in front of a local whore house in the east end of town and went right upstairs to see the girls. The carload of women from the cannery saw this poor guy go upstairs to the whore house. For the next two weeks the cannery women kidded this poor sap about where he had gone, what he had done, and how good it was. They certainly made life miserable for him for a while, and the next time he went upstairs I'll bet he looked carefully up and down the street to make certain no woman working at Seufert's cannery saw him.

CHINESE

The decision to use Chinese workers in the cannery was made in 1896. Seufert's built and operated their first salmon cannery up at The Dalles fishery. At the same time, in 1896, they took over the cannery which they had always operated down at Seuferts, Oregon. The two were about a mile apart. I believe that the cannery Seufert's built at the fishery was never used, but that the cannery at Seuferts was operated by the family from 1896 on. When they first started to operate this cannery in 1896 they used Chinese labor exclusively. The Chinese did all the butchering of salmon, the sliming, filling of cans, sealing of cans; they put them in the retorts and took them out, stacked them in the warehouse, put on the labels, put them in boxes, and loaded the boxes on freight cars. All the manual labor was done by the Chinese; the only exceptions were a white man who worked as steam engineer, a white foreman, white machinist and white bookkeeper.

All the Chinese came from Portland. They were brought out on passenger trains. In those days you went to Portland and bought tickets for the entire crew of about 50 men, notified the railroad what day they were to leave Portland. The railroad would put a passenger car on especially for the Chinese crew, and bring them up to The Dalles. The train would generally arrive in The Dalles about noon. The train then carried the car out to Seufert's where all the Chinese were then unloaded from the passenger car. The Chinamen brought all their own luggage, which was in the baggage car, and it was unloaded at the cannery when the Chinese got off. The luggage generally consisted of a three-gallon bucket for each man. In these buckets the Chinamen carried all of their clothes and personal belongings. The buckets were very important because when they reached the China house they were used as suitcases, then later as bathtubs, because a man could take a sponge bath from his bucket.

There were leaders. In the first place, all these Chinamen belonged to the same tong. If you had two tongs in a China house and a tong war broke out, you would wake up some morning with a lot of dead Chinamen on your hands, so you always made sure you had Chinamen from the same tong. They were hired through Portland, and down there the Chinese grocery always seemed to be the one the Company dealt with. These Chinese grocers hired the crew and sent them up to you, and they also supplied all of the food and supplies that the Chinese needed to live on for all the time they were living and working at the cannery.

The man we called the China boss was the leader of the whole crew. The whites never talked to anyone except the China boss. You told him what you wanted done, and he gave the orders to the Chinamen and saw that they were carried out. If you spoke to a good Chinese worker, he would not respond to you, and he would not take orders from anyone except the China boss. You also had to furnish the Chinese cook who did all of the cooking for the Chinamen at the China house. And you had to furnish a Chinese bookkeeper who kept all of their accounts. You also had to supply the Chinese with pigs and ducks. These were always bought from local farmers in the spring; the Chinese raised them all summer and butchered them as needed. The Chinamen had a hog pen, and the hogs were never permitted to step on the ground. The hog pen floor was covered with boards, and these boards were thoroughly washed and cleaned every day.

In those days you hired the Chinamen just like you hired the crew of a ship. They were hired to go to work in April, generally about the 25th, and then they were to work until the 15th of October. They were not paid at all during that time; on the last day they got their entire six months' pay in one lump sum, always in cash. As a rule they wanted 500 or 1000 dollar bills. As far as the pay of each individual was concerned, the Chinese boss and bookkeeper had all of the accounts, and if anyone deserved more pay because of particular extra work, the account was turned in and you paid it. When the crew was paid off, you went down to The Dalles, bought the tickets for the entire crew, notified

the railroad and the passenger train was flagged at the cannery on whatever day you sent the crew back to Portland.

The Chinamen lived in what we called the China house. Each had their own quarters, for the house consisted of several parts. First of all there was the bunk house, generally a wooden structure where each Chinaman had his own room. Each room had a bed but no bed *ever* had a mattress. The Chinese would only sleep in a bed on boards. In fact, one time the Company thought they would do a good turn for the Chinamen and put springs and mattresses in the China house. The next morning every spring and mattress was outside, and the Chinese slept on boards. These boards were 1x12s, cut as long as the bed, laid on the iron bed, and then were covered with blankets on which the men slept.

The Chinamen also had their own cook house with a Chinese cook. He cooked all of their meals. Most meals consisted of rice; and then of course they were great eaters of duck and pork. When the Chinese cooks made something out of meat, usually chicken or pork, they would always use peanut oil in their cooking. You could always smell it from outside. All Chinamen seemed to have a great sweet tooth. Every day the grocery trucks or wagons from The Dalles would come out with all kinds of pastries which were sold to the Chinamen.

In the early days, up until World War I, the hours were from six in the morning until six at night. The men went to work at six, worked until noon, had an hour off, went back to work at one, and worked until six. That was an eleven-hour day. By the 1920s and on into the 1930s this dropped to ten hours, and then later to eight. They worked six days a week. It was up to you to keep them busy, since they got full pay whether or not they worked; if they worked overtime, they were paid for it.

The only night-time activity I ever saw a Chinaman do was to gamble. They were great gamblers. They gambled every minute when they weren't working. They played dominoes and fan-tan mostly, but they were also quite active with the mah-jongg set.

There were no women around at all. No Chinaman ever brought his wife along, and of course there were no provisions for women down at the China house. The China foreman had his own little house, but he never had a wife that we knew of, or if he did, he never brought her along. The men came up for the entire six months and had no relations with women in that time.

In those days the relationship between Indians, Chinese and whites was very clear-cut. Each man tended to his own business and didn't interfere with the rights of others. The Indians all stayed at the Indian camp, the Chinese all stayed down at the China house, and the whites all stayed at the white bunk house. None of the whites was ever permitted to go down with the Chinese, and of course the Chinese never came up around the whites. And the whites were never permitted around the Indians. It was always assumed that a white who went down around the China house or around the Indians was only looking for trouble, and no one ever permitted any of the whites to go down and bother the Indians or Chinese in any way.

Across from the mess house the Chinamen had a bath house. It was just a plain little building probably ten or fifteen feet long, plain wood inside with a long

bench against one wall. Outside alongside this building there was a stove, with an open water tank on top. The Chinamen could fill this tank with water, fire up the stove with four-foot slab wood, and have all the hot water they needed to bathe in. I don't know exactly how they bathed. Of course some took sponge baths. I always thought that they somehow or other managed to make a steam bath in this little bath house.

One of the big deals at the China house was pig butchering day. This was always a Sunday afternoon. It was both work and for some Chinamen a lot of fun. The fun of course was reserved for the Chinamen who were spectators. The whole China crew would collect outside and back from the pig pen. This group would be in high spirits, full of fun and even more full of free advice. The group who did the work consisted of a few Chinamen who got into the pig pen and cornered the hog. The hog would not cooperate, and protested loudly, and this only added to the fun. Anyway, somehow the Chinamen would up-end the hog and hogtie him. Then the China butcher, generally the China boss himself, would take a long knife and, while the hog squealed, he would slit its throat. This always brought out another Chinaman with a dishpan which was held under the hog's throat to catch all the blood that gushed forth. This was as far as I ever got at the Chinese hog butchering; from there on I really don't know what happened, although after the butchering the China boss would give me the pork tenderloin, which was really good eating.

The last few days of the canning season the Chinamen were paid in cash for their summer's work. On pay day itself there was no work in the cannery. This was a holiday. Late that afternoon sometimes a big

102

fancy car would drive up from Portland and in it would be three well-dressed Chinamen and a couple of attractive white girls in the back seat. The China boss said they came up for a visit. Anyway they would drive directly in back of the cannery to the China house and of course we would not see them again. By the next morning the big car and its occupants would be gone. But all that next day for some reason you never saw a more jolly, contented bunch of Chinamen.

Chinese cannery labor was not cheap labor. The Chinamen working in a salmon cannery received the same wages as men working outside the cannery—the fishwheel workers and the fish house workers. The Chinamen were used in a salmon cannery because a Chinaman has hands as nimble as a woman's, and he also had the power in his fingers and wrists of a man. Packing salmon all day into a tin can was hard work and needed nimble fingers and strong wrists.

The Chinamen were anticommunist, and had great faith in the American navy because it had just beaten the Japanese. One day, about 1947 or so, when the Chinese communist army was approaching Shanghai, and the American naval force was anchored in the harbor, these cannery Chinamen were quite sure that the American navy was going to take on the communist army and put them in their place. Then the news came that as the communists approached the city the American fleet pulled up anchor and sailed away. The morning that this was in all the newspapers the China boss came up to me and asked, "What is the matter with you fellows, you no fight?" Well, there wasn't much to answer.

One time in the 1930s while I was in Portland I visited the China boss at the Portland tong headquarters. It was north of Burnside down toward Union Station; the tong building was probably two or three stories high, drab and old. I entered and asked for the China boss, and in a bit he came out of the back room and greeted me. Then he took me into the back, just the back room of a Chinese store, then up a narrow stairway. At the head of the stairs was a door with a peephole. The door opened and we walked toward the front of the building. We were now on the second floor. We went down another narrow hall. On each side of the hall were open narrow bunks, open to the hall but partitioned up to the ceiling between bunks. Each cubby hole had a curtain across the front of it. Some curtains were pulled, and I assumed that Chinamen were asleep on their bunks. Others had the curtains back and were empty. We came out of that narrow hall into a room that ran all the way across the front of the building. Here there were plain wooden tables and benches, and Chinamen smoking, talking and gambling. The air was so stuffy I don't believe a window had been opened for a long time. The room had been painted long before. You knew you were in a room full of Chinamen from the smell of food. Anyone who has been in a Chinese mess house will know what I mean. I assume there were cooking quarters off to one side of the room.

The China boss took me into another room opposite the bunk hall. I wasn't in the least prepared for what I saw. Here was this long room, beautifully finished, I would say in teak, black lacquer and gold, probably brass, and at the end was a teak altar, beautifully carved, all in black teak, and on it sat a bigger-than-life buddha, all polished brass. In the half-light it was breathtaking. The whole thing was so impressive, so unexpected, I have never forgotten it.

Quite a few Chinese cannery workers would return and work for Seufert's year after year. It was always quite a thing for us at the cannery to wait out in front of the office for the train to arrive from Portland with the new China crew to see which Chinamen were returning to the cannery for another salmon canning season, and to see the new men arrive too. Of course all these Chinamen worked for all the companies canning salmon on the Columbia River, one year for Seufert's, the next for Barbey, then the next year for CRPA. Then they would probably come back and work another year for Seufert's. Only the China bosses came back to the same company year after year. When you had a good China boss you kept him. Seufert's never thought of getting a new China boss as long as the regular China boss was ready and willing to come back.

In the late winter when you were thinking about opening the cannery for the coming season and you needed a China crew you just wrote your China boss a letter and told him to get you a China crew for the coming season. He would generally come up to The Dalles from Portland on the local passenger train and in the Company office he would tell you what the going wages were to be for the new season. You could argue about the crew's wages but whatever the China boss said he would have to pay the China crew was about what you were going to have to pay to get your crew. Then you decided how many men you needed, and what jobs were to be filled. After you and the China boss had decided on that, the China boss then returned to Portland on the train and down in Portland signed up the crew for you. When you were ready to open the cannery and start your canning operation, the China boss would bring the crew up for the new season.

I want to talk now just a little about the Chinese salmon butchers. A Chinese butcher could butcher a 30-pound Chinook salmon in 45 seconds, and the Company expected each man to butcher at least ten tons of salmon in a ten-hour day, or roughly one ton per hour. Three Chinese butchers could handle 30 tons of Columbia River salmon per day, which would produce at least 900 cases of 48 one-pound cans per day. On such a day the Company always had at least two men, usually white, who did nothing but pick up salmon from the fish room floor and put the fish on the butchering tables, always with the heads facing the Chinese butcher. The Chinese were hired to butcher, and they were too busy to stop and pick uncut salmon off the floor and heave them up on the tables. The Chinese butchers were the elite of the Chinese cannery crew.

The Chinese butchers always used a heavy knife of imported Sheffield steel. These were the finest butcher knives available. They had long heavy blades, curved at the end. They held a fine sharp edge, and the heavy blade would not nick when the butchers cut into the heavy backbone of a big Columbia River Chinook salmon. While the Chinese butcher was working he would sharpen his knife on a steel from time to time. Also these Chinese never washed the butcher knives in hot water. The knives were first wiped off on a wet burlap sack, then thoroughly washed in cold water, and then the knife was honed on an oil stone. Then the knife was put away by the Chinese butcher until the next day's work began.

These fine knives were hard to get after World War I, and by the 1930s it was nearly impossible to buy one. Price was no consideration as far as the Company was concerned; but the knives were just not available. The Company always bought the knives, but once the Chinese butcher was given his knife it became his personal property. He kept it in order, and when he left in the fall of the year and went back to Portland he took the knife with him.

There was always a grindstone down by the closing machines in the cannery. It sat on a wooden frame, and was pumped by one's feet while sitting on a little bicycle seat. There was a little tin can on the frame so you could put water on the stone while you were sharpening a knife. These stones were used for the big heavy butcher knives the Chinese used; they would take nicks out of the blades. They could also be used to sharpen a pike pole, but usually it was easier to sharpen those on an emery wheel.

We also butchered salmon in the cannery with a machine called an "Iron Chink." The machine got its name because it replaced Chinese butchers. The Iron Chink Seufert's used was purchased in 1918 and was still in use until the salmon cannery stopped operating. An Iron Chink would butcher about 15 salmon per minute, but it could only handle small salmon, so it was only used in the fall. Even then it was only used when the cannery was so busy you had all the salmon you could possibly handle in a day. It was used to butcher such small fish as jack salmon, small Chinooks and steelhead. The Iron Chink stood about seven feet high. It only took two Chinamen to operate it; one white man would feed salmon to the Chinamen who operated the Iron Chink. These two Chinamen were always butchers. The first fed the salmon onto a butchering table where a knife on the side of the Iron Chink cut off the head. The first Chinaman passed the salmon on to the second, who fed the salmon into the Iron Chink tail first, belly up. The Iron Chink was basically just a large revolving wheel some six feet in diameter. The wheel seized the salmon and while the big wheel revolved slowly making one complete turn, the Iron Chink cut off the fins and tail, slit the belly open and removed the entrails. When the big wheel completed its revolution the salmon came out completely cleaned and butchered.

The Iron Chink, using two Chinamen to feed it and one white man to pike salmon to the Chinamen, would butcher as many salmon in a day as ten Chinese could butcher by hand. The Iron Chink was noisy, and it threw salmon guts all over the place. Sheets of tin covered the Iron Chink to keep the salmon guts around the machine. The shortcoming of the machine was that it tended to tear the salmon meat, and also that it was limited as to the size of fish it could handle. It was never used to butcher a fancy Columbia River Chinook salmon; these were always butchered by hand so you were always sure of getting a nice fancy pack. Also, the Iron Chink was wasteful. When you butchered by hand you could save more of the salmon weight, so as long as the three Chinese butchers could butcher by hand all the salmon the can fillers needed, the Iron Chink wasn't used; but in the fall when you were running fall Chinooks and packing by automatic filling machines, then sometimes you had to use the Iron Chink to keep enough butchered salmon on hand for the automatic filling machines to stay busy.

Each day the Chinamen would gather up all the broken and smashed cans in the cannery, put these smashed cans in a box, walk out of the cannery to the side of Fifteenmile Creek, and throw the whole works over the fence into the creek. Later in the afternoon, if I had nothing to do after the cans had been thrown over the fence, I would take a .22 rifle and shoot at some of the cans that would come floating down the creek out into the Columbia River. It was good target practice, and of course when you hit a can you could see the water splash behind it, and then the can would sink and you could be sure you had hit your target.

There was never any goldbricking among the China crews who labeled cans and loaded cars. They all worked and each did his own share of the work. These Chinamen would just naturally go to work as a group on a job, with each man taking the job he was physically capable of doing. The old men all labeled cans and the middle-aged men stacked the salmon cases after the Chinese laborers had filled them with labeled cans. These middle-aged men also saw to it that each laborer had a full case of unlabeled salmon cans at his side, and took away the cases of labeled cans. They also manned the hand trucks and trucked the salmon cases ready for shipment in the freight cars. The young Chinamen and the husky ones did all the piling and stacking of the canned salmon cases into the freight cars. If there was a pile of canned salmon in the warehouse to be taken down onto the warehouse floor for labeling, it was the young men who lifted the cases down. Once in a while when you had to move some cases in the warehouse, but the distance was not far, instead of using a hand truck a number of young Chinamen would line up in single file and pass the cases down the line, one case at a time. It was surprising how many cases of canned goods a China crew could move this way.

When the China crew walked from one job to an-other in the cannery they would invariably line up single fine. The board walk in back of the cannery boiler room to the China house was probably a hundred yards long or so. This walk was constructed of 2x12s set on end on the ground, with 2x12s cut 30 inches wide nailed across. The Chinamen used this board walk twice a day, coming up to the cannery and going back to the China house. Through the years these Chinamen walking single file down that walk wore a path in the wood. Many of them walked with their hands clasped together behind their backs.

I grew up around the Chinamen, and although I never learned to speak Chinese, as a kid I soon learned to talk pidgin English. The China boss could speak that, and any of the Chinamen who could speak any language besides Chinese could speak it. Using pidgin English you could carry on a conversation with the Chinamen without any trouble. Of course this led to considerable arm waving by you and by the Chinaman, but this just helped the conversation along. To a white person who had no knowledge of pidgin English, your conversation with the Chinaman was just so much mumbo-jumbo, but then the Chinamen and I understood each other, and that was the important thing.

During the 1920s there was a big Chinese tong war on the Pacific Coast. During this time several Chinamen were shot and killed in the big coast cities. The tong that all the Chinamen in the cannery belonged to was involved in this war. The Chinamen came to work each day at the cannery, but you could easily tell that they were a nervous bunch. They talked little, and from the way they walked you knew that they were all on edge. As soon as the work in the cannery was finished each day, the China crew rushed back to the China house, had supper, and then each man went to his room and locked the door. One Chinaman stayed out of sight but on guard all night, and he was armed. And I might add, that at a time like this only a fool would have gone near that China house. The China boss seemed to have been a marked man during that particular tong war, so every night as soon as he had had supper, he came up to the cannery and had himself locked in the label room for the night. He just moved his bedding into that room, and was locked in each night for the duration of the tong war. As soon as word was sent that the war had been settled, then everything returned to normal immediately, and a day or so later you would never have known that just a few days before your Chinamen had been afraid for their lives.

In the 1920s Seufert's China house was a wooden bunk house that sat on the river. One night a Chinaman went to bed leaving a candle burning. Somehow during the night the candle was knocked to the floor, and the China house caught fire and burned to the ground. The next morning the Company had to go to all the stores in The Dalles and buy clothes for some 50 Chinamen who were lucky to get out of the fire alive. They had been able to save nothing, since they had been in bed when the fire broke out. The next morning they had only the clothes they had worn to bed. The poor Chinaman who slept in his underwear that night was lucky! Anyway, Seufert's clothed the entire crew with new clothes the next morning.

Soon, word reached the office that the man who was responsible for the fire would be lucky if the China crew didn't kill him, so several of the white men at the cannery were sent down to the China house to bring the frightened Chinaman back to the cannery. Up at the cannery they locked the Chinaman in the label room and left one of the white men outside as a guard. That night the Company took the Chinaman by car to The Dalles and bought him a railroad ticket to Walla Walla. It was hoped that the Chinese in Walla Walla would at least take this man in. After the Chinaman was put on the night train no one around the cannery ever saw him again. I never heard what happened to him.

As a general rule, if the Chinamen had any differences among themselves, they were settled down at the China house, and we seldom heard anything about it. Several times, though, the China boss would have a difference of opinion with a Chinaman in the cannery. The China boss would stand some ten feet away from the other Chinaman, look at him, and give him a tongue-lashing, and then turn around and walk away. Then the other Chinaman would follow behind the China boss, staying some ten feet behind him all the while, and proceed to give the China boss a piece of his mind. Then the China boss would stop and turn around. The other Chinaman would stop, turn around and walk away, and now the China boss, still staying some ten feet away, would follow the Chinaman and really give him a piece of his mind. After the China boss followed the other Chinaman for some 15 to 20 feet, giving him a tongue-lashing, the China boss would stop talking and the other Chinaman would keep on walking, never stopping or looking back or saying another word. Then the China boss would turn around and walk away, apparently having won the argument.

The only time I ever saw Chinamen use violence on another Chinaman was one time when the canning season was over but the Chinamen had not left for Portland yet. I was down by the closing machines near the retorts. Five Chinamen came walking past. There was a flash of tember, and one Chinaman gave another a real tongue-lashing. The one being lashed started to answer, all in Chinese, and was apparently holding his own verbally, when suddenly all four Chinamen moved in on him, each grabbing an arm or a leg. I have never seen a man upended, thrown to the ground and given a good thrashing so quickly. The whole episode was over in a minute or so. When the four Chinamen were through beating the fifth, they let him up. No one said a word. The four stood together, and the beaten man quietly walked off toward the China house. I have no idea what it was all about.

In the 1920s when everything was still shipped in wooden boxes, the China crew made all the wooden salmon cannery cases. Also in those days all labeling was still done by hand, and the China crew did this. Of course hand labeling was slow and took a large number of men to label a car of salmon by hand, but then you had to pay the crew whether or not they worked, so they might just as well be in the cannery warehouse labeling cans as being down at the China house doing nothing. The China boss picked the crew; you had nothing to do with it. The men the China boss brought up from Portland were the ones you took, and no ifs about it. Before the days of our present social laws, the China crew always had a couple of old men, possibly as much as 80 years old, but the Chinamen's attitude was that a man should work, although he was not expected to do more than would be reasonable for his age. These old men got full regular wages and were hired as salmon fillers; but about all they could do was to sweep the floor. There were always one or two real

old men. They kept the cannnery floor clean and I must add that they might have been old and slow, but never could you find fault with the job they did.

These China crews were dependable, and hard workers, and once you signed a labor contract for your China crew, that worry was over for the season. The China boss always came with his crew the day you wanted them to arrive. He had all the men specified in the labor contract, and the men could and did do their jobs well, and the labor boss followed the contract to the letter. There was never any question of the honesty of the boss, or of the willingness of the crew to carry out all the provisions of the contract. And of course we also followed the labor contract right down the line. If there was ever a question about anything, you and the China boss discussed it, and when the China boss left he was satisfied. And I must emphasize that never under any conditions would the Company ever do anything they hadn't agreed to do in these Chinese labor contracts. In 58 years of salmon canning operations, Seufert's had only six China bosses. Five came from the same family, and during all those years I never heard of a disagreement between the China boss and the Company over a contract once it had been signed.

For some reason Chinese labor was always referred to as contract labor, with the hint that there was something bad about this. I never could understand why this was, at least in this day and age with labor contracts playing such an important part in our industrial labor relations. The China boss would meet in the Company office early in the spring and tell the Company what the China labor would cost for that coming season. You might argue about various Chinese labor costs, but when it was all over the China boss' ideas would prevail. These labor discussions were always friendly, although there could be arguing and some shouting. But the whole discussion never lasted more than an hour. By then you knew what the China crew would cost for the year and that was that.

Next the labor contract was drawn up, which was just a copy of the one used the previous year. You decided how many men you wanted on each job and marked it in the contract. You always needed three salmon butchers, and then you had to decide on the number of slimers you would need to handle the butchered salmon. Then there were the fillers who packed the salmon into the cans, the patch fish men, the cooler men, the test tub men and the retort men. The China boss also had to have a Chinese cook and a Chinese bookkeeper. (You always agreed to furnish all the wood needed in the China mess house.) This made up your crew for the coming year. Chinese labor of course included board and room. You had to purchase so many sacks of rice from the Chinese grocer in Portland, and then you bought some pigs from the local white farmers up the creek. There was also a bonus provision in the contract. Any Chinaman filling more than 3,000 cans of salmon in a standard working day got a bonus. The China boss kept these records, and you paid a bonus to whomever he said. You also agreed to purchase railroad tickets from Portland to Seufert's for each man. In the fall when you closed the cannery you agreed to purchase tickets for each man from Seufert's back to Portland.

All of the Chinamen who came up with the China boss were of course all from the same tong, and they all came from the same district in China. All the Chinamen who worked for Seufert's were Cantonese.

When the China crew arrived from Portland on the passenger train, they got off at the cannery and went directly to the China house. They spent the rest of the day getting settled. No one expected them to go to work on the day of their arrival. If the following day happened to be a Friday, the China crew would refuse to start work. They belived it would bring bad luck, not only to them, but to you also. All you could do was go along with them. It might be just a Chinese superstition, but why take a chance? Of course the crew got a full day's pay for that Friday, but then, one day's pay for the China crew wasn't going to make that much difference to you.

Once in a while we had a Chinaman in our crew who was out of the federal penitentiary on parole. Generally such men would be sent down from McNeil Island. The Company was always asked if we would accept a man on parole. If the China boss approved, the Company agreed. The men on parole were doing time for dope smuggling, and without exception we always recognized them as men who had worked for Seufert's before. Every so often during the summer the parole board would write the Company a letter of inquiry about the Chinaman on parole, asking whether he was behaving himself, tending to business, and so on. I don't remember a single man we couldn't make a good report on. When the season ended, the Chinaman out on parole went back to Portland with the rest of the China crew. After the crew left we would hear no more about this man, but in another year or two we could have another man out on parole, and once in a while we would get the same man back again; he had been sent up to McNeil Island a second time. Occasionally, after the China crew had left for Portland we would find an opium pipe down in the Chinese bunk house, but as far as we were concerned, we never did see any of the Chinese use any kind of dope.

The clothes the Chinamen wore in the cannery were blue denim bib overalls. If the weather was chilly, they might wear a blue denim coat. They nearly always wore cloth caps. The Company furnished the China crew with knee high gum boots. I can always remember ordering these gum boots. You had to be sure to order small sizes. The Chinamen had smaller feet than white men. The Company also furnished each Chinaman with an oilskin apron and cotton gloves. With a pair of cotton gloves on, you had no trouble picking up and holding an unbutchered salmon fresh from the river. And of course it was easy to hold raw butchered salmon also.

The China boss would write letters to other China bosses at other canneries along the Columbia River, and vice versa. This exchange of letters was an important source of information about how the salmon were running at the other canneries. The China boss would stop you in the cannery and tell you he had just gotten a leter from Astoria from Barbey's cannery, which meant the China boss there. He would proceed to tell you how much salmon they were getting per day, how big the fish were, and whether the fish were all Chinooks or not.

Up until World War I, the standard day was 11 hours: 6:00 A.M. until noon, and 1:00 until 6:00 P.M.; six days a week, no work on Sundays. Any Sunday work or work after 6:00 P.M. on weekdays was overtime. By the 1920s and on into the 1930s the China crews were working a ten-hour day, six days a week: 7:00 A.M. until noon, and 1:00 until 6:00 P.M. And by the middle 1930s it was down to an eight-hour day, six days a week: 8:00 A.M. until noon; and 1:00 until 5:00 P.M.

Once in a while a Chinaman would get a toothache. Then we would take him to the local dentist to have the tooth pulled. The Chinaman would insist on the tooth being pulled without Novocaine or anything else. Afterward we would bring him back to the cannery and he would go right back to work. As the China boss always said, "No medicine, no make him sick."

The white crew always insisted that the roots on a Chinaman's tooth were shorter than the roots on a white man's tooth, so it didn't hurt a Chinaman as much as a white man when you pulled his tooth. I remember one poor Chinaman who had somehow gouged a piece of flesh out of the back of his hand. He showed it to me. I wanted to take him to a doctor, but he insisted I put iodine into the wound. I did. I poured iodine right into the hole in his hand. I can still see that iodine bubbling and boiling in the hole in that poor Chinaman's hand but he never said a word. He just sucked in a deep breath and held his hand tightly with the other hand. The treatment must have worked because the patient never came back.

If there was a serious injury, a broken leg or something that needed medical attention, we would put the man into a car and drive him to the hospital. In those days if a man was injured you could still call a doctor and he would drive out to look at the patient and then decide what to do. But we were always told to take an injured man to town to the doctor right away. As the Company put it, if you called a doctor, by the time he arrived the man could be dead.

By the end of World War II the old experienced

Chinese cannery crews began to disappear. After World War II the young Chinamen had been Americanized. They didn't want to work in a salmon cannery out in some isolated spot for six months, with little or no chance to get into town to spend their money or to have a good time. By then jobs were plentiful in Portland, so they would just not leave the city to work in a cannery. By the late 1940s it was becoming harder and harder to get any China crews at all.

All Chinese cannery workers were great tea drinkers. In fact, I don't ever remember seeing a Chinaman take a drink of water in the cannery. They always got a drink of Chinese tea from the teapot. This Chinese teapot would hold about three gallons of tea. It was just a big metal pot that was always sitting down by the test tub near the retorts. A Chinaman was always free to leave his job for a few minutes at any time during work to walk over to the teapot and pour himself a small cup. You might say they drank tea all day long, but I don't believe they had more than a few swallows at any one time. They did not seem to fill a cup and stand there and drink until the cup was empty. The Chinese just poured some tea into the cup, took a couple of swallows, tossed the rest out on the cannery floor by a water down, put the cup down and returned to work. Everyone seemed to drink out of the same cup. None of them seemed to be concerned that someone else had used the cup before him. From time to time the Chinese cook would bring a fresh pot of hot tea up from the mess house. He always took the old pot of tea back to the mess house. I don't know what he did with it then. While I never drank out of the Chinamen's teapot, I have had a lot of Chinese tea, the kind the Chinamen used, and this was far superior to anything I have seen

in the United States that passes for tea. Chinese tea was very mild. It was pleasantly sweet. You drank it straight, there was no need to add sugar, and of course it would have been unthinkable to put cream in Chinese tea.

The Chinese workers were all great smokers. If they smoked cigarettes, they smoked continuously. They smoked both American cigarettes bought in a store, and the kind one rolled, especially the older men. When a Chinaman lit a cigarette he inhaled the smoke deeply into his lungs and held it for what seemed like an incredibly long time before exhaling. I have seen a Chinese light a cigarette, take a deep long drag which seemed to pull the cigarette down at least a quarter of its length, and hold his breath, then slowly exhale, letting the smoke leave his mouth slowly and curl up into his nostrils. Then he would inhale all this smoke again deeply, and hold it a long time before exhaling. As far as I know none of these Chinamen had ever heard of lung cancer, and we certainly had a lot of heavy smokers among the Chinamen working in the cannery who lived to a ripe old age.

From time to time the Chinamen would smoke a Chinese water pipe. It was always kept down by the test tub right along side the Chinese teapot. The water pipe always sat in a three-gallon bucket of water, about half full. Halfway up the water pipe was a little pipe about a quarter of an inch in diameter and an inch or so long. It was attached at an angle, with the open end higher than the other. When a Chinaman wanted to smoke, he put his mouth over the upper end, and the lower end was below the surface of the water in the bucket. He held the pipe at an angle so that it was straight, and right in front of him. Then he would suck on the pipe, which would draw water up, and he would then take his mouth off to break the suction. The water would then drop down into the bucket from the pipe but would spill out over the end of the little pipe attached to the water pipe. This would clean out any unsmoked tobacco from the end of the little pipe. The Chinaman took a pinch of Chinese tobacco which always came in little round cans like snoose. It was cut very fine so that it looked like human hair. He would put a pinch of this tobacco into the top of the little pipe, light a match, hold the match over the tobacco, take a deep drag, and take just one mouthful of smoke. He would hold this one drag of smoke in his mouth for several seconds, and then exhale. When he lifted his mouth from the water pipe the water seemed to bounce in the pipe, flowing over the top of the little side pipe holding the tobacco. Of course the water put out the lighted tobacco and washed out the little side pipe. The whole thing was put down and left for the next smoker. All surplus tobacco, both unburned and ashes, was just flushed out of the end of the little pipe and into the water bucket. I never saw anyone empty that bucket, so I don't know who did.

All the Chinamen smoked cigarettes (I do believe that once in a while we would have a Chinaman smoke a pipe, but he was a rarity), but I never saw one smoke a cigar and I never saw a Chinaman chew.

The gravel bar above Rabbit Island on the Washington side of the Columbia River was part of the Washington school land. All gravel used in building Bonneville Dam came from that bar. On these seine bars around Celilo on both sides of the Columbia, Chinamen years ago panned gold, but the amount of gold taken was so small that the operation didn't last long. But in the depth of the Depression in the winter men would go out on these seine bars and pan again. They were lucky to get a dollar or so a day, and after a short time this attempt was so obviously unprofitable no one bothered to try it again.

As far as handling the mail for these employees, whites and Chinamen alike just brought their letters into the office, sealed and stamped, put on one end of the desk and that evening I took all the mail with me on the way home, stopped at the post office and mailed it. Now I must add that there was never a post office at the cannery. Several times the post office had suggested it to the Company but the Company would not have it. The Company felt that having a lot of farmers living up the creek running in and out of the Company office to pick up their mail would be a nuisance as the Company only wanted people in the office that were there on Company business.

Seufert's handled all the mail for their employees through the cannery office. The Company had a mail box at The Dalles, P.O. Box 541. The Company picked up its mail each morning there. My dad always did this chore until I took it over in the later years. The mail was picked up and then driven to the cannery office. In the busy season Seufert's Cannery office would handle the mail for at least a hundred people, perhaps as many as a hundred and fifty. Each morning there was a whole armful of mail. It was just picked up and carried, but it was never put into a mail sack. At the cannery it was separated according to camp, then given to one of the fish truck drivers to be delivered. Mail for white employees living at the cannery was put into a mail box on the cannery office counter. These employees generally picked up their mail during the noon hour. We also handled all the mail for the Chinamen, and at that time

Seufert's also had a Japanese family running the cherry orchard, so we handled the Japanese mail also. It was surprising how quickly one learned to tell the Japanese newspaper from the Chinese. All the Chinese mail went directly to the China boss in the cannery. The envelope would have his name written in English, plus ''Seufert's Cannery, The Dalles, Oregon.'' On the left side of the envelope, running from top to bottom, were Chinese characters. I do not know what the characters said, but it must have been the name of the particular Chinaman the letter was meant for.

The Chinese newspaper was important to the Chinamen, and during the Sino-Japanese War in the late 1930s the Chinese newspaper was always hurriedly opened and read. At that time I would take the American newspaper into the cannery, down by the retorts, and read the war news in it. Some of the Chinese crew would wait for me every noon, generally the younger men. They could not read English, so they would all gather around me in a circle, sitting on their haunches. Then I would read the war news from the American newspaper. Everything would be perfectly quiet except for my reading, and then all of a sudden one Chinaman would jump up and give an excited opinion about what I had just read, all in Chinese. Then just as suddenly he would squat down again and rejoin the circle. I would be interrupted a dozen times in my reading. When the story was complete I would say, ''That's all,'' and they would all nod their heads and get up and go back to business.

If the Chinamen used liquor we never saw any evidence of it, although of course they had Chinese liquor down at their house. This was generally In-ga-pay, a Chinese wine about the color of red lacquer with a god-awful taste. It came in one-pint crocks. Then there was Chinese gin, which was clear and came in one-fifth bottles and tasted like ham grease. It was god-awful too.

The only Chinaman I ever saw drink American liquor was one of our China bosses. One day he asked me to bring him a fifth of American whiskey from town. It was in the morning, and the cannery was full of fish, and this China boss was working as a butcher helping the other Chinese butchers keep up. I got the fifth of whiskey and gave it to him. He stopped butchering, walked over to a little cupboard, took out a standard water glass, filled it to the brim, threw his head back, took a couple of swallows, and the glass was empty. He filled the glass a second time, threw his head back, took a couple of swallows and the glass was empty. He did this a third time, and when the glass was empty again he wiped his mouth on the back of his sleeve and turned to me and asked if I wanted a drink. After watching him I sure didn't. He went right back to butchering salmon after drinking three water glasses of whiskey, as if it was just routine; and as far as any show of effect, it must have been just routine because if I hadn't seen him work that fifth of whiskey over I wouldn't have known he had taken a single drink.

This same China boss one time invited me to come down to the China house for supper. He was going to fix something special. He had at one time worked in the kitchens of big Portland hotels. At the China house he prepared an excellent salad, lettuce and various oils, and then took raw sturgeon and sliced it paper thin and put it in. Surprisingly enough the raw sturgeon was good eating once you got the first bite down. Then he brought out another salad with baby octopus the size of a half dollar. He had cut each of them in half, but so help me, they looked just like babies' hands, and it was too much for me. I certainly passed that dish up.

The Company always had to furnish the Chinamen with a Chinese garden. Back of the cannery the Chinamen had an acre of land that was kept just for them, and they raised their own Chinese vegetables there. It was always called the Chinese garden. When they were working in the garden they always wore large coolie hats with wide brims, and carried their vegetables in baskets: two baskets, one on each end of a pole, and the pole balanced on their shoulders. When a Chinaman carried a pole like that he always ran with a funny gait; he never walked.

Surrounding the China garden was a high solid wood fence, probably nine or ten feet high. Since it was solid, it served not only to keep animals out, but also as a windbreak (down behind the cannery the west wind howled all summer long). The China boss and one or two other Chinamen did all the work in the garden. Of course when the cannery was busy these Chinamen all worked in the cannery, but when it was not busy, the Company never said anything about a China boss who kept one or two cannery Chinamen busy in the garden.

The garden raised all the vegetables needed in the China mess house. And from about July on, the China boss would ship several hundred pounds of Chinese vegetables by express to Portland six days a week. They were sent to the Chinese grocers in Portland. Whatever the China boss received for these vegetables was none of the Company's business. This was just one of the

sidelines the China cannery foreman had going for himself.

Another sideline was the salmon head sale. When there was not too much salmon being butchered in the cannery the heads were tossed onto the floor under the butchering table. They were collected at the end of the day. When the Indians wanted salmon heads they went to the China boss and bought as many as they wanted for 50 cents a sack. When the cannery was real busy there was no time to save the salmon heads for the Indians, and they were floated down a flume and dumped into the river.

The China house mess hall was a large bare room, which the Company whitewashed once a year. There were six wooden tables, for about ten men per table, and benches to sit on. The tables were bare. Above the tables wire pot holders hung from the ceiling to hold large metal teapots. When a Chinaman wanted tea he just stood up and took the pot from the holder, poured his bowl of tea, set the pot back on the holder and then sat down and drank his tea. The Chinaman ate with two bowls. The large one held rice and the smaller one his tea. He ate with chopsticks.

The kitchen was at one end of the mess house. It, too, was just a bare room with running water from a faucet into an open water tank. The water was cold. The cook stove was a square concrete box. It had a fire door where the cook fired his stove with four-foot slab wood, but no grates. The top of the stove was also concrete with four large round openings. Into each opening the cook put a pan the size of a large wash pan, but these were Chinese pans and had pronounced sloping sides. The Chinese put rice in these pans, then set them

114

in the openings on top of the stove, actually almost into the fire. Then he took another pan the same size and inverted it over a rice pan. Next he took a towel or sugar sack, soaked it in water and wrung it out, rolled it up tight and placed it around the edges of the pans. This made a tight seal for steaming the rice. If the cook wanted any hot water, he just dipped some cold water from his water tank into one of the large pans and put it over the fire.

There was only once that the use of dope by a Chinaman caused us any trouble. One day the China boss came to me and said he had a Chinaman who was sick and acting crazy. After talking to the China boss for a bit I got the picture. Over the weekend a Chinaman had gone off his rocker by using an excessive amount of drugs and was crazy from the effect. The boss and his crew were excited and frightened and did not know how to handle the situation, so they had come to me for advice on what could easily become a nasty situation for all concerned.

I certainly couldn't call the police. Down at the China house it was a tense situation, and a uniformed policeman approaching the China house at that time could lead to any number of unpleasant possibilities. Someone might even start shooting.

I told the China boss to put the Chinaman who was high on drugs in my car and I would take him to the doctor. So he and a couple of the China crew put the man in my car. I only hoped he wouldn't cause me any trouble on the trip into town. He didn't, he just sat in a daze. I took him to a local doctor and explained I had a problem. The doctor took one look at the patient and said, "You sure as hell do. Take him out to the

County Hospital." So back in the car for the Chinaman and me, and out to the County Hospital. I told the attendant I had a patient from the local doctor. The attendant took the patient down the hall and I gave the clerk the Chinaman's name and the cannery address and left.

A couple of days later I got a call from the hospital. They wanted me to come and get the patient. I said I could not do that. The party on the other end of the line said they couldn't keep the Chinaman because he was a hophead who had to be watched all the time; when their backs were turned he would go through every drawer and cabinet in the hospital looking for morphine so he could have another fix. I replied that I was sorry, but that was the hospital's problem. I had delivered the Chinaman on doctor's orders and the hospital would have to work it out with him. I never did hear any more about the matter. One thing was sure: our China boss at the cannery was certainly glad to be rid of him. And he never showed up in our China crews again.

One time the salmon cannery was working nights. We had a Chinaman up in years taking salmon cans from the closing machines and racking the cans up in coolers. This Chinaman must have been nearly blind. His glasses had lenses so thick that when you looked at him his eyes were magnified. Once in a while when we were working at night the cannery machinery would stop. Then this old Chinaman would begin to do a Balinese dance, first one leg and then the other, with all the necessary postures required of a Balinese dancer.* The other Chinamen would pay attention to him, but because the whole thing was happening in the dim light, and the dancer was not concerned with anyone about

*Probably T'ai-chi-chuan, a dance-like traditional Chinese exercise.

him, it made the hair on the back of your neck stand on end. Then the cannery machinery would start to operate again, and everyone would go back to work, including the dancer, just as if nothing out of the ordinary had happened. This Chinaman would put on his dance several times during the evening, but never during the day. I was fascinated by it. I could not help wondering if as a young man he had been trained as a dancer somewhere in the Far East, and then I would wonder how under the sun he had ended up as an old man working in a salmon cannery on the Columbia River.

The last China boss Seufert's had was Yee Gum. He had come to the United States from China as a young man, in the 1890s. One day in the cannery we were talking and he told me when he first came to the United States he got off the steamer in Portland. As a Chinaman he couldn't get employment then, since the country was in a great depression. In order to make enough to live on he managed to get a ripsaw, and with the saw over his shoulder, he walked the streets of Portland's residential districts, looking for work sawing slab wood into stove length. He was paid 50 cents per cord for sawing. He would shake his head when he remembered how hard he had to work to earn 50 cents.

SHIPPING

When an order was received from New York City to ship a car on a certain steamship company steamer leaving Portland, you telephoned to Portland and talked to the steamship agent and reserved cargo space. The Company would have cargo on the Portland docks ten days before the steamer sailed. We always tried to have our shipment on the dock several days before sailing. When you shipped by steamer you had to put an identification mark on the case on the end opposite the end with the brand name. You could make up any mark so long as it was clear. We generally used A over NY, but if 100 cases of Wasco Choice Columbia River salmon were going to each of three different buyers, then on the first 100 cases you might use A over NY, on the next 100 case lot you could use S, and on the third 100 case lot you might use just the letters NY.

The steamship companies' minimum car rate was 30,000 pounds, but you could put the ten different shipments in this one car, and the steamship company would accept the ten shipments as one. They made one bill of lading covering the entire shipment, and then segregated each of the ten lots on the New York pier; individual buyers would each pick up part of the shipment.

About half of the shipments Seufert's made by water to New York City went by the Luckenbach Steamship Company, and the other half went by Panama Pacific Line. Panama Pacific cargo left Portland on the Pacific Steamship Company steamer for San Francisco, and was transshipped to the Panama Pacific Line ships for New York City. Since the large wholesale grocery houses we dealt with were on Manhattan Island, we had to be sure the steamship company made a Manhattan delivery as specified by the New York City wholesalers in their shipping orders. On all canned goods Seufert's shipped to New York City, a bank draft attached to a delivery order was sent to a New York City bank for collection.

When the cargo arrived at Manhattan aboard the steamer, the bank notified the wholesaler and presented the draft for payment. When the wholesaler paid the draft the bank gave him the delivery order. The wholesaler presented the delivery order to the dock, which permitted him to remove the canned goods specified in the delivery orders.

As far as the steamship companies were concerned, canned salmon, canned fruit and canned vegetables were all canned goods. They all went on the same bill of lading and under the same freight rate. This was not true on the railroads (at least up until the early 1930s); canned salmon went at one rate, canned fruit at another. If you combined salmon and fruit in the same railroad car on one bill of lading, the railroad would charge the higher rate. This was one way railroads did all they could to encourage you to ship by truck or steamship. When you shipped by sea, responsibility for any damage was yours. The steamship company would not pay any claim for damage done while the goods were moving by sea. This was maritime law, which was entirely different from law on land. When you ship by sea you protect yourself against damage, provide and pay for your own insurance policy. You contact the marine insurance agents in Portland, give them the name of the vessel and the cargo you are putting aboard. We had the agent issue our maritime insurance, and then war insurance that protected us against acts of war. Then we got an all-risk marine insurance policy which took care of anything you forgot on the other two.

We shipped all the canned goods from the cannery to New York City by steamship until World War II. During the war we of course shipped everything by rail. After the war was over and the steamships started to operate again between Portland and New York, we again shipped by steamship until maritime unions put the steamship companies out of the intercoastal busi-

ness. Then we had no choice but to go back to shipping by rail.

In the late 1930s Seufert's was using the Port of Portland to ship salmon to New York; in some years the entire tonnage of canned salmon moving across the Portland public docks came from Seufert's Cannery.

In 1950 we had a car of canned goods to be shipped to New York City. The car had been loaded at the cannery and shipped to the dock in Portland. I had handled all the shipping documents. I had also written a letter to the marine insurance agents in Portland to put the required amount of different marine insurance on this particular shipment. Shipment was made aboard one of the Luckenbach Steamship Company's vessels. Well, instead of mailing the letter requesting the marine insurance agency in Portland to issue a policy against the shipment, I left the letter lying on the seat of my car. After all, there was no hurry. It was a Thursday afternoon, and I could mail the letter on Friday and it would reach the maritime insurance people by Monday morning. The ship would have sailed the previous Friday afternoon, but everything would be taken care of. Well, Friday evening, with the letter still undelivered to the marine insurance agency in Portland, the phone rang at my home. It was my dad. He asked if I had placed marine insurance on that shipment going by Luckenback. I said I had. Then the roof fell in. My dad said he had just heard over the radio that one of the Luckenbach ships had been sunk in a collision off the coast. Then he said that since I had put marine insurance on the cargo, there was nothing to worry about. When he hung up I was one scared boy. I listened all the rest of the evening to all the radio reports, trying to learn the name of the vessel. About midnight the report came through. It was the *Mary Luckenbach* that had been in the collision off the Golden Gate, not the ship our cargo was on. Believe me, I was one relieved boy. Never again did I delay getting marine insurance on a cargo after a vessel had already left port.

In shipping canned salmon from the cannery warehouse to the New York City wholesalers, the old-time salmon packers would never make shipment of any canned salmon until it had sat in the warehouse for at least 30 days. This was to make certain that the entire packing operation of that particular block of canned salmon was all properly sealed and cooked. If anything went wrong, it would show up within 30 days. The can would start to swell, and you would then know that something was wrong, and the can would be destroyed. Of course by the 1920s and 1930s it was rare to have anything go wrong, but the Company, in order to protect its customers, always left the cans sitting on the warehouse floor, just to be sure. I might add, it was a good practice then, and it is now.

FRUITS & VEGETABLES

Seufert's also canned fruits and vegetables in the salmon cannery building, one of the very few firms in the United States that ever canned both. This combination was extremely rare. The Company had the salmon cannery. Salmon runs came in May and September, and the other three months the cannery wasn't busy. You had to have a big crew on hand, and the crews were paid whether or not they worked, so by canning fruits and vegetables you could keep the crews busy. In those days the crews would much rather be working than just sitting around twiddling their thumbs.

The first fruit orchards around The Dalles or Wasco County were planted about 1852 in the creek bottoms. A number of years later farmers found they could grow fruit on the hillsides around The Dalles. The third step in growing and developing fruit orchards in Wasco County came in 1885 when F.A. Seufert planted orchards along the shores of the Columbia River on land that at that time was considered a blow-sand area. F.A. Seufert purchased the land at Seuferts because of the water rights on Fifteenmile Creek that went with the land. Seufert's immediately irrigated their orchards as soon as they were planted. Under irri-

gation the so-called blow-sand along the Columbia River was highly productive when plenty of water was available. F.A. Seufert planted his orchards in the winter of 1885 back of where the salmon cannery was to be built.

My grandfather told me that in the winter of 1886 there was an extremely heavy snowfall. He and the hired men had to tramp a path in the snow around each tree so that the deep snow would not break down these young trees.

These early orchards were not planted like the orchards of today, with a block of fruit trees all bearing the same kind of fruit. In those days Seufert's was still shipping fresh fruit by rail from Wasco County. Seufert's planted many varieties of, say, peaches in their orchards so they would have peaches ripening over a long picking and shipping period.

As soon as they planted orchards along the bank of the Columbia River it became evident that windbreaks were needed if the fruit trees and their crops were not to be beaten to pieces by the heavy west winds around The Dalles. F.A. Seufert planted rows of Lombardy poplar along the west side and river side of his orchards. These Lombardy poplars were an excellent windbreak; the trees grew rapidly, they did well when planted close together to form the windbreak, they took little or no care, they were a tough, hardy tree. But more important, they were tall, and their branches grew close to the trunk, and more or less straight up. All in all they were by far the best trees for windbreaks around The Dalles country.

Seufert planted his Royal Anne cherry orchard by the late 1890s, but didn't start to can Royal Anne cherries until about 1905; from then on Seufert's always canned those cherries, until the cannery was closed in 1954. They also bought most of the Royal Anne cherries they canned from the local cherry growers around The Dalles. In all the years that Seufert's owned and operated a cherry orchard, they had lots of Indians come year after year to pick for them. The Indian families would either come down from Celilo or the Indian reservation, pitch their wigwams on the edge of the orchards, and set up camp. All the Indian men and women, old and young, plus all the kids, went into the orchards and picked cherries. They would stay until the entire crop was picked, then they would break camp. Some would pick cherries for other local farmers around The Dalles, while others returned to Celilo or went back to the reservation.

One time, about 1905 or 1907, it was probably the last part of June, Seufert's were picking their Royal Anne cherry crop. They were using Indian pickers as usual. Mr. Benjamin Gifford, the famous photographer, came down to Seufert's cherry orchards. He hired a couple of young Indian men, Henry Thompson was one, I am sure, and took them up to Fivemile Rapids where he had them take off their clothes and put on loincloths. Mr. Gifford took the Indians out on the rapids and posed these noble men, naked except for loincloths, spearing and dipnetting salmon from the rocks of the Columbia River. Mr. Gifford got some nice pictures and I am quite sure that the glass plate negatives are now among the collections of the Oregon Historical Society.

When it came to canning fruit, Seufert's only canned a fruit that took very few people to prepare. Canning Royal Anne cherries was almost an entirely mechanical operation. The cherries were delivered in wooden lugs by the farmers to Seufert's Cannery and were unloaded on the cannery floor. The cherries were held in the lug boxes until you were ready to can them. Then the fresh Royal Anne cherries were poured onto a picking table. A moving belt carried the cherries along this table and white girls sorted over the cherries, removing any that were damaged in any way and not fit for canning. Next the cherries were washed in cold water, elevated to a cherry grader, sized by grades for uniform size. They were graded in three sizes: extra large were fancy; large were choice; and standards were small. From the grader the sized fruit went to an automatic filling machine. This machine also put the proper amount of syrup in the cans, filling the cans automatically to the top. Next the cans entered an exhaust box, a steam box with the cans carried through on a chain. The steam heated the cans, and when a top was put on, the heat in the cans would produce a vacuum when they cooled. Next came the closing machines which put on the lids. Now the cherry cans were ready for the retorts. After cooking, the cans were taken to the warehouse where they were stacked, later to be labeled and shipped.

The big market for Royal Anne cherries was in the industrial East. You sold Royal Anne cherries between Chicago and New York City. For some reason, the rest of the United States was not much of a market. If you shipped into the Chicago market, you shipped by rail. The New York City market always had its cherries shipped by steamer, at least as long as the steamships were available and running.

In the cannery you would use boys and white women and once in a while an Indian woman to stack cans in the warehouses. The women would stack the cans and the boys would pick and remove the empty coolers after the women had emptied them of cans. When the boys weren't doing this, they were expected to stack cans too. When I first went to work in the cannery stacking cans in the 1920s, 25 cents an hour was good pay and a ten-hour day would make you $2.50. You fed yourself on this, and by pooling a car, a group of workers would have a way to get to the cannery and return home to town at night. At the start of the season often some poor devil wouldn't have any transportation, so he would walk the three miles each way to and from work. But just as soon as the group of cannery workers found someone didn't have transportation, they would bring him along the next day.

If an Indian man wanted a job in the cannery during the cherry season, that was fine. The Indians were good doing manual labor in the cannery. They were used to hard work and could hold their own with any of the whites. The only trouble with an Indian was when you hired him you could never be sure he would come back the next day. After all, the Indian had more important things to do than work in Seufert's Cannery; but when you were busy and short-handed, you never hesitated to give an Indian a job if he wanted it.

The Chinese cannery workers were hired to can salmon, and when you had salmon to can, that is what the China crew did; but when they weren't busy canning salmon, they were put to work canning cherries. A Chinaman could not tell what we would call a good piece of fruit from a bad one, so you never used a Chinaman on the picking belt. Only white women. But down the line on the filling machines and the syruping machines you could use Chinamen as machine operators, and I have never seen people who could operate a piece of machinery as efficiently as Chinamen. A Chinaman would operate a machine all day long, day after day, and have no trouble; but put a white man on the same machine, and it was either breaking down or jamming up or breaking cans all day long.

Down on the retorts and closing machines, the Chinamen handled both jobs just as they handled both jobs when canning fish. The Chinamen never resented being put to work in the fruit cannery. Maybe they knew that Royal Anne cherries were always considered the elite of all the fruit packed in cans in the United States. In fact, years ago our broker in New York City, Ed Skiffington, an old-timer in the food business, told me he only liked to sell three things, and handling these three he could make a better-than-average living. The three things he wanted to handle were fancy Columbia River salmon, Royal Anne cherries and Japanese crab meat.

In the cannery the fruit was graded on what was called an Allen grader, a shaker grader. The fruit was shaken over a riddle, a perforated galvanized sheet, the fruit falling through certain sized holes that determined the fruit size. The riddles were shaken by an eccentric. This grader was built in the 1920s for Libby, McNeil and Libby's big fruit cannery in The Dalles. This cannery was closed in 1927. In the early 1930s I bought this grader and installed it in Seufert's Cannery. The grader was a good one, and present-day fruit graders still use the same shaker principle. The thing that impressed me about this grader was that the Libby's crew built it from parts of a Model T Ford, because a person would always be able to get parts for a Model T.

The sugar syrup was made in the cannery's sugar room. This room had six large galvanized tanks. Each tank held 200 gallons of water. If you wanted to make 40-degree syrup for fancy cherries, then you dumped five 100-pound sacks of sugar into the tank holding 200 gallons of water and this would produce the syrup of the desired density. To help mix the sugar and water, the men in the sugar room used an oar, one that had been used on a seine. The oar had been cleaned, and with a sawed-off handle, it made a good mixer. There was a steam coil in the bottom of the tank to heat the syrup so it would mix better. The sugar came from the California and Hawaiian Sugar Refinery at Crockett, California. The sugar was brought up the coast in steamships and unloaded on the docks in Portland and brought to The Dalles by railroad. The sugar always came in 100-pound sacks, a cotton bag inside a burlap sack. Burlap sacks were used around the cannery to sew fresh sturgeon for shipments, and any burlap bags you didn't need were sold to the local grain dealers in The Dalles. The cotton was washed at the cannery and used as towels in the Company's mess houses. The cot-

ton sugar sacks that the Company didn't need went to Portland companies whose business was buying and reselling cotton sugar sacks.

Seufert's big cherry orchard below the cannery was always irrigated. You took irrigation water to the orchard in an open flume. The flume had a round hole in the side opposite a row of fruit trees. The hole was closed with a plug. When you wanted irrigation water you just pulled out the plug and a regulated amount of water would run out of the hole into an irrigation ditch. Just below the hole and in the flume itself you would put a little partition across the irrigation flume. All the surplus water not flowing out of the hole in the side of the flume would flow over the top of the partition and continue on down the flume. The irrigating water flowed through the orchard in a ditch, or really, a furrow plowed with a horse team. This type of irrigation was restricted to fairly level ground, and Seufert's had one of the few orchards around The Dalles where the land was level enough for irrigation. This all changed by the end of World War II. Then, irrigation pipe made of aluminum was light enough so that a man could pack a 20-foot length over his shoulder and use it with a sprinkler system for water in the orchards. From then on it was just as easy to irrigate a hillside as a piece of level land.

In the 1920s Seufert's planted the hay field above the cannery into an apricot orchard. There were some 100 acres of apricots. This orchard was all dry land. The first year you would get a crop of apricots, say, 100 tons. The second year, no crop to speak of, perhaps 10 or 15 tons. The third year you would get a crop of some 30 or 40 tons. Then the fourth year you would get 100 tons again. Then the crop yield would repeat itself. After World War II Seufert's put in a sprinkler system to water this apricot orchard. Then it immediately started to produce 300 or 400 tons of apricots every year. This is what happened: A tree bears fruit, and this takes the vitality out of it just after the tree has produced the fruit. Then the tree bears the fruit buds for next year's crop, and it is at this time, right after the crop has been picked, that the tree needs strength to form the fruit buds for the coming year. By watering the land and giving the tree all the nourishment it needs at that critical time, the tree is assured of having plenty of vitality to have a heavy set of fruit buds for the coming year. The orchards were watered all summer, but you only put enough water on the land to keep the trees healthy. If you watered and then stopped, the trees would die back. In other words, a tree's root system can support just so many branches from the trunk. If you took the water from the fruit tree, then it would die back, that is, the outer limbs. This is nature's way of assuring that only enough branches are left on a tree that can be supported by the root system. All dead branches have to be cut off, which adds to the expense, and dead branches produce no fruit. So, once you start irrigating, you have to keep it up if you want the orchard to keep bearing fruit.

On canned fruit and vegetables Seufert's used the following labels: Royal Anne cherries Wasco Brand for fancy cherries; Merrimac Brand on choice cherries; and Klondike Brand on standard cherries. On purple plums Seufert's used Wasco Brand on fancy purple plums; Merrimac Brand on choice purple plums; and Klondike Brand on standard purple plums. On peas, either Merrimac or Wasco Brand on fancy peas; and Klondike Brand on standard peas. On pitted, red sour cherries, Seufert's used only a water pack, as with all of their pie cherries, so they used only Klondike Brand. Only Merrimac Brand was used on tomatoes, and asparagus center cuts were sold under Klondike Brand; but the spears were all labeled under Merrimac.

The one big reason Seufert's packed fruits and vegetables was the fact that Wasco County raised fine Royal Anne cherries, apricots, prunes, pie cherries and peas. Asparagus could be shipped in from the Walla Walla country. And another reason for packing fruits and vegetables was that your brokers had more items to sell; and since the brokers all worked on commissions, the more you packed the more they had to sell, and the more valuable your account was to them.

There was a third reason, too: by packing fruits and vegetables you had more tonnage to ship, and the more tonnage, the more often you shipped, and the better service you gave your buyers. One last reason: you could sell perhaps 100 cases of salmon in Minneapolis, but how under the sun could you get it there? By packing fruit, your Minneapolis broker could always sell a carload of fruit, and then you would just put the canned salmon in your first fruit car for Minneapolis. This way you could sell and deliver canned salmon in small lots all through the Midwest, where if it weren't for the canned fruit, you would never have enough canned salmon to make up a carload. While I don't believe any canner ever made any money packing purple plums, the darned things were a good seller, and you could always sell a car of canned prunes in just about any market in the United States.

In the 1930s Seufert's canned pitted, red sour cherries. There were a number of large orchards around The Dalles raising these sour cherries then. The local farmers delivered them to the cannery in fruit lug boxes. The cherries had to be dumped into tanks of fresh cold water to firm up the fruit. In fact, once in a while when we were short of water tanks to hold the cherries, we would use the old mild-cure salmon barrels from the basement. These barrels would hold at least 200 gallons of water, and they were clean, since they had never been used; so they came in handy when you were short of tanks. After the cherries had sat in the cold water for a short time they would become firm, and then we would take the fruit from the tanks, and run them over a picking table, with white girls picking over the fruit to remove the cherries that were not fit for packing. Then the cherries went into an automatic pitting machine. The fruit was dumped into a hopper, the pitted fruit came out the bottom and the pits came out of the side of the machine. The cherries then went to the automatic filling machines to be put into cans, and from there to the syruping machines, which filled the cans with water. The automatic filling machines were run by Chinese machine operators. Next the filled cans went from the syruping machines through the exhaust boxes to the closing machines to have a lid sealed on, next to the retorts for processing, then to the warehouse to await labeling and shipping.

All the pitted, red sour cherries were packed in water in a No. 2 or a No. 6/10 can. They were all sold either in San Francisco or Portland. Those that went to Portland went by truck, and those for San Francisco were sent by sea. Since they were considered pie fruit, most of the 6/10 cans went to bakeries, although the No. 2 cans went to grocery stores and were sold to housewives.

In the early 1930s there was a considerable acreage of tomatoes across the Columbia River at Grand Dalles. These tomatoes were planted by both whites and Japanese. The tomatoes were raised both for the fresh vegetable market and for canning. Tomatoes were delivered to the cannery in fruit lug boxes. Canning tomatoes were first washed in fresh water at the cannery, then passed into a scalder. This was an endless belt carrying the tomatoes through a steam bath to scald and loosen the skins. Then they went through a fresh water bath again. This cooled the tomatoes and cracked the skins so they could be peeled easily. From here the tomatoes were placed in pans, delivered to white girls who peeled the tomatoes. The peeled tomatoes were put into a can and sent through the exhaust box. The cans were sealed, taken to the retorts, and processed; then they were removed to the warehouses where they were held for labeling and shipping. The tomatoes that Seufert's packed were either sold locally or in Portland, although once in a while you might sell a carload in New York City. All tomatoes packed by Seufert's were what was called solid pack. Nothing was put into the cans but tomatoes. Seufert's canned good tomatoes, and they had excellent flavor, but around The Dalles the nights were too cold for tomatoes to develop a blood red color, and it was this lack of color that made Seufert's give up canning tomatoes. Buyers bought tomatoes on color and not taste, and I have to admit California tomatoes did have better color, although they did not have near as good a flavor.

About 1932 The Dalles area raised a lot of fresh peas for the market. These were picked by hand. Peas in pods were handled in gunny sacks, packed in local packing houses and shipped to the fresh vegetable markets in the Pacific Northwest. When this market broke, the farmers had no other way to market their peas, so in 1932 the Company put in the equipment to shell and can these hand-picked peas. The market for canned peas was good, but to stay in the business it was necessary to plant and harvest peas as the other packers did. Seufert's got a couple of wheat farmers west of Dufur and toward Mount Hood to plant peas for canning on the high moist farming land between Dufur and Friend. The peas were planted in the grain fields like wheat, with a seed drill, and then when the crop was ready to harvest, the pea vines were mowed and raked into windrows which were picked up with a hay loader and hauled in trucks to the viners.

Seufert's owned and operated the pea viners. The viner station was around the Dufur country close to the pea fields. The vines were fed by men with pitchforks, and went into the viners to be threshed. The shelled peas came out one side of the viner and the vines came out the other end. The farmers kept the vines to be used for silage. The peas were placed into fruit lug boxes and hauled to the cannery. After unloading, the peas were dumped into a fanning mill to be cleaned; and the mill would also remove seeds, leaves, sticks and so forth. Next the peas were washed in fresh water. From there the peas went into a blancher, a machine full of hot water. The peas were in the blancher about ten minutes so the hot water could remove the starch and any bitterness. From the blancher the peas were dumped into cold water, which not only cooled them but also set the green color. Then the peas went into a machine full of salt brine, and this grader graded peas for tenderness by adjusting the density of the brine. You could operate the machine so the tender sweet peas would float to the top of the machine and the hard, tough peas would sink. You canned the tender sweet peas in one can and the hard, tough ones in another one. After the sweet tender peas came from the salt brine machine they went into cold water again to wash off the brine; from there they went over to a picking table so the white girls could remove any not suitable for canning. From there the peas went to the filling machines, which filled cans with peas and also with a mild salt brine. Next the cans were sealed and taken to the retorts for processing, and from there to the warehouse for labeling and shipping. The Company's pea pack was sold either in Portland or San Franciso. San Francisco sales all moved by steamship usually on the Coastwise Line.

Seufert's canned prunes in late fall. The Dalles-Mosier area raised excellent prunes. They were delivered to the cannery by farmers using fruit lug boxes. In the cannery the prunes were canned just as the Royal Anne cherries were. The fruit was dumped onto a picking table, inspected by white girls, then washed, graded by the shaker for size, filled into cans, put through the syruper, run through the exhaust boxes; the cans were then sealed, moved to the retorts for processing and then taken to the warehouse to be labeled and shipped. Prunes were shipped all over the United States: to New York City, Chicago, Minneapolis, and Memphis, Tennessee. Also you would stop cars en

126

route at various smaller cities for partial unloading.

Seufert's canned apricots until the cannery closed. They only canned their own apricots, and never bought from local farmers. The apricots were picked in the Company orchards by both white and Indian pickers, and were hauled to the cannery for processing. At the cannery the apricots were poured out of lug boxes onto a picking table. Here white girls picked over the fruit as it was carried along on a picking belt. The girls removed any trash or fruit not good enough for processing. Next the fruit was washed and passed over the shaker grader.

After the filler automatically filled the apricots into the cans, the filled cans went to the syruper, then through the exhaust boxes, and then had lids sealed on by the closing machines. Here the Chinamen took the sealed cans to the retorts for cooking. Then the Chinese retort crew took the processed cans to the warehouse for labeling and shipping.

All the small apricots, those too large to be canned whole, and any over-ripe fruit were separated on the shaker grader and then went to an automatic pitting machine. You just dumped the apricots in a hopper and they came out below, pitted. Of course the fruit was crushed, but this made no difference since these apricots were going to be used for jam or pies. We always referred to this type of pack as pie apricots. After coming from the pitter, they went through a steam box carried on a chain. In this box the steam preheated or precooked the apricots. Then they were put directly into No. 10 cans which were sealed and taken to the retorts to be cooked; then they were taken to the warehouse to be labeled.

There was a good market for pie apricots all over the United States. Seufert's shipped to New York City, and cars were also moved down through Oklahoma City into Texas. Whole, unpeeled apricots were generally sold either in Portland or in New York City.

One time I figured the cost on canned apricots. My cost figures showed apricots to be a profitable item. The next January I was again figuring the costs for inventory, and discovered that the summer before I had forgotten to figure in the cost of sugar. No wonder canned apricots showed such a nice profit! The next time I figured the cost of canning apricots you can be sure I included the sugar costs.

Seufert's also canned asparagus. This was raised at Walla Walla and sent to The Dalles for canning. Asparagus was shipped by railway express. The car was loaded in the evening at Walla Walla and early the next morning the asparagus was unloaded from the passenger train at the express company station at The Dalles. The express company would deliver by express truck so the asparagus reached the cannery the first thing in the morning. It came early, in April, so you had plenty of time to can asparagus before the spring fishing season opened. It was also shipped and delivered to the cannery in cannery fruit lug boxes, with the asparagus standing upright in the boxes, and packed tight, so it could not fall over.

In the cannery when the asparagus was taken from the boxes it was washed and then inspected by white girls who removed any not fit for canning. Next Chinamen put the asparagus into little boxes, laying the asparagus on its side. The boxes were run through a circular saw which cut off the hard wooden butt end of the stalks, which was discarded. The boxes were emptied into a blancher, a tank of hot water which had a chain with paddles attached which moved the asparagus through the hot water. The asparagus was removed from the lower end of the blancher after ten minutes, and from there it went into a cold water bath to be cooled and so that the green color would be set. Next it moved down a belt and the white girls removed the different sizes of asparagus from the belt and put them in pans of water. It was graded by the diameter of the stalks. Chinamen put the asparagus into cans. These men had nimble fingers and strong hands and were by far the best asparagus packers. This was true not only at Seufert's, but for years the big California canners used Chinamen to fill the asparagus cans. It was always packed upside down, with the top or flower end of the stalk going into the bottom of the can. Filled cans went to the syrupers where salt brine was added. If you filled the cans with the flower end of the stalk at the top, the machines which added brine and put the lid on would mash the delicate flower and ruin the appearance of the asparagus. After the cans went through the closing machines they went to the retorts to be processed and were then taken to the warehouse for labeling and shipping. Asparagus was sold only in the Pacific Northwest.

The Dalles was always a big Royal Anne cherry growing area, but even by the time that Seufert's closed their cannery in 1954, the market for canned Royal Annes seemed to be dying. The greatest demand was during the height of the Great Depression and after World War II. Why the demand dropped off, I don't know. Personally I don't believe price had anything to do with it. Until after World War II the United States

government still made fruit packers use the same density of syrup in canned fruit as they had done years ago, but then fruit packers were allowed to add one-third corn syrup. Corn syrup is thick but has no sweetness and just does not have the good flavor that canned fruit had before World War II. Whether or not this affected the demand, I don't know. One thing I will say, however, is that as long as Seufert's canned fruit they always made the syrup only from pure sugar. The buying public did know the difference, since Seufert's would constantly get letters from housewives all over the United States saying how much better their canned fruits were than those of other packers.

There was quite a tonnage of red, sour pie cherries around The Dalles at one time, but they were a pie fruit that brough a low price to the grower. After World War II those growers pulled these out of their orchards and replanted with Royal Anne cherries. As far as I know there are no red sour cherry orchards left in The Dalles area.

Peas interested the wheat growers during the 1930s, but high wheat prices and prosperity took away any desire to continue growing peas in Wasco County. After World War II no one was interested in growing peas, so that, too, came to an end.

Prunes around The Dalles were excellent. They were firm, sweet, and had a fine flavor, but the farmers just could not stay in business raising prunes at the prices the fruit sold for in the orchards. Around The Dalles and Mosier a crop bearing two tons to the acre was good, but around Salem the farmers were producing seven or eight tons per acre. The dry-land fruit grower just couldn't compete, so by the end of World War II prune orchards were coming out and Royal

128

Anne cherries were going on to the land as replacements.

Apricots that were grown on irrigated land around The Dalles could compete with Yakima apricots, but when Seufert's closed their cannery, there was no market left for the old cannery apricot orchards. So, the people who took over the orchard pulled it out and put the land into wheat.

Asparagus canning had run out for Seufert's by the time World War II began. The big canneries in the Walla Walla country wanted the asparagus for canning, and it become more profitable and perhaps just more convenient to deliver asparagus to the canneries there, rather than box and ship to The Dalles by express. As far as Seufert's was concerned, they could no longer get enough asparagus, so they just stopped canning it.

All in all, fruit canning around The Dalles area after World War II was just no longer practical, and for economic reasons the farmers pulled out all their orchards except for Royal Anne cherries. It was a change with the passing of time.

Soon after World War II, I took the Pacific Great Eastern Railroad to the railhead in British Columbia. There I took a bus over to the mining town of Wells. While sitting in the lobby of a local hotel, an old prospector walked in, sat down beside me, and wanted to know if I was the local dentist. I told him no, I wasn't, that I was just in town for the trip, and that I was an American from Oregon. The old man said he had a tooth that needed fixing, and it was the dentist's day to visit town.

After a bit, the old prospector said that when he was a young man he had worked in Oregon on the Columbia River for a contractor who was going to blast out part of a river channel. Nearby a man had an orchard, and during the noon hour, the men on the river job would walk over the rocks to the orchard and pick fruit. After a day or two, the owner came down to the river and told the men working on the blasting job that he didn't want them to climb his trees because they were breaking branches. He said if they would stay out of his trees, he would put a lug box full of fresh fruit on the edge of the orchard every day, and the men could help themselves. The old prospector said, "You know, that is just what that man did. We helped ourselves to the fresh fruit every day, but none of us ever climbed one of his trees again." I told him that it was quite a coincidence, since the man he was talking about was my grandfather, F.A. Seufert. This was the contract put out by the Army Engineers to blast off the outer end of Covington Point. My reason for telling this story is not so much my chance meeting with the old prospector in British Columbia, but how old-timers like my grandfather handled situations. They knew men and how to handle them.

STURGEON & OTHER CREATURES

Seufert's fishwheels and fishwheel scows always caught some sturgeon. A 100-pound sturgeon was common, a 200-pound sturgeon was not uncommon, and once in a while they would be much bigger. The No. 3 Fishwheel used to catch sturgeon regularly, and in the fall of the year, the seines would also occasionally catch a large sturgeon. They were taken to the cannery where the Chinese butchered them.

Butchering a sturgeon was an entirely different proposition from butchering a 30-pound salmon. First, the head was chopped off over a chopping block, with a large knife like an axe. The blade was at least a foot long and just as deep. This cleaver had a handle a foot long, enough so that a man could grasp it in both hands. The Chinese butcher swung the cleaver like an axe and a 200-pound sturgeon might take several blows at the back of his head before you could cut it from the body. Then the butcher would slit the sturgeon's belly and remove the entrails. Then he would cut around the tail clear to the backbone, and then grasping the tail he would start to pull. The backbone, actually a thick gristle-like substance that was very limber, would be pulled from the sturgeon's body at the

tail. After pulling about a foot of the backbone out, the butcher would actually wrap the slippery backbone around his wrist just as a man might wrap a rope. With a piece of the backbone around his wrist he would pull some more, and the entire backbone would come out. It looked like a gray piece of rope, about as big around as your finger. Of course as the Chinese butchers were pulling out the backbone, the sturgeon would move and flop around as if it were alive. Then the butcher would wash the sturgeon in fresh water until it was clean. Then he sewed it into a burlap sack. A regular gunny sack would be used if the sturgeon was small, one sack over the front part and another over the back, sewed together at the middle of the fish using a regular grain needle used to sew up grain sacks.

Next, the butchered sturgeon was weighed to get the dressed weight and a shipping tag was attached that showed the shipping address (before World War I it was S. Schmidt and Company, Astoria, Oregon; later on into the middle 1930s, the Doty Fish Company in Kalama, Washington). The butchered and wrapped sturgeon was loaded on an express hand truck. The express company in those days had at least two of these

130

hand trucks at Seufert's Cannery at all times. When the passenger train westbound for Portland would pass Seufert's Cannery in the early afternoon, it was flagged down. When the train stopped you backed the express hand truck up against the baggage car and the dressed sturgeon was placed in the baggage car for shipment.

Once in a while a big sturgeon would be full of eggs. These sturgeon eggs were in great demand as caviar, but they had to be in the right stage of development or they were no good. As long as the eggs had not separated, they were placed in a cannery case for shipment. If the eggs had separated, they were no good and then you had to throw them away. Some of the big sturgeons might be carrying 30 pounds or more of eggs. These eggs were placed in a salmon cannery case, the lid was nailed on, a shipping tag attached, and the box was shipped to the same people the sturgeon went to. Later they would pay you for the eggs, but the price would depend on the condition of the eggs.

Seufert's bought sturgeon from any fisherman who wanted to sell them. One man in particular who fished for sturgeon at The Dalles for years was Henry Wickman. He fished between Threemile Rapids and Big Eddy directly in back of the cannery. Wickman fished in September. In the fall he would not be operating the scows because the river was too low, but he just loved to fish for sturgeon using a fishing boat and a sturgeon line. A sturgeon line was several hundred feet long with heavy fish hooks attached, spaced a few feet apart. The line had heavy weights at each end holding the line on the bottom of the river; another came to the surface where a barrel was attached to act as a marker. Wickman sold his sturgeon to Seufert's at the union fish price and of course all fishermen who sold sturgeon to Seufert's always received union price.

Eels were used as bait to fish for sturgeon. Sturgeon just seem to love eels. Eels were thick in the Columbia River around The Dalles. Any time you wanted eels for sturgeon fishing you just went out on the river and you could find eels along the bank sticking to the sides of the rocky shore. They were thick around the lower end of the spillways from The Dalles-Celilo Canal and down in Fifteenmile Creek just opposite the cannery. In order to catch eels all you had to do was walk down, reach out and grab one in your hand and pull real hard. Fishermen usually put their eels in a gunny sack and carried them down to where they were going to fish. Then they took a knife and chopped the eels into two- or three-inch lengths, just like chopping up a rubber hose. If you wanted the eels to be really attractive to the sturgeon, you lay them out in the hot sun for two or three days, and then the sturgeon couldn't resist them.

In the 1920s Henry Wickman was coming up the river one day during high water, and saw that a raven had built a nest on a high sheer bluff overlooking the river. There was a young bird in the nest. This young raven was a good-sized bird but still had not learned to fly. Moving the pick-up boat nearly against the bluff, Henry Wickman used a dipnet and took the young raven from the nest and brought him up to the cannery. The men put this young raven in a cage and named him Jiggs. In a short while the young bird had become everyone's pet. The next year the raven was full-grown so the men took him from his cage, clipped one of his wings, and then turned him loose in the yard in front of

131

the cannery. By that summer the raven had learned to talk, and could say a number of words, such as "hello." By then the raven had the run of the place and earned his keep by keeping the road in front of the cannery clean. When Fat Charlie was driving the gut wagon past the front of the cannery several times a day, the bird's work at keeping the road clean was much appreciated.

The thing I remember most was that anything loose, such as a key or a coin, or anything that sparkled in the sun, the raven would pick up and put it in the middle of the road, cover it with leaves and sticks right before your eyes. In a moment or so the raven would have camouflaged the shiny object so that it looked so natural against its surroundings that you would have a hard time to walk over and find the object. One day F.A. Seufert was sitting on the bench in the yard in front of the cannery. Jiggs was sitting alongside him. The raven spotted F.A. Seufert's diamond stud on the front of his shirt sparkling in the sun. The bird made a quick peck at the sparkling diamond and missed. After driving the bird away, my grandfather said, "Lucky for you, Jiggs, that you missed, or we would have had an operation right here and now." By the third year the raven, with his wing still clipped, started to wander away from the cannery during the daytime, although he always came home at dark. One day the raven wandered away down to Fifteenmile Creek in back of the barn. A couple of kids from The Dalles found the bird, and as soon as they realized he couldn't fly they killed him.

In the 1920s and 1930s Fifteenmile Creek had water flowing in it all year round. It was lowest in the middle of summer, but even then it was a good-sized stream. Floods generally came in late winter or early spring when the Chinook Winds came and melted the snow cover in the wheat fields to the south of the cannery. Fifteenmile Creek could then become a raging torrent, but in summer there was always good trout fishing between the cannery and the ice dam. Down by the cannery there were any number of muskrats living in the river. If you stood very still you could watch them swimming in the creek down below. The falls at Fifteenmile Creek directly under the railroad bridge were covered in summer with eels hanging to the rocky sides of the falls on their way up creek to spawn. It was also full of crawfish. We never fished for them, but you could stand on the rocky banks of the creek and watch the crawfish in the deep pools. The creek was so clear you could easily see the bottom. It was fun to stand on a rock above the creek over a quiet pool of water and fire a .22 bullet into the creek. In less than a minute you would be surprised how many trout would swim over to investigate the place where the bullet had struck the water.

Beavers in the creek were a nuisance. About a mile up the creek the Company had a small diversion dam across the creek, and then on the south side there was a pipeline down to the cannery to bring irrigation water to the Company orchards. The beavers thought this diversion dam was a fine place for a home. Every night the beavers would plug the water pipe with sticks and brush to stop the leak in their pond, and every day the Company would send a man up the creek with a shovel to remove the beavers' industrious efforts. The poor beavers always lost, because after this went on for a week or so and the beavers showed no sign of giving up, the Company would call the game authorities and report their troubles. The Game Commission would come and trap the beavers and move them to a new home where there wasn't such a conflict of interest.

At dusk mother skunks and their young would come out and play along the banks of the creek, and romp about. If you kept real still the little skunks would play with each other just like kittens. Of course you always kept very quiet, so there was no problem.

Now all this has changed. The creek is no longer a nice little stream flowing down toward the cannery; the fish are gone, the eels are gone, the crawfish are gone, and so are the muskrats and beavers. Now the creek is dry by the middle of summer, and the water left in the pools is stagnant and covered with scum. At such times Fifteenmile Creek stinks, and at times I cannot help wondering if some of our so-called progress doesn't stink, too.

LIVESTOCK

Once in a while a Seufert Company horse would cut himself on a barbed wire fence. Some of these barbed wire fence cuts were deep, and the poor horse would bleed profusely. Around the cannery the men used what they called Monsol salts. This was a yellowish powder, and a handful on the cut on the horse's leg would stop the bleeding immediately. We always kept some Monsol salts back by the engineer's desk, near the retorts. Whenever you cut yourself shaving a pinch of Monsol salts would stop the bleeding immediately.

Seufert's had a barn where they kept cattle. The cows were kept for milk for the crews. Of course horses were taken care of there also. The man who took care of the barn was always referred to as the cow man.

The Company owned some 3,000 acres of grass or rangeland back from the Columbia River. This rangeland ran from the back of the cannery up to and back from No. 5 Fishwheel. Here the Company would run some 50 head of beef cattle. These were just turned loose to take care of themselves. The rangeland was good and there was plenty of water, so the range cattle would do well. As the months went by they became wild; they were never in a barn and would not go into

one. To protect the cattle from the bitter east wind in the winter, the Company would build a three-sided open barn, the open side away from the wind. The cattle could seek shelter here if they needed it.

Seufert's had one man who knew livestock, and the cattle were his responsibility. They also kept just one saddle horse, but the man in charge of the cattle owned his own saddle. This man would decide when the cattle were to be sold and when the time came he would bring these cattle in and help load them on a truck for market.

The Company at one time kept their own bull. The bull was kept on the river side of The Dalles-Celilo Canal. This made an ideal bull pen. Of course the bull could not cross the canal, so there was no worry about the bull getting with the cattle until one wanted him to. Also on the river side of the canal every few miles there would be a spillway for the canal so you always had plenty of water for the bull. The spillway would also irrigate a considerable acreage of alfalfa that furnished feed for the bull.

If you had an unusually late and bitter winter and the calves were born then, the man looking after the

134

cattle would often bring these calves into the cannery, wrap them in blankets and lay them down before the stove and get them warm again so they could survive. I can always remember how these calves only a few hours old would shiver from the cold. Once in a while one of the cows would get too close to a bluff, fall off and be injured, and then of course someone had to take a rifle up the river and destroy the injured animal. This was one job I was always sure to avoid.

Once in a while the Company would buy a work horse. Often the Company would find this horse so mean that no one around the cannery could get near him, let alone harness him for work. This horse was just put into pasture. Then at least once a year the Indians would come down from the reservations to break horses. They would come to the cannery and offer their services. The cannery crew would round up the mean horse and put him into the corral at the barn. The group of Indians who came to break the wild horses would consist of three men, the rider and two helpers. The Indians would get this horse against the corral fence and blindfold him, put a bridle on him, then one of the Indians would mount the mean horse to break him in. The mean horse, when turned loose, would make several efforts to throw the Indian rider. The Indian would give a yell, slap the horse on the rump with his hat, and the horse would just quiet down and let the Indian ride him around the corral. We always gathered to see the fun, but there never was much excitement. These Indian riders would break these horses in not more than a minute, then the fun was all over. The Indians would then go to the Cannery office and collect their fee. The fee came to $2.50 per horse. The men all thought that good pay for a few minutes' work. Of course none of the cannery crew would think of getting into the corral with the horse for that amount of money. These men around the cannery had all been around horses and could drive a team, but they were just not horsemen.

GRANGES & SPORT FISHING

Around The Dalles area the fishwheel and salmon industry contributed both money and jobs to many people, and local businesses and most people in the area always supported and helped the upper river fishing industry.

But also around The Dalles and Hood River there was always a group who opposed the local fishing industry at every opportunity. A number of these people were active in the local Granges. Why the upper river fishing industry bothered these people so much, I don't know, unless it was just sour grapes. It just seems to bother some people no end to see others a success in business.

The Grange, especially in the Hood River Valley, knew nothing about the fishing industry on the Columbia River, but were more than willing to join the Astoria Fisherman's Union to try to destroy the salmon fishing industry around The Dalles area. The Oregon State Grange was one of the main groups sponsoring the initiative measure on the Oregon ballot in 1926 to outlaw fishwheels in Oregon.

In the commercial fishing areas around The Dalles there were any number of sportsmen angling for

salmon each fall. The one thing I want to point out was that Seufert's never in any way interfered with these sportsmen fishing on the Company's property or with sportsmen passing over Company land going or coming from the Columbia River while sport fishing.

On the Washington side of the Columbia River in an eddy above Seufert's Washington seine bar and just below the SP&S railroad bridge was the one place downriver from Celilo Falls where these sportsmen fished from boats. They would anchor their boats in this eddy to fish.

The only other place the sportsmen fished was at Celilo on the Oregon shores below Downes Channel and down to the Tumwater Fishwheel. The sportsmen would be thick along the river bank. The site was easy to reach. When one of these sportsmen fished and caught no salmon, he could always walk up to Downes Channel and buy a salmon from an Indian and go home and show the big salmon he had gotten at Celilo. The Indian fisherman was always glad to sell a sportsman a salmon, always at least twice the price being paid by the salmon canneries.

This reminds me that when the cannery wasn't

busy and you wanted to kill time, you went into the cannery, got a few salmon eggs, a fishing pole and a fish basket, and walked up to the ice dam on Fifteen-mile Creek, probably an eighth of a mile above the cannery. You could fish down to the cannery. Often in an hour you could get five or six nice rainbow trout, and of course in those days you didn't need a license as long as you fished on Company property.

TELEGRAPH, TELEPHONE & RAIL

For the cannery business all communications between The Dalles and the cities the Company was doing business with was done by telegram. All sales, sales confirmations, new prices, numbers and initials of box cars shipped, and both our brokers and suppliers, all communicated with the Company by telegram.

When, for instance, we had information for our New York City broker it was all written down in a telegram. I would take the telegram to the telegraph office that evening on my way home. These telegrams were always sent as a night letter. This way we sent our telegrams at a cheap rate but knew they would be delivered in the New York City office in the morning. We always made a copy of the telegram, put it in an envelope and mailed it the same night by regular mail. This way if there was an error in the transmission of the telegram, in less than a week's time the New York City office would have an exact copy so the telegram could be checked for any errors in transmission.

This practice of using telegrams for communications and then mailing a copy by surface mail continued up to about 1950. By then the use of telegrams started to fall off and the Company was relying on air-mail for most of their communications with the brokers. On airmail letters between the Company's office and the Company's broker's office, the letters were mailed at The Dalles post office in the evening. But we always put a duplicate copy of the airmail letter in a separate envelope and mailed it the same night by regular mail. After all, we weren't sure that the airplane was going to get there; the railroad mail service was considered much more reliable and dependable. By the end of World War II the Company was sending most of its communications by airmail and by that time no one thought it necessary to play it safe by sending a copy by surface mail.

In the late 1920s a long-distance telephone call from New York City was considered quite an event. (Then no one thought of just picking up a telephone, placing the call with the long-distance operator and talking with your party on the other end of the line in a minute or so.) In those days a telegram for my grandfather would come from New York City saying that so-and-so wanted to talk to him about a car of salmon. The call would be made on such-and-such a day at such-and-such an hour. On the appointed day and hour my grandfather, my dad and I, plus the book-keeper would collect in the office. Everybody sat on a chair, talked in hushed tones waiting for the phone to ring. When it did my grandfather would get up, walk across the office and take down the receiver and answer the call. The rest of us all sat around in silence, you could have heard a pin drop. When the telephone call was completed my grandfather hung up the receiver. The first thing my dad would ask was, well, could you hear him. When my grandfather said he could hear them just as plain as talking to The Dalles, the next question my dad would ask, well, what does he want. By that time everybody had relaxed. Then my dad and grandfather would talk about the business that had been involved in the long-distance telephone call from New York City.

In later years, about World War II, we had a large Jewish house in New York City that always bought a straight car of Wasco Brand choice Columbia River Chinooks from the Company each fall. These would always be one-pound flats. This wholesale house was owned by an elderly Jew, named Abe Krasne. He always called my dad personally, the two of them making the deal, the number of cases involved and the price. After the opening pleasantries, such as, "How are you, Abe," the dealing would begin. Both would start shouting. You wondered why the long-distance call was even necessary. They could have heard each other without a telephone. After this went on for five minutes or so, a deal was agreed upon. After saying goodbye my dad would always turn to me and say, you know, that old Abe is not a bad guy.

One of the first telephones put in at The Dalles was built by Seufert's about 1900. It ran from the cannery office, some three miles to The Dalles and there was put into the Western Union office. This was put in so that when telegrams came for the Company, the Company could be called and the telegram delivered immediately by telephone. The Company operated probably some 15 miles of private telephone service. The telephone lines from The Dalles were part of the regular Bell System; Seufert's Cannery was listed as a The Dalles telephone and listed in The Dalles city directory.

Seufert's Cannery had a unique telephone number. It was Suburban 0. This number was used by Seufert's for at least 40 years and was changed only when The Dalles exchange went over to the dial system.

In the cannery office Seufert's had their own switchboard, and from this switchboard you could talk to different phones in the cannery or up the river. Here I must add that Seufert's always used the old battery-operated, hand-cranked wall-hung telephones. Down in the cannery, of course, we each had our own ring, but this was surprisingly efficient. Any man working in the cannery that heard your ring would call it to your attention even if you didn't hear the phone ring, and it was only a minute or two before someone told you the office wanted to talk to you.

Seufert's had, of course, their own telephone line up the river. There was a telephone at old No. 3, No. 4 and No. 5 fishwheels. There were also phones across the river in the mess house at the Cyclone Wheel, at the mess house at the fishery, upriver there was a telephone in the office at the Tumwater fish house, and on down at the Oregon landing. Each fishwheel, fish house and mess house had its own ring, so there was no question about which outfit you wanted to talk to when the phone rang.

The telephone poles and glasses came from either Western Union Telegraph or the Bell System. When either of these two big companies replaced their poles they always came into the cannery office to ask if Seufert's needed any new poles. Seufert's sent out a crew to pick up the replaced poles. Of course, for Seufert's telephone line, any telephone or telegraph pole that was discarded by the big companies would serve for years.

In the 1920s the Union Pacific ran a little local passenger train past Seufert's Cannery. This train consisted of a baggage car and a chair car. It was called the Portland-Pendleton Local. It was generally just referred to as No. 2 if eastbound and No. 1 if westbound. It did all of the local work. It passed the cannery eastbound about 11:15 in the morning. If you wanted to ride this little local to Tumwater, you just stood on the edge of the tracks in front of the cannery and as the train approached you would wave your arms. As soon as the engineer saw you, he would give two short toots on his whistle. This was the engineer's signal that he saw you and would stop and pick you up. When the train stopped, you got into the chair car, told the conductor you wanted off at Tumwater, and he collected the fare. If I remember right, the fare was 25 cents for an adult, although I have forgotten what the half fare was. When you approached Tumwater the conductor signaled the engineer on the air whistle on the locomotive cab, and the engineer would signal the conductor with the locomotive whistle that he had received the conductor's

signal. The train would stop at Tumwater fish house, and here we got off and had dinner in the Tumwater mess house with the men. About 1:10 P.M. the westbound Portland-Pendleton Local would be due, and you would stand beside the track and wait for the little train to approach and repeat the entire episode over again, getting back to the cannery at Seuferts in about 20 minutes.

Up until 1921 when the Columbia River Highway was completed between the cannery and Celilo, the salmon were all hauled from Tumwater fish house down to the cannery in boxcars. When the salmon fishing season was about to start, either in the spring or fall, the Company would notify the railroad. The railroad would then set aside some five or six box cars for fresh fish hauling service. These cars were always old, dilapidated cars and were to be scrapped. These cars were assigned to the fish service then between Seufert's and Tumwater.

At the Tumwater fish house side track one of these old cars would be spotted. You loaded salmon into the car generally late in the day. The salmon were just piked onto the car's floor, not over one or two fish deep. You then turned a water hose into the car. This was to wet the fish down and to be sure that the car floor and sides were wet. This was done to keep the car cool and the salmon fresh. You then notified the railroad agent at The Dalles that the car of fresh fish at Tumwater was ready to be hauled to the cannery. Sometime during the night the train dispatcher would issue orders to a westbound freight to pick this car up, and in the morning the car would be sitting on the cannery siding at Seufert's.

In the fall when the weather was hot, I can still remember the men opening the boxcar door on one of these salmon cars. The smell after being closed all night was a smell to remember. If it didn't make you toss your cookies, nothing would. You then got into the salmon car and piked all the salmon out by hand into little iron cars. You hauled the salmon in these little cars through the warehouse into the fish room where they were dumped, the salmon falling on the fish house floor, later to be canned. A carload of salmon in one of these old salmon cars weighed about two or possibly three tons, so four or five boxcars could haul all the salmon down from Tumwater fish house every day without any trouble.

And what became of the boxcars put into the salmon hauling business between the cannery and Tumwater? Well, in the fall when the cannery closed and there was no more need for these boxcars, the railroad did the only thing it could do with them. The railroad hauled these cars to Albina and burned them.

Seufert's bought land along the Columbia River to build fishwheels, and purchased the shoreland from the state; eventually they owned a ten-mile stretch of land from The Dalles to Celilo Falls. Later, the state would no longer sell shoreland to private companies. When the Oregon State Portage was built it ran almost its entire length through Seufert's property, so in the deed Seufert's reserved the right to operate their own trains over the railroad. Seufert's trains consisted of a speeder and a little four-wheel, two-axle trailer car. I can well remember riding on this little speeder. You could load a half-dozen fish boxes on this little trailer car, or probably five or six hundred pounds of salmon. When you wanted to pick up fish at Fishwheel No. 5, you called the Oregon State Portage dispatcher at Big Eddy, told him you wanted to go to Tenino, and asked if he had any trains out on the line. If he said no trains were operating, you had a clear track and nothing to worry about. But if he did have a train out, then you were responsible for keeping out of his way.

Seufert's also had a clause in the deed transferring Seufert land to the federal government for the right-of-way for The Dalles-Celilo Canal. The clause stated that if the U.S. government ever abandoned the canal, the land would revert to Seufert's. However, by the time The Dalles Dam was built and filled the canal, the government had already bought out Seufert's.

When Seufert's Cannery was built in 1886 the OR&N Railroad built a siding into the cannery at no cost to Seufert's, and agreed to keep it in repair, an agreement which had not been made by railroads for years. At present if a railroad builds a siding into your plant, you must pay the cost, plus the cost of keeping it in good repair.

EXPORT

Down at Memphis, Tennessee, the Company was represented by Jacob J. Peres and Company. The Peres family were Dutch Jews and had been in the food brokerage business since before the Civil War. The family one generation after the other continued in the business until the family finally sold the brokerage business about 1960. The Peres family had represented the Seufert Company since 1906.

About 1906 or so Seufert's packed Columbia River eels. The eels were caught in the fishwheels, cleaned and cut into lengths to fit a one-pound tall can. The eels after being put into the cans were then processed just like a can of salmon. The eels were canned for the salmon trade in New York City. These eels were packed and sold as eels in jelly. (The Oregon Historical Society has some of these labels in its archives.) The Company packed about 500 cases that year but discontinued the canning of eels after several seasons. The Company didn't have time to pack eels during the salmon season.

One thing the Company did pack that was delicious was spiced salmon. You always used choice Chinook when you were packing spiced salmon. A choice Chinook was not so rich in oil and this grade of salmon was preferred. Spiced salmon was always packed in half-pound cans. The can of salmon contained not only salmon but salt, pepper, bay leaves, cloves, cinnamon, allspice and a slice of lemon. The product was delicious, although you either liked the pack or you didn't. I thought it was one of the best products ever put up. In other words, I loved spiced salmon. The Company never packed very much of this item each year. It was a slow, time-consuming process so you didn't fool with spiced salmon until late in the fall when you weren't busy.

Seufert's had a number of excellent labels that had high consumer acceptance. These were Merrimac, Wasco and Klondike brands. Seufert's started and registered the brands with the patent office under copyright from the years 1896 and 1898. These brands are still in use today by the successor of Seufert Brothers Company, Francis A. Seufert and Company.

Once, on Seufert's Merrimac brand the label printer carelessly printed the United States flag flying at the *Merrimac*'s stern. This was promptly brought to the Company's attention from southern patriots. The *Mer-*

rimac flew the Confederate flag all through her career as a Confederate warship and never flew the stars and stripes, never. The next order of labels specified that the stars and bars be shown as the flag of the ironclad *Merrimac* and the Confederate battle flag has flown ever since on Seufert's Merrimac brand. (The original copyrights issued on these brands are now in the possession of the Oregon Historical Society.) Merrimac brand was chosen because in 1896, when Seufert's started canning salmon, Seufert's started selling canned salmon around Waco, Texas, and Memphis, Tennessee. The Civil War had not been over too many years and the ironclad *Merrimac* was a well-known Confederate warship, loved throughout the South, so Seufert's used this popular and well-known name, Merrimac, on their canned salmon. Today, Merrimac choice canned salmon is still a big selling brand of canned salmon in the Memphis, Tennessee, market.

Wasco brand [see endpapers] was chosen by the Seufert's because of Wasco County and the Wasco Indians and it was a well-known name in Oregon. The label has always carried a picture of an Indian, and some of the warehouse employees in the big cities of the East who were either illiterate or foreign-born, could identify the brand by the Indian on it. Wasco salmon was always a big seller in New York City. Today it is still used on pink salmon in the Memphis, Tennessee market.

Klondike brand was taken and copyrighted by Seufert's in 1898. It was of course, during the gold rush to the Yukon Territory. The label has always been a good one but is now used throughout the south on chum salmon. After all, people know salmon comes from Alaska and Klondike brand is appropriate.

Seufert's also had Annie's Favorite brand; Annie was F. A. Seufert's wife, and my grandmother. This brand was used on fancy Columbia River Chinooks only and sold in the New York City market. The brand is still in use but because of the shortage of really fine salmon, it is difficult to find any salmon that are appropriate for the brand.

From time to time Seufert's used Celilo brand and Tenino brand, both Indian names from around The Dalles. But these two names simply never caught on with the buying public, so both brands were used on odds and ends that sometimes turned up around a cannery.

About 1910 or 1912 Seufert's had a Lusitania brand named after the famous ship crossing the North Atlantic. This brand was used on fancy Chinooks in the New York City market, but the day that the German submarine sank the *Lusitania* during World War I, with heavy loss of life, completely destroyed any usefulness of using the brand. So Seufert's just quietly and quickly removed Lusitania brand from the grocery shelves.

Years ago the swastika was used by label companies on many labels to fill in blank spaces. Packers and buyers years ago felt a label should have no blank spaces on it. (Today we would say their label design was busy.) Of course the rise of Hitler on the European scene completely destroyed use of the swastika in the United States.

I have mentioned that while Seufert's never entered the export market, Seufert's salmon was exported by the New York City wholesalers to Europe from time to time.

In the export canned salmon business it was very important that the salmon label vignette be just right.

The salmon had to be leaping up a waterfall; in other words, the head higher than the tail, the salmon was standing on his tail. This position showed the customer that the salmon was fresh when canned.

If the label showed the salmon with the tail higher than the head or the body arched down instead of up, this indicated to the European canned salmon buyer that you had, as they said, canned a dead fish, meaning you had canned salmon that was not fresh. You can understand the European reasoning if you can imagine a salmon out of the river a number of hours, then placed on the corner of a table. The head and tail would droop down over the edge of the table, the salmon drooping more and more the longer it was out of water.

So when you designed your salmon labels you had to be sure that your salmon in the vignette was shown leaping with his head higher than his tail, thus assuring your European customers that you only put fresh salmon in your cans.

About 1910 Seufert's decided to mild cure salmon. Seufert's had Italian immigrants build a thick rock basement wall under the cannery warehouse floor on the north end of the building. It was here that Seufert's was going to hold the mild-cured salmon while it was being processed. Later it was shipped down to the ice plant that Warren's had at Goble, Oregon, where it was held awaiting shipment. Seufert's eventually felt this business was not very profitable, and they quit after a year or two, and never put up any more of the mild-cured salmon. Years later, some of the old barrels used for this were still stored, empty, in the stone room, which was surprisingly cool even on the hottest days of August. We eventually set up a stitching machine down there for the Chinamen who were making paper boxes. It was cool and comfortable to work down there even on blisteringly hot days.

Henry Wickman once told me the blacksmith at the cannery used eel oil to temper the cutting ends of rock drills, and felt it was the best thing in the world for tempering an edge. To make this oil you had to get at least a gunny sack full of eels, which was no problem because the fishwheels would catch eels right along with salmon. The eels were put in a barrel and then you put the barrel out in the sun and let nature take its course for 30 days or so. When you pulled the wooden plug on the bottom, the oil would have settled to the bottom of the barrel and would drain out into a container. In the blacksmith shop the rock drill ends were heated to a cherry red in the forge and then were dipped in the can of eel oil, which would temper the drill to the proper hardness for drilling rock. Imagine the stink that rose from the can of eel oil when the red hot tip of the drill touched it! He swore by the process, but said blacksmiths didn't like to go out to get the eels.

One time Wickman had five scrawny chickens he wanted me to can for him. He wanted to eat them the following winter, and my share was to be one can. Henry killed the chickens and dressed them, and when time came to singe them I offered to get some newspaper to use as a torch. Henry said there was no need for that. He went into the machine shop and got a gasoline blow torch, lit it, and proceeded to singe the chickens. Then he cut them up and put them into cans; I sealed the cans and put them into a retort for processing. When the cooking was complete, Henry gave the steam engineer and me each a can of chicken. About a week later the cans had cooled and had been sitting, so the engineer and I decided to open ours. Well, when

144

we opened the can the odor of gasoline was so strong. We certainly weren't going to eat chicken that smelled like a blowtorch. So I put the stuff in a pan and set it out for the cannery cats. They came running up, but after one sniff, they all turned their backs and walked off.

I have always liked cats, and always had a pet cat at home. One day as I was sitting at my desk in the Company office, I looked out the window and saw that one of the cannery cats had caught a mouse and was playing with it, tossing it up in the air and catching it and letting it run off and then pouncing on it. I decided to go out and take the mouse away from the cat. I put the mouse in the bushes where it would be safe and told the cat to go about its business. Some of the men saw me and I took a lot of kidding, but all the same I'm glad I rescued the mouse.

In reference to the Seufert records now in the archives of the Oregon Historical Society: starting from the fish runs of 1884, 1885 and on until 1954, these records are invaluable. The records show the fish runs of every day of every year for that entire period. I don't believe there is any place where such a record exists other than the Oregon Historical Society.

These records have tremendous significance today because they show what the runs were in the past, and we often hear a lot of political bunkum about the runs of today. If we go back over these old records and the records of today we are often surprised at how they show that the same pattern of salmon runs exists now as then. There may have been more salmon in the earlier days than there are now, but the pattern for the runs, when they came and so on, is definitely the same.

I would say that a fishwheel was by far the most fascinating fishing gear that was ever invented. There was something about the wheels dipping into the water and coming out with the fish that fascinated people no end. Around The Dalles years ago the local sports would often stand on the deck of a fishwheel and bet silver dollars with each other on how many salmon would come up in each dip as it emerged from the river. You placed a silver dollar on the railing and said one fish, or no fish, or two fish and the other man called your bet. If you called it wrong, then he took the dollar. It was great sport although expensive.

AFTERWORD

Seufert's salmon canning and fishing operations were unique. Their salmon cannery was farthest from the sea, and was located behind two mountain ranges. Seufert's operated fishwheels the farthest up the Columbia River. Their seining operations were above any others on the river. Their fishermen fished the Columbia River farthest above the mouth of the river. And the Celilo Falls Indian fishing grounds were the richest for their size of any fishing grounds in the world.

This closes a recording of personal memories going back over some fifty years of Seufert's Columbia River fishing and canning operations. Personal memories of men and women, close personal friends, acquaintances and others whose names I no longer remember. Personal memories of an era now long gone, never to return, an era that today is just history.

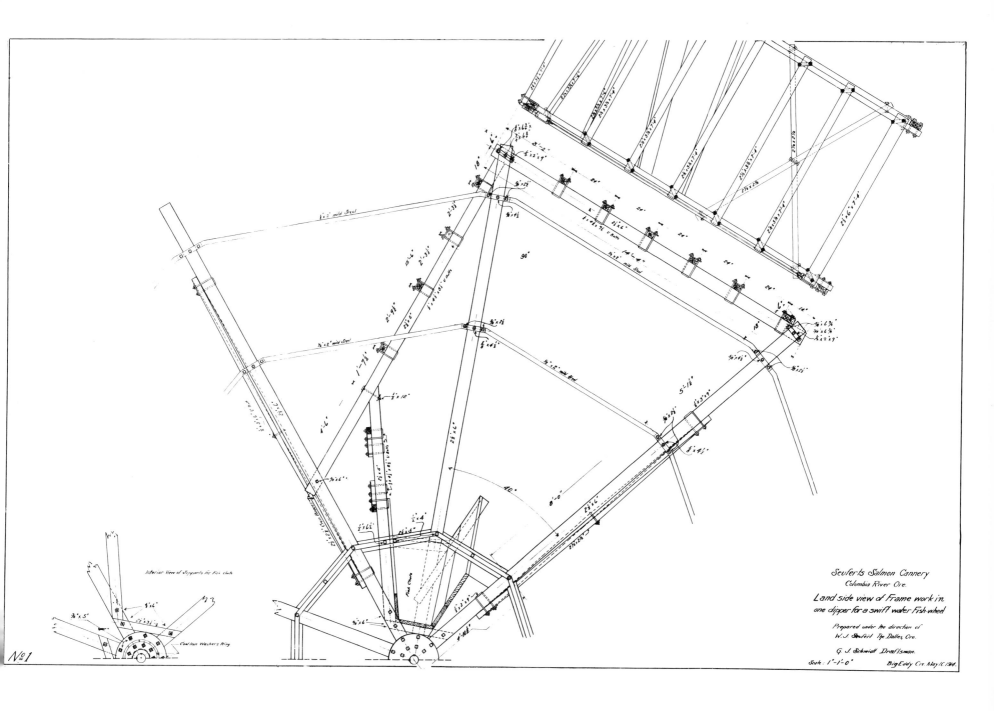

Seuferts Salmon Cannery
Columbia River Ore.

Land side view of Frame work in
one dipper for a swift water fish-wheel

Prepared under the direction of
W. J. Seufert The Dalles, Ore.

G. J. Schmidt Draftsman.

Scale: 1"-1'-0"   Big Eddy Ore. May 10. 1914.

Interior View of Supports for Fish chute

Cast Iron Washer's Ring

No 1

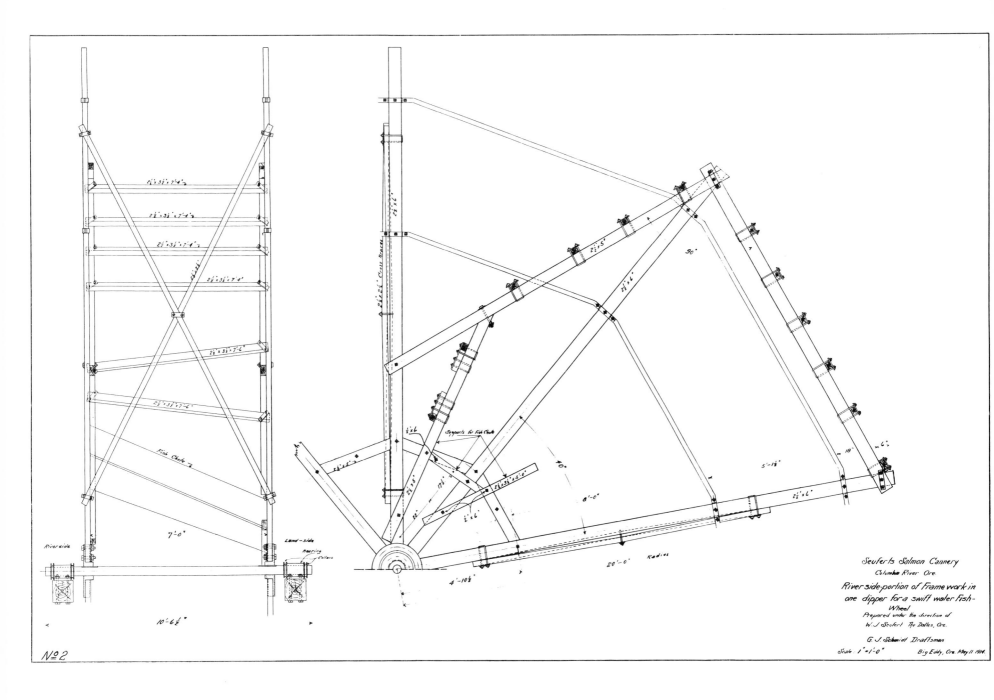

Riverside

Land-side

Bearing Collars

7'-0"

Fish Chute 3

10'-6 1/2"

2 1/2"x 3 1/2"x 7'-4 1/2"
2 1/2"x 3 1/2"x 7'-4 1/2"
2 1/2"x 3 1/2"x 7'-4 1/2"
2 1/2"x 3 1/2"x 7'-4"
2 1/2"x 3 1/2"x 7'-6"
2 1/2"x 3 1/2"x 7'-6"

2 1/2"x 6"

2 1/2"x 5 1/2" Cross Brace

2 1/2"x 5"

2 1/2"x 6"

Supports for Fish Chute

4"x 6"

4"x 6"

2 1/2"x 3 1/2"x 6'-0"

90°

40°

6'-0"

5'-1 1/2"

18"

2 1/2"x 6"

20'-0" Radius

4'-10 1/2"

Seuferts Salmon Cannery
Columbia River Ore.

River side portion of Framework in
one dipper for a swift water fish-
Wheel
Prepared under the direction of
W. J. Seufert The Dalles, Ore.

G. J. Schmidt Draftsman

Scale 1"=1'-0"   Big Eddy, Ore. May 11, 1914.

N° 2

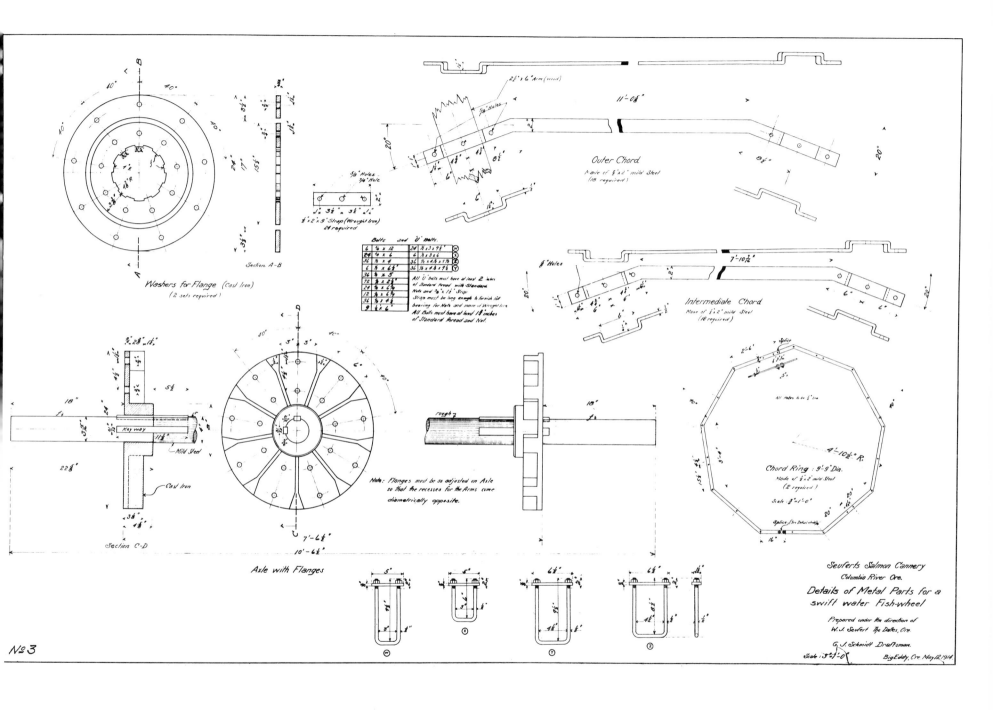

Washers for Flange (Cast Iron)
(2 sets required)

Section A–B

⅛"×2"×9" Strap (Wrought Iron)
24 required

2½"×6" Arm (wood)

Outer Chord
Made of ⅜"×2" mild Steel
(18 required)

Intermediate Chord
Made of ⅜"×2" mild Steel
(18 required)

Bolts and U Bolts.

6	¾ × 12		24	⅜ × 3 × 9¾		
24	¾ × 6		6	¾ × 3 × 6		
36	½ × 6		36	½ × 4½ × 5¾		
6	⅝ × 6½		36	½ × 4½ × 5½		
36	⅝ × 5					
72	½ × 2½					
12	¾ × 6½					
36	⅝ × 4½					
9	¾ × 6					

All U bolts must have at least 2 inches
of Standard Thread with Standard
Nuts and ⅜"×1½" Strap.
Strap must be long enough to furnish full
bearing for Nuts and made of Wrought Iron.
All Bolts must have at head 1½ inches
of Standard Thread and Nut.

Section C–D

Mild Steel
Key way
Cast Iron

Axle with Flanges

Note: Flanges must be so adjusted on Axle
so that the recesses for the Arms come
diametrically opposite.

rough

Splice
All Holes to be ⅝" Dia.

Chord Ring : 9'-9" Dia.
Made of ⅜"×2" mild Steel
(2 required)
Scale ¾"=1'-0"

4'-10½" R.

Splice (See Detail sheet)

Seuferts Salmon Cannery
Columbia River Ore.

Details of Metal Parts for a
swift water Fish-wheel

Prepared under the direction of
W. J. Seufert The Dalles, Ore.

G. J. Schmidt Draftsman.

Scale ½"=1'-0"   Big Eddy, Ore May 18. 1914.

No 3

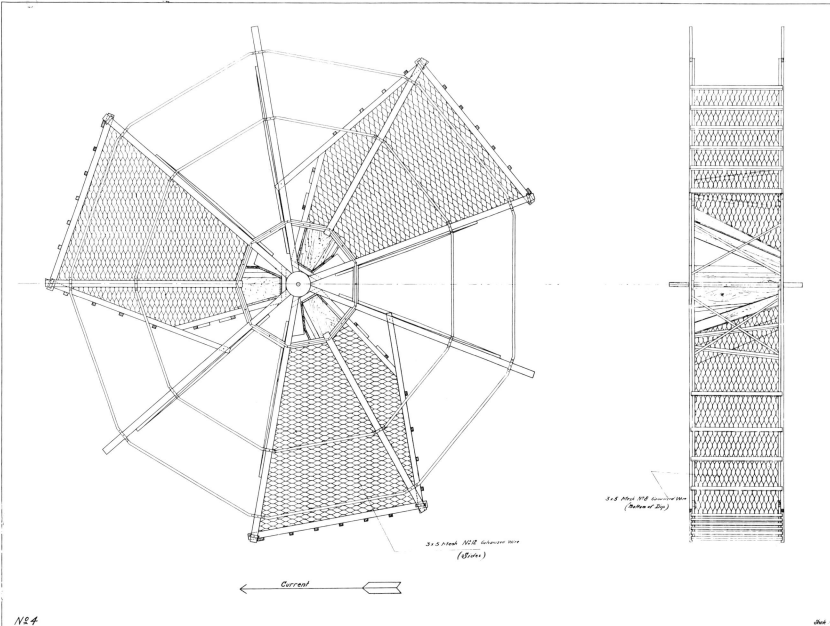

3 x 5 Mesh N°.12 Galvanized Wire

(Sides)

3 x 5 Mesh N°.8 Galvanized Wire
(Bottom of Dip)

Current

Seufert's Salmon Cannery
Columbia River Ore.

General Plan of a swift
Water Fishwheel

Prepared under the direction of
W. J. Seufert The Dalles, Ore.

G. J. Schmidt Draftsman.

Scale: ½"=1'-0"   Big Eddy Ore. May 15 1914

N°. 4

PHOTOGRAPHIC PORTFOLIO

BY

GLADYS SEUFERT

Channel on the Washington side of Celilo Falls. (Gladys Seufert photo)

154

Downstream bird's-eye view of the Columbia at Celilo. (Gladys Seufert photo)

Upstream view at Celilo. Tumwater Fishwheel at left foreground. (Gladys Seufert photo)

155

156

Celilo Falls at dusk. (Gladys Seufert photo)

Another evening view of Celilo Falls. (Gladys Seufert photo)

157

158

Overview of Celilo Falls and Indian dipnetters. (Gladys Seufert photo)

Celilo Falls fishery from cable way cart. (Gladys Seufert photo)

Celilo Falls from Chief Island. Big Island is at the left. (Gladys Seufert photo)

Successful Indian dipnetter at a small horseshoe falls at Celilo. (Gladys Seufert photo)

162

Section of Celilo reached only by cable way carts. (Gladys Seufert photo)

Downstream view at Fivemile Rapids. (Gladys Seufert photo)

164

The most famous and productive Fishwheel, No. 5 at Fivemile Rapids. (Gladys Seufert photo)

Fishwheels No. 6 (center) and No. 5 (left background). (Gladys Seufert photo)

166   The wheel furthest upstream, the Taffe at Celilo. (Gladys Seufert photo)

(Left) Indian dipnetting at Celilo. (Gladys Seufert photo) (Right) Seufert Bros. salmon labels. (OHS Coll.)   167

Seufert Bros. salmon can labels. (OHS Coll.)

Seufert Brothers China House on bluff just upstream from Seufert Brothers Cannery. The China House burned and was replaced in a slightly different location. The fishwheel is No. 1; at its base is a fishwheel scow. (Gladys Seufert print)

Fishwheel No. 1 during high water. Picture taken in 1902. The top of a beached fishwheel scow can be seen beyond the footbridge. (Arthur Seufert photo)

Fishwheel No. 1, high and dry during low water, was located behind Seufert's Cannery. This 1901 view looks east. All fishwheels required constant repair and reconstruction. No. 4 Fishwheel was rebuilt in November 1916. The wall outside of No. 3 was rebuilt November 1918. The Phelps wheel channel was deepened 6 ft. in November 1919. No. 5 channel was deepened at the mouth 6 ft. in 1919. Phelps wheel was rebuilt in the winter of 1921. The wooden crib at No. 3 was replaced by a cement wall in 1921. All fish scows were rebuilt in 1922. A new cement wall was built at No. 2 in 1922. The last year Covington wheel fished was May 1921, and was then abandoned. (Arthur Seufert photo)

(Left) Fishwheel No. 4 on the Oregon shore at The Dalles fishery. The No. 4 wheel was built in 1886, destroyed in 1894, and later rebuilt. Taken in late 1880s, this is the oldest known picture of a Seufert fishwheel. (Gladys Seufert print) (Right) Seufert's Fishwheel No. 3 at Big Eddy, Oregon. Picture taken during high water of May, 1948. The Columbia River continued to flood, and about a week after this picture was taken the Columbia River carried away Fishwheel No. 3. The concrete block (just above the water) was the counter weight that equalized the weight of the wheel. The spiked wheel on top of the large vertical gin posts was called the bull wheel. A rope passed around the bull wheel and hung down to the fishwheel deck. This rope raised and lowered the wheel. (Gladys Seufert print)

172

Fishwheel No. 3, looking east up the dry channel at low water. (Arthur Seufert photo)

173

Fishwheel No. 3, about 1900, looking upstream. The wheel can be seen turning in the channel. The Columbia River in this picture has not yet reached flood stage. (Arthur Seufert photo)

174

A channel in the Columbia at low water, looking upstream toward Fishwheel No. 3. The bluff on the left is the south side of Mema-loose Island. The picture was probably taken about 1901. (Arthur Seufert photo)

175

Picture taken at fishery. A view of Fishwheel No. 4 (foreground), and the Cyclone Wheel in Washington (background). The building (foreground) was the Oregon terminus of a cable car across the Columbia River to the Cyclone Wheel. (Arthur Seufert photo)

176

Seufert's Fishwheel No. 4, fall 1949. The water in the foreground is The Dalles-Celilo Canal. Just east of No. 4 Fishwheel Seufert's had a cable way across the Columbia River to the Cyclone Fishwheel and fish house. (Gladys Seufert photo)

177

Picture taken last week of May 1948 when the Columbia River was at flood. This same high water destroyed Vanport, Oregon. Looking west down The Dalles-Celilo Canal, Big Eddy Wheat warehouse (left center), Seufert's Fishwheel No. 4 (right center), and the fish house and engine house for Seufert's cable way (both right center) that crossed the Columbia River here. (Gladys Seufert photo)

Rock-filled timber crib of Seufert's Fishwheel No. 5. These cribs gave support and stability to the wheels. Picture taken in 1952. (Frank Seufert photo)

179

Fishwheel No. 5. Probably tak-
en about 1900, looking downstream. Fishwheel No. 5 was located at the upper entrance to
Fivemile Rapids. (Arthur Seufert
photo)

180

Seufert's Fishwheel No. 5 and entrance of Fivemile Rapids, October 1956. (Gladys Seufert photo)

181

(Left) Seufert's Fishwheel No. 5. This was the most famous of all the fishwheels on the Columbia River. It caught the most fish and made the most money. It was located at the head of Fivemile Rapids on the Oregon side of the Columbia River. Picture taken in 1947. (Gladys Seufert photo) (Right) Seufert's Fishwheel No. 6 at Tenino, Oregon, 1956. This wheel was located at the head of Fivemile Rapids just outside of The Dalles-Celilo Canal locks. The footbridge went over the Seufert's Fishwheel No. 5. No. 5 was some 300 feet to the left of No. 6 on the edge of the bluff overlooking the Columbia River at the head of Fivemile Rapids. (Gladys Seufert photo)

182

Mainline of the O.R. & N. looking east. Fishwheel No. 5 is on the point, Fishwheel No. 6 is between No. 5 and the railroad, on its own channel. Photograph taken about 1902. (Arthur Seufert photo)

183

Seufert's Fishwheel No. 6 (foreground) and Fishwheel No. 5 (background). Fishwheel No. 6 was built to fish during extremely high water, and 1948 was the only year there was enough water to operate it. But, in 1948, No. 6 could not run because Oregon had outlawed fishwheels. Picture taken in May 1956 during high water. (Frank Seufert photo)

184

Fishwheel No. 6 was built after the flood of 1894. It was built to operate if another massive flood occurred. But the river was not high enough to put any water in No. 6 channel until the flood of 1948. (Arthur Seufert photo)

185

(Left) Seufert's China Pete Fishwheel, 1909. Built by The Dalles Packing and Canning Co., and purchased by the Seuferts in 1907. Seufert's operated the wheel from 1907 to 1927. Soon after purchasing the China Pete Wheel, Seufert's started to replace the wooden cribbing with concrete. China Pete was destroyed by high water in 1916 and rebuilt; high water again destroyed the wheel in 1917, and it was rebuilt. China Pete was completely rebuilt in 1922. (Gladys Seufert print) (Right) Seufert's Phelps Fishwheel (1959), opposite The Dalles Dam. The wheel was first operated in the late nineteenth century, rebuilt in 1921, and burned and removed by the U.S. Army Corps of Engineers, June 5, 1963. (Gladys Seufert photo)

186

Phelps Fishwheel, looking up-stream approximately one mile downstream from the cannery. Built in 1886, the wheel was named after a family who owned the property at the time Frank A. Seufert purchased it. The Phelps Fishwheel remained fishing during the flood of 1894, when other wheels were destroyed. The wheel kept F.A. Seufert from going bankrupt during the flood; it usually was not a good wheel, but during the high water of 1894 it fished well. (Arthur Seufert photo)

187

Seufert's Phelps Fishwheel. This was the last of the many fish-wheels on the Columbia River. All the others were destroyed by the time this picture was taken in April 1959. The massive structure of The Dalles Dam fills the background. Compare the resultant changed landscape with that in the facing photograph. (Gladys Seufert photo)

Seufert's Little Wheel at Fivemile Rapids, on the Washington side of the Columbia. This wheel was built by The Dalles Packing and Canning Co. The Seuferts purchased the wheel in 1907 and operated it to 1934. Picture taken 1908. (Gladys Seufert print)

189

Seufert's Cyclone Wheel, named so because the summer west winds blew a gale here. The Cyclone Wheel was located about halfway up Fivemile Rapids. The wheel was built by The Dalles Packing and Canning Co., and was sold to the Seuferts in 1907. Seufert's rebuilt the wheel with huge concrete piers in 1909. The gin posts on top of the channel walls are 40 feet high; the concrete channel walls are much higher. (Gladys Seufert print)

190

Big Tumwater Fishwheel at Tumwater, Oregon, sometimes called Tumwater No. 1. The main channel of the Columbia can be seen in the background just beyond the Little Tumwater, or Tumwater No. 2 wheel, which was always removed before high water. Photograph taken about 1906. (Arthur Seufert photo)

Covington Fishwheel, looking west toward The Dalles with Mt. Hood in the background. Taken from the back of Seufert's Cannery in about 1900. (Arthur Seufert photo)

192

Covington Fishwheel. Looking west toward The Dalles. Picture was taken during high water, a short distance below Seufert's Cannery on the Oregon side of the river. (Arthur Seufert photo)

193

Seufert Brothers Covington Fishwheel. Probably June when the Columbia was high, looking upstream on the Oregon side, about 1900. (Arthur Seufert photo)

194

The Cement Wheel. Picture taken from the Oregon shore looking upstream; in the distance fishwheels No. 5 and No. 6 can be faintly seen. Probably taken about 1915. (Arthur Seufert photo)

195

Taffe Fishwheel at Celilo, Oregon. The channel from the fishwheel down to the channel mouth was known as Downes Channel. Picture was taken in September 1953. (Gladys Seufert photo)

196

(Left) The Bay Wheel on the Washington side of the Columbia, just above Big Eddy, 1906. The base of this wheel was constructed out of stone by Italian immigrants. A few years later high water destroyed the stone base; it was replaced by concrete. (Arthur Seufert photo) (Right) Early 1920s view of a fishwheel scow being towed upriver to a fishing site. The towboat without a deck house is the salmon tender *Hyak*. (Gladys Seufert print)

197

A Seufert fishwheel scow being towed upstream by salmon tenders about 1916. (Gladys Seufert print)

198

One of Seufert's scow fishwheels just above the mouth of Fifteen-mile Creek on the Oregon side of the river, looking upstream toward Big Eddy, about 1901. A fishwheel scow was tied to the bank and the wheel was lowered into the water and the wheel slowly revolved with the current. Scow fishwheels could only catch fish on days when the river was muddy and the salmon could not see clearly; in clear water salmon had only to swim around the fishwheel to avoid it. (Arthur Seufert photo)

Fishwheel scows on a beach just below The Dalles. (Gladys Seufert print)

200

Seufert's fishwheel scows tied up for the winter, just below the Phelps Fishwheel. The house just showing on the rock bluff was part of Lone Pine Tree Indian Village. The launch in the picture belonged to the Seuferts and was named *Lilly*. (Gladys Seufert print)

This view, taken about 1900, shows an Indian village just above the mouth of Fifteenmile Creek. The camp was just below and opposite Seufert's Cannery. (Arthur Seufert photo)

202

(Left) Indian woman and her child sitting alongside the railroad spur and wagon road at Seufert's Cannery (taken about 1900). (Arthur Seufert photo) (Right) Henry Thompson, son of Celilo Indian Chief Tommy Thompson, pictured at Celilo, Oregon, in April, 1966. (Gladys Seufert photo)

203

(Left) Hannah Yallup (left) and Lily Heath at the May 1967 Indian Festival held in Celilo Park to raise money for the longhouse in Celilo Village. (Gladys Seufert photo) (Right) Indian girls at Seufert's Cannery. This picture was taken about 1900 in the road looking toward the Columbia River between the Cannery and the Company office. (Arthur Seufert photo)

204

View of Indian skulls on Mema-loose Island just above Big Eddy, Oregon (probably about 1899). The wooden buildings in which the Indians laid their dead were partially destroyed by the high water of 1894. The bones were later placed in big pits. (Arthur Seufert photo)

205

Indian cemetery at Spedis (Klickitat County, Washington) overlooking Horsethief Lake. Taken in June 1966. (Francis Seufert photo)

206

About 1916 this view was taken of Seufert's seining operations from the S.P. & S. Railroad bridge down the Columbia below Celilo Falls. The closest operation is Seufert's Washington Seine Bar Two. The tents along the shore are living quarters for the seine crew. On the opposite side of the river is Seufert's Oregon Seine Bar One. (Gladys Seufert print)

A seine boat at the upper end of Seufert's Oregon Seine Bar One, 1939. The S.P. & S. Railroad bridge is in the background. The seine is piled on the stern deck of the seine boat. The crew is just shoving the boat off the beach to begin to make a lay. (Francis Seufert photo)

208

Seufert's Oregon Seine Bar One below Celilo Falls. The seine crew has just completed a lay and the lower end of the net has been landed. The running team (out of the picture on the left) is starting to haul the seine ashore, the man in the boat is releasing the net, and the team in the foreground will help land it. Picture taken in September, early 1940s. (Gladys Seufert print)

The seine crew (pictured on a September day in the 1940s) has just completed the haul at Seufert's Oregon Seine Bar One, and the men are picking the net up from the beach, restacking it on the seine boat. The seine's "cork line" is on the right edge, and the "lead line" on the left. (Gladys Seufert print)

Looking downriver at Seufert's Oregon Seine Bar One in 1939. The seine has just been landed and the men are dragging it up on shore. Salmon beat the river to a froth trying to escape. The seine boat may be seen in the background just off the beach. Francis Seufert, in the business suit, is walking down the beach. (Gladys Seufert photo)

Seining for Columbia River salmon at Seufert's Washington Seine Bar Two, in 1906. After first being laid in the river from the deck of a seine boat, moved in a circle to corral the salmon, the seine was pulled up on the banks of the river by teams of horses. This bar was located a short distance below Celilo Falls. The main Columbia River channel was located across the river below the bluff. This picture was taken in September. (Arthur Seufert photo)

212

Taken the same day as the preceding photo, this pictures the seine crew starting to make the lay. The shore end of the net is being held by the anchor team (outside of this picture). The seine boat makes a half circle to lay the net, and the boat comes ashore downriver. The lower tail end of the seine is attached to the running team, which will drag the net onto the beach. After the salmon are removed, the net will be carefully reloaded in large folds back on the boat. The men reloading the net in the stern of the boat were "swiping the net." (Arthur Seufert photo)

213

The seine has just been landed at Seufert's Oregon Seine Bar One, and the crew is picking up fall Chinooks from the beach, and tossing them into the ferryboat (right), to be taken to the landing. There they will be loaded into trucks and hauled to the cannery. Picture taken in September 1944. (Gladys Seufert print)

214

The landing on the Oregon side of the Columbia River about a mile below Celilo Falls. At this spot fish were brought by ferry from Seufert's Oregon Seine Bar One, Washington Bar Two, and Clantons Bar (the latter downstream about one mile from Bar Two). Salmon were piked from the ferry into the cribs (or fish boxes) at the edge of the roadway, then were piked into wagons, such as the one shown, and hauled to the fish house at Tumwater. (Arthur Seufert photo)

In front of Seufert's Cannery, Seufert, Oregon, 1917. The men in the picture were both fish-wheel operators and seine fishermen. The man in the center is Guy Whipple who for years ran Seufert's seines at Celilo, and at one time operated Seufert's fish-wheel scows. In the mid-1930s he became Seufert's cannery superintendent. The others are unknown. At this time the cannery building was one story high on the south end. In 1919, this part of the cannery warehouse was jacked up, turned around so it ran north and south, a hollow-tile one-story wall was built, and the cannery warehouse was set on top. This end of the cannery warehouse was then two stories high. The door marked with the numeral 1 in the picture can still be seen inside on the second floor of the old cannery warehouse. (Gladys Seufert print)

216

View from rim rock of the Oregon side of Celilo Falls: Big Island (at left), Tumwater Fishwheel (lower middle), and The Dalles-Celilo Canal (bottom). In 1955 (the year this photograph was taken), the old cable way from the Tumwater Fishwheel to Big Island was gone. Channel just inside of the rock point, outside of Tumwater Fishwheel, is the channel that was blasted for Seufert's Tumwater Fishwheel No. 2. (Francis Seufert, Jr., photo)

Celilo Falls and S.P. & S. Railroad bridge. Half of the Columbia River flowed through channel (bottom) and half flowed over falls (at the center) and under far side of bridge. The Dalles-Celilo Canal (lower left). Washington Seine Bar Two can be seen (flat, sandy area above bridge). The concrete wall (to act as a buffer for barges under the S.P. & S. Railroad bridge) is being placed in preparation of the flooding of the Columbia River by The Dalles Dam. August 1956. (Francis Seufert, Jr., photo)

218

View of Celilo Falls, taken from The Dalles-Celilo Canal. On this 1940s spring day, the falls are just reappearing after the spring flood. (Gladys Seufert photo)

A very early view (the picture was taken in early 1880s) of Indians dipnetting for salmon at The Dalles Fishery. Seufert's Fishwheel No. 4 was later located here. (Gladys Seufert print)

220

Tourists stand along the right side of the river in this 1950 photograph. They are watching the Indian dipnetters at Celilo. Some of the visitors brave the precarious footbridge in the foreground. (Gladys Seufert photo)

221

A big fall Chinook netted by an Indian fisherman at Celilo Falls, 1952. (Gladys Seufert photo)

222

Celilo Falls, Indian dipnet fishermen. Tourists stand on rocks (at
right) watching Indians fishing at
Celilo. The fish box on a Seufert's
cable way is taking Indian fishermen from the Oregon shore out
to Chief Island. There is also a
temporary footbridge. Picture
taken 1952. (Gladys Seufert
photo)

223

Two fish boxes on Seufert's cable way at Celilo in the fall of 1956. The cable way boxes carried the Indian dipnet fishermen to and from Chief Island. The bottom of the fish box was hinged, and locked shut by a lever. The Indian placed his salmon in the fish box, the box was carried across the river to the head of the cable way. There, by releasing the lever, the hinged bottom was opened, dropping the salmon onto a floor. The salmon was then piked onto a scale, weighed and the Indian was paid in cash for his catch. (Gladys Seufert photo)

224

In 1954, Indian dipnet fishermen stationed on their precarious scaffolds at Celilo Falls. The main falls is in the upper background at the left. (Gladys Seufert photo)

Sitting almost serenely on his fishing scaffold, this Indian dip-netter is a tiny figure before the massive power of Celilo Falls. Picture taken 1956. (Gladys Seufert photo)

226

Pictured in the fall of 1941, Indian dipnet fishermen, catching salmon in raging Celilo Falls. Chinook Rock is at the left, and Chief Island at center right of picture. (Gladys Seufert photo)

227

Seemingly more precarious than the scaffolds at Celilo Falls were these boxes (pictured in 1956) attached to a cliff over one of the two main channels on the Washington side of the falls. (Gladys Seufert photo)

228

Indians dipnetting in Downes Channel at Celilo Falls in the fall of 1950. (Gladys Seufert photo)

229

Original Seufert's Cannery office, Seufert, Oregon, later the home of one of the employees. (Arthur Seufert photo)

Oregon, Railway and Navigation mainline and loading platform of cannery at Seufert's, Oregon (about 1898). (Arthur Seufert photo)

231

Looking west at Seufert's Cannery showing wagon road bridge across Fifteenmile Creek, about 1900. (Arthur Seufert photo)

232

Looking west across Fifteenmile Creek, and Seufert's Cannery. Cannery was sometimes called "The Ranch Cannery" by the Seuferts. The building on the left, by the small bridge, is part of the cow barn. The small white building near the railroad bridge is the cookhouse, the office is just beyond the cookhouse. (Arthur Seufert photo)

233

Seufert's Cannery, Seufert, Oregon. Picture taken in summer, about 1901. (Arthur Seufert photo)

Seufert's Cannery behind the new O.R. & N. Railroad bridge, looking west toward The Dalles and Mt. Hood, about 1926. (Gifford photo)

235

An advertising leaflet used for Seufert Brothers Company.

Established 1886

SEUFERT BROS. COMPANY
THE DALLES, OREGON

Packers of—ANNIE'S FAVORITE, MERRIMAC, WASCO and TENINO BRAND

COLUMBIA RIVER SALMON

WASCO and MERRIMAC BRAND ROYAL ANNE CHERRIES

SELLING AGENTS:

Jacob J. Peres & Co., Memphis, Tenn.
Francis H. Leggett & Co., New York, N. Y.
S. T. Southgate & Co., Norfolk, Va.
B. H. Voskamps Sons Co., Pittsburg, Pa.

H. A. Dreves & Co., St. Paul, Minn.
R. C. Williams & Co., New York, N. Y.
Austin Nichols & Co., New York, N. Y.
Reid Murdoch & Co., Chicago, Ill.

236

A 1973 view of a section of Seufert's Cannery, Seufert, Oregon, which at one time had held the machinery for canning salmon. (Gladys Seufert photo)

237

The sad end of an important industry, and the end of an era. The burning of the Seufert Brothers Company Cannery at Seufert, Oregon, by the U.S. Army Corps of Engineers on February 4, 1975. (Gladys Seufert photo)

238

(Left) Boiler Room, Seufert's Cannery. In 1953, at the end of the fall salmon canning season, the boiler room fireman shut off the fires under the big boiler for the last time. He took off his gloves and overalls, laid them in top of the fuel oil pipes by the oil burner's blower, and went home. In September of 1973 the overalls and gloves were still there. Never again will a fireman in Seufert's boiler room wear them and light the fires under the big boiler for the start of another fall canning season. (Francis Seufert photo) (Right) Francis A. Seufert & Company office door in the U.S. National Bank Building, The Dalles, Oregon, 1962. (Gladys Seufert photo)

239

The Oregon State Grange was one of the groups to sponsor the initiative measure on the Oregon ballot in 1926 that outlawed fishwheels in the state. This company statement remained for years on the Seufert barn. (Gifford photo)

240

Salmon saltery at the Seufert Brothers Fishery, about 1900. (Arthur Seufert photo)

Chinese butchers gutting and fileting salmon, preparing the fish for canning. At Seufert's Cannery, only Chinese were used for this work, for they were the best butchers, fast and precise in their butchering of the fish. (Joe Gildersleeve Photo, Dr. Ralph A. Prose Coll., OHS)

242

Seufert's Cannery, Seufert, Oregon. Fresh Columbia River salmon on fish house floor. Chinese are slimming salmon. Picture taken September 1947. (Gladys Seufert print)

243

Iced salmon ready for butchering on the fish house floor of Seufert's Cannery. Ice was placed on the fish the night before to keep them fresh. The machine in the middle right hand side of the picture is the "Iron Chink." This butchering mechanism worked well with small fish; large salmon always were butchered by the Chinese. Salmon butchering tables are in background. This picture was taken on an early September 1946 morning. (Gladys Seufert print)

This picture was taken about 1901 in the fish room of Seufert's Cannery. The salmon on the floor are fairly large. Large salmon were generally caught in the month of June and were known as "channel fish," because it was thought that they always followed the main ship channel up the Columbia River. (Arthur Seufert photo)

Seufert's Cannery. Chinese cannery workers filling half-pound salmon cans. The man in the center is operating belt-driven salmon gang knives. The gang knives were on a large wooden drum about three feet in diameter. On top of the drum were circular wharp knives that cut the salmon into exact can-sized pieces. Steel fingers on the drum carried the whole salmon past the knives. The large fish on the table by the gang knives are sturgeon. The wooden tanks in the foreground hold slimed salmon. Picture taken between 1910-1918. (Gladys Seufert print)

246

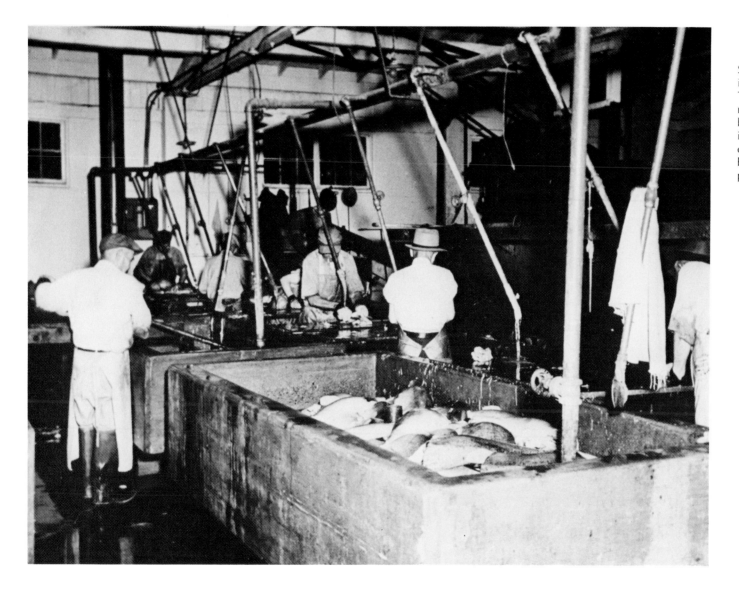

Seufert's Cannery. Chinese sliming salmon, September 1944. The sliming operation was so named because the Chinese butchers cleaned the slick coating off the salmon, and thoroughly washed and cleaned the belly cavity. (Gladys Seufert print)

247

Interior of Seufert's Fifteenmile Creek Cannery looking toward the front, or west end of the building. Much of the salmon canning process can be seen here. The salmon butchering tables are just beyond the low wall in the background. Barely showing at top center are large concrete tanks where the salmon were placed after the Chinese had butchered them. Then the Chinese finished cleaning the fish. The salmon were next put through a gang knife. The cut salmon were then carried in wooden boxes to the filling tables in the foreground. (Arthur Seufert photo)

248

Interior of Seufert's Cannery, about 1900. On table (middle background), salmon were packed by hand. The filled cans were placed on a belt that carried through a washer, where the outsides of the cans were cleaned. The lids were seated on top and crimped into place. The cans were then tipped on their sides and run through a small trough containing acid and a trough containing molten solder (the acid cleaned the can so the solder could hold the lid tightly in place). The soldering machine is shown at the left foreground. (Soldering machines were replaced by the sanitary can closing machine on the Columbia River in about 1910.) (Arthur Seufert photo)

Interior of Seufert's Cannery, about 1900. The retorts used to cook the canned salmon are at the rear. The cans were put in the tray coolers, which were then stacked on the little railroad cars (see cars on near track, and stacked coolers on left track). The load of coolers was then rolled into the retorts where the salmon was cooked at 240°. If they were big one-pound flat cans they were cooked 90 minutes, if little one-half pound cans, 75 minutes. The cans shown are one-pound cans. (Arthur Seufert photo)

250

The cans on the cooler racks are readied for cooking in the retorts (background). Picture taken in 1944. (Gladys Seufert print)

China House. The Chinese crews working for Seufert's lived in this house, which was just above the river on a point of land north of the cannery building. Picture taken in the middle 1960s. The Dalles Dam looms in the background, along with its fish ladder. (Gladys Seufert photo)

252

Steam bath, used by the Chinese crews, located near the China House. The basin's water was heated by a fire built in the brick structure. Picture taken in the 1960s. (Gladys Seufert photo)

253

A man and his dog hunting along the Columbia River back of Seufert's Cannery (probably taken about 1900). In the center background is the Bluejay Fishwheel. (Arthur Seufert photo)

Union Pacific rail crossing at Celilo Park, Celilo, Oregon. Taken
in January 1974, this is the last
picture taken by Francis Seufert.
He had a lifelong interest in railroads, their operations and their
locations in passes, so it was fit-
ting that his last picture should be
of a railroad.

255

(Left) Frank A. Seufert, founder of Seufert Brothers Company, and pioneer salmon canner on the Columbia River. This photograph was taken about 1890 by his son, Arthur Seufert. (Right) Arthur Seufert (1878-1954), son of Frank A., and father of Francis. (Gladys Seufert print)

256

The Frank A. Seufert home on Fourth Street in The Dalles, about 1900. (Arthur Seufert photo)

257

(Left) Annie Isabella Seufert (1855-1928), wife of Frank A. Seufert. (Gladys Seufert print) (Right) Francis Seufert, about 1950. (Gladys Seufert photo)

258

Francis Seufert and Gladys Seufert, with their son Frank. Taken in Portland, Oregon, March 1949, when the Seuferts were on their way to Los Angeles by train. (John Fries photo)

259

COLOPHON

The text face for *Wheels of Fortune* was set in Hermann Zapf's Optima, often described as either a calligraphic roman or a modified sans serif. The display type is Eric Gill's Gill Sans, a derivative of the fine face designed by Edward Johnston for the London Underground Railway. The text was set by Irish Setter, and the display by Comgroup, both Portland firms. The book was printed and bound by Publishers Press of Salt Lake City.

Designed by Bruce T. Hamilton.